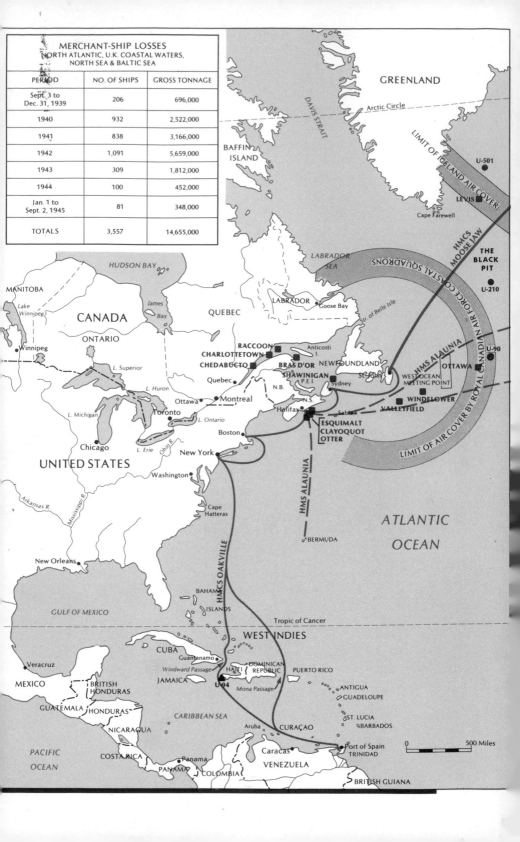

MERCHANT-SHIP LOSSES
NORTH ATLANTIC, U.K. COASTAL WATERS, NORTH SEA & BALTIC SEA

PERIOD	NO. OF SHIPS	GROSS TONNAGE
Sept. 3 to Dec. 31, 1939	206	696,000
1940	932	2,522,000
1941	838	3,166,000
1942	1,091	5,659,000
1943	309	1,812,000
1944	100	452,000
Jan. 1 to Sept. 2, 1945	81	348,000
TOTALS	3,557	14,655,000

GREENLAND

Arctic Circle

DAVIS STRAIT

LIMIT OF ICELAND AIR COVER

U-501

LEVIS

Cape Farewell

THE BLACK PIT

U-210

BAFFIN ISLAND

LABRADOR SEA

FORCE COASTAL SQUADRONS

HMCS MOOSE JAW

LIMIT OF AIR COVER BY ROYAL CANADIAN AIR

HUDSON BAY

James Bay

LABRADOR

Goose Bay

Str. of Belle Isle

HMS ALAUNIA

U-90

OTTAWA

MANITOBA

Lake Winnipeg

CANADA

QUEBEC

Winnipeg

ONTARIO

RACCOON

CHARLOTTETOWN

CHEDABUCTO

Anticosti I.

NEWFOUNDLAND

WEST OCEAN MEETING POINT

Quebec

BRAS D'OR

SHAWINIGAN

N.B.

P.E.I.

St. John's

Sydney

L. Superior

Ottawa

Montreal

WINDFLOWER

VALLEYFIELD

Toronto

L. Huron

L. Michigan

L. Ontario

Halifax

N.S.

Sable I.

ESQUIMALT

CLAYOQUOT

OTTER

Chicago

L. Erie

Ohio R.

Boston

UNITED STATES

New York

HMS ALAUNIA

Washington

Arkansas R.

Mississippi R.

Cape Hatteras

ATLANTIC OCEAN

BERMUDA

New Orleans

HMCS OAKVILLE

GULF OF MEXICO

BAHAMA

ISLANDS

Tropic of Cancer

WEST INDIES

CUBA

Guantanamo

Windward Passage

JAMAICA

U-94

HAITI

DOMINICAN REPUBLIC

PUERTO RICO

Mona Passage

ANTIGUA

GUADELOUPE

MEXICO

Veracruz

BRITISH HONDURAS

ST. LUCIA

BARBADOS

GUATEMALA

HONDURAS

CARIBBEAN SEA

Aruba

CURAÇAO

NICARAGUA

PACIFIC OCEAN

COSTA RICA

Panama

PANAMA

COLOMBIA

Caracas

VENEZUELA

Port of Spain

TRINIDAD

0   500 Miles

BRITISH GUIANA

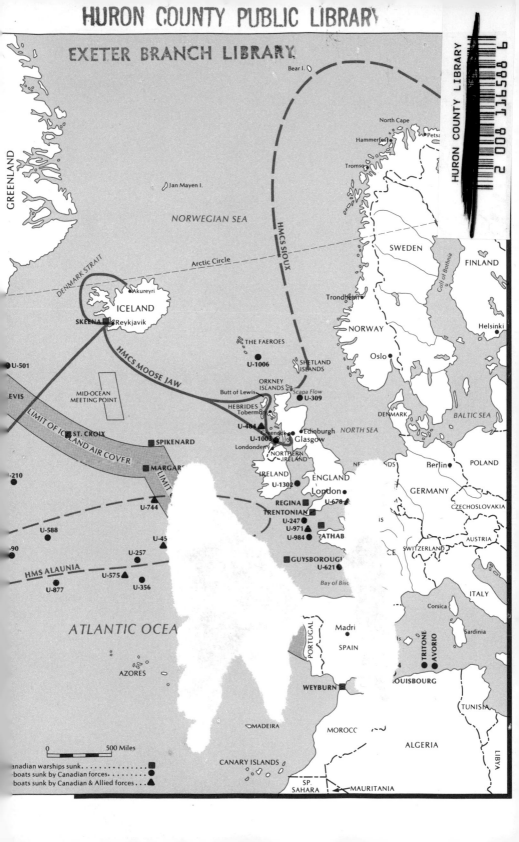

GREENLAND

Bear I.

North Cape

Hammerfest

Petsa

Tromso

SWEDEN

FINLAND

Jan Mayen I.

NORWEGIAN SEA

Gulf of Bothnia

HMCS SIOUX

Arctic Circle

DENMARK STRAIT

Trondheim

Akureyri

ICELAND

SKEENA

Reykjavik

NORWAY

Helsinki

Oslo

THE FAEROES

HMCS MOOSE JAW

U-1006

SHETLAND ISLANDS

MID-OCEAN
MEETING POINT

ORKNEY ISLANDS

Butt of Lewis

Scapa Flow

U-309

DENMARK

BALTIC SEA

LEVIS

HEBRIDES
Tobermory

NORTH SEA

U-484

Edinburgh

ST. CROIX

LIMIT OF ICELAND AIR COVER

SPIKENARD

U-1003

Glasgow

Londonderry

NORTHERN
IRELAND

NE

DS

Berlin

POLAND

-210

MARGAR

IRELAND

ENGLAND

GERMANY

LIMIT

U-744

U-1302

London

U-678

REGINA

CZECHOSLOVAKIA

U-588

TRENTONIAN

U-247

U-971

AUSTRIA

U-45

U-984

ATHAB

SWITZERLAND

U-257

CE

HMS ALAUNIA

GUYSBOROUGH

-90

U-575

U-621

ITALY

U-877

U-356

Bay of Bisc

Corsica

Sardinia

ATLANTIC OCEA

Madri

PORTUGAL

SPAIN

Is.

TRITONE

AVORIO

AZORES

OUISBOURG

WEYBURN

TUNISIA

MADEIRA

MOROCC

ALGERIA

LIBYA

500 Miles

CANARY ISLANDS

anadian warships sunk . . . . ■

-boats sunk by Canadian forces . . . . ●

boats sunk by Canadian & Allied forces . . . ▲

SP.
SAHARA

MAURITANIA

Hal Lawrence

A BLOODY WAR

One Man's Memories of the Canadian Navy 1939-1945

The Nautical & Aviation Publishing Company of America

8 Randall St., Annapolis, Md. 21401

Macmillan of Canada/Toronto

Reprinted 1979

CANADIAN CATALOGUING IN PUBLICATION DATA

Lawrence, Hal, 1920-
A bloody war

ISBN 0-7705-1734-X

1. Lawrence, Hal, 1920-   2. World War, 1939-
1945 – Naval operations, Canadian.   3. World War,
1939-1945 – Personal narratives, Canadian.
I. Title.

D811.L39   940.54'59'71   C79-094222-4

Charts prepared by
William R. Constable, C.C.
National Defence Headquarters
Ottawa

Printed in Canada for
The Macmillan Company of Canada Limited
70 Bond Street, Toronto
Ontario M5B 1X3

Contents

Preface

This is a story about the sea and about the first five and a half of the twenty-five years I spent in the Royal Canadian Navy. These years coincided with Canada's fighting in the Second World War, and though they were few in number, I believe them to have been part of a brave naval tradition that originated in the England of Queen Elizabeth I with Blake, Raleigh, and Hawkins, was inherited by the Royal Canadian Navy some three hundred years later, and flourishes now in the reign of Queen Elizabeth II. When I was a midshipman I served with sailors and marines who fought in the Great War of 1914-18, in the South African War of 1902, and in the Boxer Rebellion of 1890-92. I come of a military family: my father was a professional soldier for thirty-six years and fought in the First World War and the Second World War; my grandfather fought in the Afghanistan Wars of 1878 and at Saukin in 1885; my eldest son joined the Canadian Guards. On the Irish side of the family, my immediate ancestors enthusiastically fought the English for many years until the Easter Rebellion of 1916; then, with equal enthusiasm, they fought each other in the civil war following independence.

One of the questions that has harried me while preparing this narrative has been, why am I writing it? As it turns out, the process has been a catharsis, setting down at last the inchoate thoughts and daydreams, the nostalgia, fear, hope, and despair, that the period arouses. That's one thing.

Another is that I spent five and a half years with an interesting group of men, men who, unlike most others, faced almost daily such dilemmas as, shall we promote this man or court-martial him? Shall we rescue survivors or pursue the enemy? Shall we live or die in the effort? And, along the way, I learned about their virtues—courage, for instance, but not only the dashing, sword-waving, follow-me-men type of courage. There is another kind

vii

that forces a man to his duty, doggedly and patiently, when hope is gone and he is cold and tired, and sick and afraid.

This was not a dull group I lived with. And if what I have just said sounds grim and portentous, I can tell you that there was more laughter than tears, and that most of my life was spent in the light-hearted companionship of dedicated professional sailors who found that a robust corollary to advancing the naval art was to drink, fight, and tomcat their way around the world. Yet, nearly every one of these men put the welfare of the navy before his own; and I speak here of the Royal Navy, the United States Navy, and the Kriegsmarine as well as of the Royal Canadian Navy. So, in a sense, this is the story of a unique group of men and the laws, written and unwritten, that governed their lives.

Yet now that I have finished, I think I know what it is before all else: it is a love story, or rather, it is several love stories.

Feast of St. Barbara, 1978
Ottawa, Canada   *Hal Lawrence*

Acknowledgements

My primary debt is to those officers and chief and petty officers who taught me my profession, to those captains under whom I served a fruitful apprenticeship in warships, and to those officers and men who served under me when I was appointed captain of my own sea-going command, and, later, senior officer in command of a flotilla. You will see how deep is my indebtedness in the pages that follow.

There are also those who, in their books, shared my experiences, amplified them, modified my thinking, gave me a perspective, and worked all the wonders that are the capabilities of articulate men with knowledge, perspicacity, and deep feeling.

My wife, Alma, shared the experiences I describe in this book, supported me in bad times, and rejoiced with me in good; this is a debt that can be acknowledged but never adequately repaid.

I thank Anita Firth, who typed the manuscript, at the same time turning my uncertain squiggles into correctly spelled words. I am grateful for the criticism of Professors (ex-Majors) Alphonse Campbell and Glenn Clever, colleagues of mine, I am proud to say, at the University of Ottawa. And then there is Philip Chaplin, a man who fought the war at sea and in the following years became a Senior Historian of the Royal Canadian Navy; over many years he has uncovered vital material, loaned me his books, and corrected succeeding drafts of this work.

one

A Snotty on Coastal Patrols

"Snotty! You're to join *Andrée Dupré* this forenoon. Fetch your kit and get aboard, chop-chop!"

The order was barked at me by the pale-eyed, red-faced Lieutenant-Commander in Charge of Officers' Appointments. In the six weeks since September 8, 1939, when I joined the navy, I had learned that everybody barked at midshipmen. Particularly at midshipmen of the Naval Reserve.

I wondered uneasily whether I should salute or not; if so, with or without the cap now held under my arm? I compromised by standing more stiffly to attention and snapping a "Yessir" in response. At once I realized it should have been "Aye aye, sir", and I sidled awkwardly to the door, fumbled for the knob, and slid out.

What in hell was *Andrée Dupré*? Who might I ask? Could my two suitcases be classed as "kit"? I wished then for a duffle bag—it seemed more seamanlike.

My walk down Halifax Dockyard was the usual embarrassment. My Burberry hid my rank, but sailors glanced speculatively at my face (which obviously would not need a razor for a year or so), regarded my shining new cap badge, and passed with never a salute. The petty officers were meticulous in saluting, and I think this was worse. Ignorant and miserable, I longed to learn something about this complex organization. Half the vocabulary was foreign—"kit" was recently acquired—and the customs, unwritten and centuries old, seemed familiar to everyone but me.

A short walk brought me to the berth of His Majesty's Canadian Ship *Andrée Dupré*—a tug. It was a bad moment. Though I was humble, this injury was unexpected. I had seen the cruisers of the Royal Navy's West Indies Squadron when they visited Halifax—white teak decks, spotless awnings, impassive Royal Marine sentries with red-striped trousers and gleaming buttons, the officer of the watch with his telescope under his arm, and the

1

sleek enamelled hull giving out the soft roar of ventilation fans through glinting brass scuttles.

Andrée Dupré was small, grey, and gritty, and in the drizzling rain her ragged ensign drooped. She was moored with a mongrel collection of tugs, harbour craft, scows, a floating crane, and three catamarans. I found the quartermaster drinking coffee in the wheel-house. In answer to my question he pointed and said, "First door aft."

The wardroom was small and square with a bunk on either side, its corticine deck covered with a strip of blue carpet. A bright bulb overhead made the daylight, seen through two small scuttles, even murkier. Two officers bearing thin gold bands on their arms were playing double patience at a table.

"Yes?"

"I've come aboard."

"Yes?"

"I mean, I've come to join. I've come to join this ship."

"Oh! Well, I don't know where we're going to put you."

After this unpromising entrance, I was made more or less at home. Although these two officers were as new to the navy as I was, they were not new to the sea. Both had Coasting Certificates in the merchant marine, and, on the strength of these, had been brought into the navy with warrant ranks in the RCNR.

In actuality Canada had three navies in 1939. There was, first of all, the Royal Canadian Navy, the RCN, the élite. Its officers had joined the permanent force as cadets at the age of about sixteen, had been through naval college, and had served their midshipman's time in cruisers and battleships of the Royal Navy. They returned to Canada, often excruciatingly British, when they shipped their first stripe. Then there was the Royal Canadian Naval Volunteer Reserve, the RCNVR. Its members, and I was one, usually had no knowledge of the sea and had been recruited at the outbreak of war principally from yacht clubs and universities. A few had been in the RCNVR before the war and had learned a bit during their summer training periods. Finally, there was the Royal Canadian Naval Reserve, the RCNR, whose officers came from the merchant marine. Most had Deep-Sea Master's Certificates and had commanded large merchant ships. Each organization was designated by its own distinctive stripes: the RCN, broad straight stripes; the RCNVR, thin zigzag stripes; and the RCNR, thin crisscross stripes. The patent difference between the three was exaggerated by the condescending attitude of the "Regulars"—the

RCN—who behaved like members of an exclusive club that had been forced to open its doors to a ragtag and bob-tail not previously eligible. The wry observation was made often that "the RCNR are sailors trying to be gentlemen; the RCNVR are gentlemen trying to be sailors; and the RCN are neither trying to be both!"

The two card-playing RCNR officers who were my new shipmates proved to be gentlemen as well as sailors. After cautiously interrogating me as to my nautical abilities and hiding their dismay behind a hearty "Well, we all have to start some time", they made me welcome.

We sailed that afternoon.

The Captain (RCNR) had been many years at sea and he handled his ship superbly. On that day was born in me a resolve to do likewise when my chance came. After a preliminary "slow ahead" to spring the ship off the wharf, he gave no orders except "full ahead" and "full astern" for the engine and nothing other than "hard-a-starboard" or "hard-a-port" for the helm. He backed and filled in that crowded basin, delivering his orders in a quiet, sure voice. The intent look and instant reactions of the helmsman, the measured advice of the Mate watching aft on the outboard side, the anticipatory stance of the telegraphsman as instantly he relayed the Captain's orders to the engine-room with his jangling telegraph, the surge of water under the stern that immediately followed—all this impressed the novice immeasurably.

This is the serious business of taking a ship to sea, one of the higher arts of the seaman, and, be she tug or battleship, the vessel commands the undivided attention of all who serve her, for the manoeuvres must be done safely and smartly.

The stern points at the gap. "Full astern." Three shrill blasts sound from the steam whistle and we are in the open harbour. "Stop her." There is a sudden silence as the engines pulsate slower and stop. The fittings in the wheel-house jiggle faintly from the slap of the waves under the counter. "Full ahead. Hard-a-port." The engines throb again and water rushes from the stern. We are pointing to the open sea. The Captain nods casually, "Take her out, Mr. Mate." The Mate moves quietly behind the binnacle and says to the helmsman, "Line her up on the gate vessels."

A chilly north wind, in its six-mile reach down Bedford Basin, was driving short, three-foot waves. From the lee side of the wheel-house I watched the drab waterfront of Halifax slide by; the waning autumn sun still had strength. I picked out the City

Hall, where Alma worked, and then the window of her office; it was empty. Two ungainly ferries, the lifeline between Halifax and Dartmouth, passed each other in their eternal duty. A dozen tankers and freighters lay placidly at anchor, awaiting orders which would send them out in the next convoy. Thirty more were in Bedford Basin astern of us. The lower part of the harbour was filled with big troop-ships; their soldiers had been pouring into the city for a week.

My exhilaration faded. There was the real navy, I thought: the battle-cruisers HMS *Repulse* and *Renown*, the cruiser *Enterprise*, the SS *Aquitania*, *Empress of Britain*, *Mauritania*, and *Queen of Bermuda*. The rails of the liners were crowded with khaki-clad figures. Our Mate waved and a few waved back. We came to the Boom, a steel net stretched across the mouth of the harbour from Mauger Beach to York Redoubt. Two trawlers in the middle of the net, Gate-Vessels, were the means of entering and leaving Halifax Harbour. Their winches thumped and steamed as laboriously they drew the movable section of the net to one side and we passed through. We were on our station.

In the five and a half years of war to follow, neither enemy submarine nor enemy raider disguised as a merchant ship attempted to enter Halifax. But that year, 1939, on the night of October 13-14, Kapitänleutnant Günther Prien slipped through the nets into the Scapa Flow of the Orkney Islands, base of the Home Fleet off the north coast of Scotland. He torpedoed the battleship *Royal Oak*, leaving 833 dead. The lesson was not lost on us at Halifax. For nearly six years, an Examination Vessel, of which the *Andrée Dupré* was one, bobbed on her station outside the net, and army guns-crews manned their weapons at Sandwich Battery. It was a monotonous, prosaic job, sometimes dangerous.

Jump into a dory on a dark, blustery night. After a wet pull to the mountainous side of a heaving merchantman, balance on the thwart amidships, choose the moment and leap, making a mad clutch for the swaying rope ladder, and then the interminable climb up the ship's side. Examine the ship's papers and deck log, talk to a captain who wants nothing so much as to get that gate closed behind him, clamber down to the boat again, pull back, take the watch back from your captain, envying him as he goes to his warm bunk, and hope there will be no more ships until your relief takes over. Many times in later years, when my destroyer was sweeping along at thirty knots in company with the rest of the flotilla, the guns pointed expectantly in the air, I thought of the men in the Examination Vessels. I thought of the harbour-craft, the drifters, the inner-patrol vessels, the minesweepers, the gate-vessels; and I thanked the gods of war for putting me on the bridge of a destroyer going into action.

In *Andrée Dupré* I stood two watches on the bridge each day as second officer of the watch and for the rest of the time was left to my own devices. The Captain was cold and formal, called everybody "Mister", and never spoke at all, apart from the orders required to run his ship. He lived, it seemed, with some deep-seated discontent, a sadness. Since I had no real duties in the ship except makee-learnee, we exchanged not a word. Feeling somewhat lost, I turned for solace to books, those friends who had never failed me. In this case I turned to my naval textbooks to see if I could make some sense out of all I had learned in the past two months, reading that supplemented the courses I had taken ashore before joining *Andrée Dupré*: two weeks each of Gunnery, Torpedo, Seamanship, Navigation, and Signals.

The Gunnery and Torpedo courses had no application, for we had neither guns nor torpedoes. Coastal navigation I used only self-consciously: there was no reason to take a fix. We always knew where we were just by looking. Mauger Beach Lighthouse stood tall and white about a half-mile away. Thrum Cap Shoal, Inner Automatic, Middle Ground buoy, and Litchfield clanged their bells all around us as they heaved in the swell, and at night flashed or occulted their white, red, or green lights. You could see Halifax quite clearly and one still Saturday night I heard the music from the Yacht Squadron dance. Nevertheless, I took fix after fix and learned the knack of handling parallel rulers and dividers, taking a bearing through a fogged-up prism, and adding and subtracting variation and deviation to my compass bearing to find the true bearing. This last was always difficult for me, for I had failed arithmetic all through school and variation always seemed to go one way and deviation the other. I would stare in mistrust at my figures after wrestling with them for a few minutes, cautiously put my resultant bearing on the chart, and discover that my fix put me inside the boom, not outside. Such doggerel verses as "Error east, compass least; error west, compass best" only confused me. However, I persevered and one magical day it came to me. I could snap a fix with the best.

Signals I was not self-conscious about, for we used it all day, every day. During daylight the strong white light of the ten-inch signal projector sent messages with the healthy clack of its shutters as the key was pounded. During darkness, the discreet blue light of the Aldis lamp signalled with the crisp click of the deflecting prism as the trigger was pulled.

We had one signalman by the name of Gay, who can only be described in hackneyed terms as a grizzled old seaman. He must have been over the age limit, perhaps fifty-six or so, even in those days of emergency. He wore the single anchor of a leading signalman and three good-conduct badges. These good-conduct badges represented at least twelve years of undetected crime, and it was a tribute to his experience of the navy in general and of shore-patrol petty officers in particular that he kept them, for his evenings ashore were riotous and at sea he was constantly surrounded with the gentle effluvium of rum. Early in the morning he was silent, but as the forenoon watch went on, his silence would lift as the time for the rum issue grew near. In the early part of the afternoon watch, after his tot, his demeanour was positively friendly and his light would clack patiently to merchant ships and chatter merrily to the more skilled warships. In the first dog-watch his sending was phlegmatic—just a job that had to be done; but in the last dog-watch he would soar to heights of visual-signalling rhythm.

After a while one can judge the ability of the man who is receiving by the way he flashes, and it was a matter of pride to Gay that he would talk only to the Yeoman of Signals in any warship. He would start off sedately when calling a warship and the signalman on watch in the other ship would answer confidently. Then Gay would speed up. The answering flashes would become more and more uncertain. Gay would speed up a little more. Repeats would be falteringly requested, sending Gay to top speed. There would be a fairly long silence in the other ship and one could imagine the Yeoman there impatiently shouldering aside the young signalman. Then came several long, authoritative flashes and the two experts would conduct their business.

One night, however, Gay came to grief. He had come to the bridge in a particularly strong miasma of rum. He got rid of a junior signalman in an approaching cruiser in the usual way and was talking to their Yeoman when I noticed something wrong. Gay was faltering on all words with s's in them. He went slower and slower, trying to articulate, and finally the signal-lamp in the other ship was handed back to the original operator. Gay was drunk and it showed, not in his voice but in his signal-lamp.

After three days we were relieved by *Ulna* and we steamed

back up Halifax Harbour. The window in the City Hall was still empty, but I comforted myself with the thought of the Saturday night supper-dance at the Nova Scotian Hotel.

The Saturday supper-dances in Halifax in those early months of the war were infused with a spirit of excitement and anticipation. As the clubs of Mayfair had been flooded a generation earlier by young people singing "Roses of Picardy" and the couples waltzed to "a sound of revelry by night", so we sat with bottles of rum in tables of ten or twenty, sang "Roll Out the Barrel", and thought ourselves fine fellows, engaged in the serious business of life. Afterwards we roamed the waterfront streets in search of food.

Nearly two hundred years earlier these streets had seen the half-wild Gorman Rangers, fresh from raids on the Micmacs, spend their money. They had seen General Wolfe's soldiers roister before the fall of Louisbourg, and, a year later, before Wolfe defeated Montcalm at Quebec. The British fleet and army that captured Havana celebrated its victory there in 1782. During the American Revolution the press-gangs roamed the town, and again during the war of 1812-14. Eighty years before us the streets rang to the songs of men embarking for the Crimea, and forty years before that to the songs of those bound for the Boer War, marching to Pretoria. And so we followed in the footsteps of all of them and of our parents a scant twenty-five years earlier when they sang "K-K-K-Katy" and sailed away to the mud of Flanders. The rum was strong, the girls were pretty, the money was adequate, and the future stretched ahead—endless, glamorous, bright, and ours. Yet, at that point, we did not cut much of a figure compared to our antecedent brothers-in-arms.

The Royal Navy had held the seas for hundreds of years and the Royal Canadian Navy was its child. Our navy was born in 1910, had reached maturity under the tutorship of Britishers, had acquired characteristics of its own that were distinctly Canadian, and was on its way to becoming the third-largest of the allied navies of the Second World War. The reputation we were to build as a good fighting navy was won by our own skill and sacrifice, but we had inherited a tradition of supremacy and leadership at sea right from the beginning.

The Royal Navy had been recognizable as a national force as early as the Battle of Sluys, off the Flanders coasts, in 1340. From the town of Portsmouth, King Henry V sailed with his fleet in 1415 for the beaches of Normandy and Picardy, and his campaign at

Agincourt. About 1540 Henry VIII codified the navy. James II led his fleets in person in the 1600s; William IV was in action under Admiral Rodney in the 1700s; George V was a professional naval officer in the 1800s (and a gunboat captain, among other things); George VI fought at the Battle of Jutland in 1916; the Prince Philip served at sea from 1939 to 1945 (and for a while we both served in the same destroyer flotilla). The senior officers and petty officers of our 1939 Canadian navy had fought, between 1914 and 1918, at the Battles of Jutland, Dogger Bank, and the Falkland Islands. They had fought under Admiral Beatty and Admiral Jellicoe; they were contemporaries of the soon-to-be-famous admirals of the Second World War, Cunningham, Vian, Bonham-Carter, and Fraser. The traditions of naval life—floggings and hangings; reforms surprisingly in advance of their time; an eagerness to come to grips with the enemy, to fight, win or lose, live or die—stretched across the centuries and rested, sometimes uneasily, on our shoulders.

No amount of tradition, for instance, could properly prepare a man for the discomforts of everyday life at sea. The art of making oneself comfortable in a constantly heaving vessel is one that only time and many painful lessons can teach. I still bear scars from my sea-time in HMCS *Ulna*, my next appointment after *Andrée Dupré*.

Ulna was a yacht of narrow beam. Consequently she rolled heavily even in the somewhat moderate swell outside the net. (The hands said she would roll in a heavy dew.) The toilet in the heads was high off the deck, so much so that I made mathematical computations and decided her original owner must have been 6'7", a figure based on the fact that I was 5'11" and when I was sitting on the can my feet were three inches off the deck. A hand-grip on either side gave some stability to the trunk, but to have disembodied legs swinging back and forth during this most personal function was disconcerting. A cut-down but wobbly apple box temporarily solved the problem, but the permanent solution was a solid teak grating filched from another yacht's wheel-house. A steam radiator immediately in front of and to the left of the can was a hazard that defied me to the end. It was impossible to hold on to the hand-grip with one hand, pull one's trousers up with the other, and not occasionally be flung against the burning-hot radiator.

My instructors in coastal patrols were not dapper naval officers of the RCN who spoke with refined accents, but the officers of the merchant marine. Some were rough, ignorant fellows who had "come up through the hawse-pipe" from a stinking fo'c's'le to the grubby cabin of third mate in an ill-found coastal freighter, and were content with their lot. Some from the fo'c's'le had doggedly forced on and become master mariners. And, as the hierarchy of maritime life was arranged in descending order by professional classes (the captain, the mates—first, second, and third—the bosun, the seaman), so also was it divided socially. Those from shipping lines were either "Apprentices", who received a small wage while studying to become officers, or "Cadets", whose parents paid the company for the privilege. These last had spent their schoolboy years in training ships like *Conway* and *Worcester*, which ranked with public schools like Eton, Harrow, and Rugby, and were the merchant-marine counterpart of the Royal Naval College at Dartmouth and the Royal Military College at Sandhurst. The cadets went from the training ships to one of the posh shipping lines—the Cunard White Star or the Pacific and Orient. In such companies there was perhaps more ceremony, protocol, and spit-and-polish than in a Royal Navy battleship wearing the flag of a commander-in-chief. Promotion in these lines was much the same as in the Royal Navy or the imperial army: at the top was the Commodore of the Fleet in command of a flagship like *Empress of Britain* or *Queen Elizabeth*. This position usually carried a knighthood with it. My captain in *Andrée Dupré* had evidently come from such a background.

My captain in *Ulna* had not. He drank and cursed his way through the day and a lot of the night. He slept in the owner's cabin of his yacht, of course, and for a one-month period when some repairs were being made in the living quarters aft, I shared his cabin—there was just no other accommodation. He decided I should not stand night watches.

"A growing boy needs his sleep," he said. "You can come up to the bridge with me when a ship's to be boarded."

And so, some time between midnight and 0600 the Captain's voice-pipe would rouse me as the oow called, "Captain, Captain, sir. Merchantman coming in."

Blearily I swung my legs to the deck and fumbled for my sea-boots. From his side of the darkened cabin I would hear the glug-glug-glug of the rum bottle as the Captain primed himself against the freezing winds topside. And invariably he would growl at me, "Go back to bed. You're no goddam use to me."

Yet I never saw him drunk. Liquor was just part of his life, like food and sleep and work. He and the Mate once made a bet that they would go on the wagon for a month: it was Lent and the Captain was religious. At about ten minutes past noon one day the Mate came into the cabin just as the Captain was downing a tumblerful of rum and claimed he had won the bet. The Captain was flabbergasted.

"Jesus Christ! You meant the afternoons as well?"

This put him in a bad mood for the rest of the day. Leading Signalman Gay, also transferred to *Ulna*, wisely stayed off the bridge; that left the wretched signalman, who was younger than me, had been in the service about the same time as me, and knew about as much as me—very little. Between us we handled the lamp and flag-hoists badly. It was foul weather, too: wet, blowing a half-gale, heavy seas rolling us, breaking white over the shoals that surrounded us, and cold. The Captain glowered like a pregnant volcano, and erupted. The signalman caught it first.

"Signalman, do you know what happened at your nativity? Do you know what happened? I'll tell you."

He was shouting now, purple-faced.

"At your nativity, they threw away the baby and *kept the afterbirth!*"

He swung on me and lowered his voice slightly out of deference to my officer status.

"And I'm not so sure about you."

Yet he could be compassionate. During a previous stay in harbour (it was three days out and three days in), my mother had become seriously ill and I had driven her to the hospital at three in the morning. We sailed the next day. Mother's frightened, pain-wracked face haunted me and I was sitting on my bunk, crying, when the Captain barged in.

"What the hell's the matter with you?"

I told him.

"We'll be in harbour tomorrow. Take a week off and report to me the next time we're in."

"Should I put in a leave form or something?"

"I'll be content if you just do as your captain orders you and not ask damn-fool questions."

As soon as we secured alongside I hastened ashore.

"Let me know how she is," the Captain said gruffly, and shook my hand.

When I returned to go to sea again the whole crew had moved to a ship better suited for boarding, HMCS *Citadel*, a pilot boat that had been stationed at Father Point in the St. Lawrence. From this ship we didn't have to board from a dory: we just nuzzled alongside a merchantman and the boarding officer jumped on board.

My education continued under various types of officers.

I served with one captain who had the greatest collection of pornographic songs that it is possible to imagine and he sang them with an irrepressible gusto in a powerful, sonorous baritone, slapping his palms against his belly in the more rhythmic choruses and urging us to sing louder. His hobby was seduction and he would recount each new conquest with a boyish glee (he was thirty-six). I met several of his lady friends and was forced to the conclusion that his powers of persuasion were never severely strained.

Another officer was the shortest, ugliest, and most engaging man I've ever known. Walter wore his cap at an atrociously rakish angle and viewed the world with unselfconscious good humour. His consideration of all with whom he came in contact was instinctive and heart-warming, and this deep, undemanding affection found its peak in his love for his wife. I met her once, a plain woman disfigured by an accident in which she had lost an eye; but to see Walter's face light up when he spoke of "my old woman" was moving.

He'd been at sea all his life, and for several years before the war he had been a rum-runner. This, as far as the law would allow, was a fairly friendly business in Nova Scotia, each side knowing its adversary. Our captain in this ship, HMCS *French*, was one of the navy's finest officers and gentlemen. J. Willard Bonner was his name. Before the war he had been an officer in the marine section of the Royal Canadian Mounted Police. Captain Bonner and Walter would sometimes reminisce.

"You remember that night in the Gut of Canso, Captain?" said Walter.

"Yes, I remember well."

"Bet you thought you had me that night."

"Well, yes, Walter, I thought I had."

"You know where I went?"

Before the Captain could answer, Walter was off to get the chart, and, spreading it on the wardroom table, he continued,

"I spotted you about here. I was heading southeast and I was pretty sure you'd seen me. Well, instead of running down . . ." We would butt in, for the Captain was plainly embarrassed.

"Don't tell him all your secrets, Walter. He'll be chasing you again after the war."

"Ah, Captain, not me. Not an old shipmate."

"Well, I suppose not," said the Captain, keeping his fingers crossed and counting on a long war. As it turned out he never did chase Walter again, for Willard Bonner went down with his ship a few years later, not far from where he and Walter had broken lances. He drowned when HMCS *Charlottetown* was torpedoed in the St. Lawrence River, near Quebec City.

Some of these merchant-service officers, with reflective minds and a gently insistent curiosity, were among the most educated men you could meet. The long, placid voyages gave them much time for reading, and in addition they knew the countries of the world as shore folk know their own towns. Their deep knowledge of people and places made me feel a little silly about my freshman philosophy, imperfectly learned. It always seemed to me, however, that there was a faint air of melancholy about them all. The sea is a fine life for the young when the blood runs thick and fast and turbulent; but later, with a wife and children at home, there are the long night watches in which to brood on the months remaining in the voyage, the slowness of promotion, the certainty that one mistake will break you forever, and the despairing knowledge that it is now too late to start all over again ashore. This incubus they all lived with. Some, perhaps good shipmates and perhaps not, solved the problem with rum, referred to all natives with a skin even slightly darker than their own as "wogs", and visited brothels when necessary. Others went slightly mad in harmless ways.

One captain had a mania about getting the ship's latitude at noon by meridian altitude, a natural enough routine to the navigator. When this was impossible because the sun was obscured, the captain would fly into a tantrum, berate the navigator with a pungency and fluency that was awe-inspiring, and threaten to beach him when the ship next touched land. One cloudy day, just before noon, the captain was glowering on the bridge when up to the foremast yard-arm was hoisted a round, red, Danish Edam cheese. The navigator raised his sextant, carefully got a cut, and disappeared to work out his sight. The captain grunted, mollified, and went below. From the best of these merchant-service officers I learned valuable sea-lore, and from the worst, how to live and work cheek-by-jowl with men I actively disliked.

After eight months of examination work I was appointed to HMCS *Acadia*. We patrolled the approaches to Halifax Harbour and acted as a training ship. We had a gun but were a little chary of using it: the first time we fired it in trials all the wooden slats fell out of the bridge, the glass windows shattered, and the anchor let go. She was an old and ladylike hydrographic-survey ship who didn't fancy her new war-time role and seemed perpetually indignant.

I came to know the Nova Scotia coast from Chebucto Head to the Gut of Canso. In Pilotage I was as good as any, in Signals perhaps better than our signalmen, and I knew the Rules for the Prevention of Collision at Sea backwards. I started shooting sun-sights and star-sights. I was infallible at determining the ship's latitude at noon by meridian altitude—an easy computation but one that requires a knack with a sextant. I was at home in a small boat in a gale and once landed on Sable Island in heavy surf. My merchant-service officers taught me all they knew; and some of them were inexhaustible cornucopias. In brief, I was at home at sea. It was with a sense of gratification that I watched each time the shore lines were slipped and we pointed our nose seaward. It seemed I had found my niche in life, and I reflected with some satisfaction on the events that had brought me to it.

There were few complaints during that last peacetime summer of 1939. Although my father had not missed a newscast since Neville Chamberlain had made his arrangement with Adolf Hitler at Munich, and although our cautious Prime Minister had, during the summer, referred in an oblique way to theoretical Canadian participation in a possible war, life continued its pleasant round. The four-oared shell in which I assiduously practised every day had won all its races and I had hopes for a place on the Canadian Olympic team the next year. My tennis had improved. Alma was now giving me undivided attention after a contest that ranked in severity with clashes between stags in rutting season. My university, St. Mary's, had won the Maritime Rugby-Football Championship the year before; I had played full-back. There was no reason to suppose that we could not win again next year, and, since I had failed most subjects in my freshman year and had to repeat, the academic burden would be light.

But in September even our giddy crowd took notice when the Censorship Regulations were invoked and the Wartime Prices and Trade Board was set up. For the first time, the Canadian Officers' Training Corps, of which I was an enthusiastic member, had an irrevocability about it that I had not counted on. At age fifteen I had been destined for the navy, but when our family doctor assured my father and me that mother's cancer would not leave her long with us, I had withdrawn my application. A Canadian naval officer's early training was with the Royal Navy in England. The doctor had, however, neglected to tell my mother, and, with a stubbornness which is seldom attributed to the Irish but which they possess in full measure, she refused to die. As year followed year we gratefully forgot her illness and I slowly forgot my naval aspirations. Now they returned in full force. As Father pointed out, I could hardly continue to play college boy with war imminent.

On September 3, 1939, Britain declared war and within twenty-four hours *Athenia* was sunk. By the end of September about forty ships had been sunk around the United Kingdom. The German pocket battleships *Deutschland* and *Graf Spee* were at sea. The formidable bulk of the British battleships *Revenge*, *Resolution*, *Barham* and *Malaya*, *Repulse* and *Renown* from time to time towered above the piers behind the Halifax hotel where we danced. Their shore-side commander was Rear-Admiral S. S. Bonham-Carter, Royal Navy, and his headquarters was a yacht— HMS *Seaborn*—moored at a down-town jetty. Bonham-Carter was the first admiral I ever laid eyes upon; regarding his rows of war ribbons and heavy gold braid, I used to wonder what extraordinary combination of experience and class-room knowledge could take an officer so high. I thought dolorously of my failed courses at St. Mary's.

My best friend was Bob Gauvreau and his father was in the navy. Was Bob joining? Yes. Could his father get me in? Perhaps. He did.

My naval training commenced at the Gunnery School in Halifax. Besides teaching the science of naval gunnery, the gunnery branch taught parade training; and parade training was the first subject given to recruits.

"Instant and automatic obedience to orders is what I want from you gentlemen," said the Chief Petty Officer Gunner's Mate to our squad that wretched first morning when we fell in awkwardly on the barrack square.

Our squad numbered twenty and ranged in age from eighteen to fifty years. There were only a few midshipmen: Dan Hanington, Peter Chance, Bob Gauvreau, Bill Hanson, me; some acting probationary sub-lieutenants, Rammy Nairs, Bud Boyer, and "Tuffy" McKnight, who argued about everything. About half the class were RCNR just recruited from the Merchant Navy; three of these had been captains of their own ships and had had to exchange their four Merchant Navy stripes for two of the navy's. They looked outraged at what was happening to them. The rest of the class, like me, were RCNVR and came from business, universities, and the yacht clubs. A variety of trades were represented: there were stock-brokers, accountants, and real-estate and life-insurance salesmen. Somehow I couldn't visualize any of us leading our men into battle, and this impression was reinforced by the three chief petty officers who ran the Gunnery School. They made us feel properly humble and unworthy.

Chief Petty Officers Green, Bingham, and Prisk were gunnery instructors—the highest rating below warrant officer—and had spent the last fifteen or twenty years in the navy, joining at about age sixteen and working their way up. Possessed of immaculate appearance and impressive bearing, limitless knowledge and an implacable hatred of all who didn't know at least a part of what they knew, they were required to remove from us all trace of sloppy civilian behaviour, and to expel the notion that we had any intrinsic worth or dignity apart from our naval function.

This was, of course, the military's time-honoured method of conditioning a man for the stresses ahead. Parade training is the first step in inculcating an instant obedience to orders upon which lives and the safety of the ship will almost certainly depend, and the process has been known and practised for centuries, long before Pavlov's dog and "conditioned reflex" became household words. A man doesn't die in battle for his country, or for democracy, or to protect his womenfolk at home. He may have come to the scene of his death for these reasons, but when the moment arrives and the primal urge of self-preservation would send a man diving for cover, he does his duty and in doing it he dies. He dies because a petty officer told him to do this or that. The habit of obedience triumphs over inherited instincts. After taking away most of one's self-esteem the navy gives it back in ample measure, but in altered form. It is the gift of discipline, a gift that makes bearable monotonous, arduous patrols and sustains and strengthens in moments of danger. It is self-abnegation for the good of the ship and for your shipmates, and you know they feel the same way. If he has to, the captain will die, and, quite simply, he expects it of everyone else. This is all rather magisterial rhetoric for what starts on the parade ground. But that's where it starts, too true!

Bawling orders to a squad of officers-under-training, some of them twice one's age, is not easy to learn. I suffered the usual inarticulate agony when in charge of grinning classmates at parade-ground drill, the same inexpressible feeling of relief when I was again allowed to melt into the blessed anonymity of the ranks, and the same delight at the discomfort of the wretch who had taken my place out front. We heard the jokes that had served for generations, including the one about the panic-stricken sub-lieutentant who was marching a squad of trainees down the jetty and couldn't think of the next order. As they approached the brink, the instructor murmured, "Say something, sir, even if it's only 'goodbye'."

Or this: "What's the first thing you do before you clean your rifle?"

"Open the bolt, Chief, to make sure it's not loaded."

"No."

"Take out the magazine, Chief."

"No."

"What, Chief?"

"Look at the serial number to make sure you're not cleaning some other bastard's rifle!"

We grinned appreciatively; it seemed best to do so. I told the story to Father that night. Mother shot him a warning glance. He gazed at me compassionately for a moment and said:

"Open the bolt."

"No."

"Well, take out the magazine."

"No."

"What then?"

"Look at the serial number to make sure you're not cleaning somebody else's."

After suitable chagrin and a forced chuckle, Father's mind drifted back, I now suppose, to his first parade ground of thirty years ago. Mother said, "Very clever, dear."

Green, Bingham, and Prisk reported to another inscrutable, implacable figure, the Gunnery Officer. He was H. F. "Herr von" Pullen, a task-master who presided over the clanging breech-blocks and shouted commands in the gun battery, the forming and

re-forming squads on the parade ground, and the thoughtful
silences of the weekly written test. How I envied him, his
knowledge and assurance, even his view of life!

"You've got to *want* to see the scuppers run red with blood,"
he roared at us on our graduation parade. He didn't make it clear
if he meant the enemy's blood or ours.

"You've got to *want* to come to grips with the enemy. No captain can go far wrong by putting his ship alongside that of the
enemy. Board them. Give them a taste of cold British steel. Shoot
them. Club them. Subdue them!"

Well! All RCN lieutenant-commanders seemed so—how shall I
put it?—icy, bellicose, choleric.

I worked a fortnight for Staff Officer (Operations), who had
the distinctly naval name of Horatio Nelson Lay. He seemed
dangerous and I stayed very quiet. I worked with Staff Officer
(Signals) for a fortnight. He had been axed out of the navy some
years previously during an economy drive; then (it was said) he
had worked for the rum-runners for a while, setting up their communications system. Along with most of the rum-runners, he
signed up again at the outbreak of hostilities.

The Torpedo School was more gentlemanly. The sleek, deadly
torpedo was a one-shot weapon but it was the only weapon that
put a Canadian destroyer (the largest ship we had) on a par with a
German battleship.

"You will live to see the day," said the Torpedo Gunner's
Mate, "when one of these beauties, just one, will be the cause of
our sinking Germany's most powerful capital ship—*Tirpitz,
Scharnhorst, Bismarck,* I don't know. But one; at least one. So
learn your lessons well."

The Seamanship School was a tangle of knots and splices,
bends and hitches, sheaves and bearings, standing and running
rigging, blocks and tackles. A brisk young torpedo gunner taught
us the mysteries of the collision mat. He leaped about, he crackled, snapping orders, exuding a sense of urgency.

"The for'ard fore-and-after is manned by the fo'c's'lemen and
the after fore-and-after is manned by the quarter-deckmen, the
topping lift by the foretopmen and the bottom line by the main-
topmen. Right? Right! Now. . . ."

"Who's he?" I asked.

"Name of Budge. Pat Budge. Came up through the hawse-pipe
from boy seaman to warrant officer. Not bad."

"What's the bastard trying to do?"

"I dunno. Be an admiral, I guess."

In the Navigation School we learned a little about Pilotage
—terrestrial navigation. Celestial navigation was considered too
exotic for the RCNVR and the RCNR knew it, of course. In the Signals
School I felt more at home, thanks mainly to three years in the
Royal Canadian Corps of Signals as a boy-soldier.

I attended my first mess dinner at Admiralty House, where I
was living in one of the third-floor bedrooms. While formal mess
dress had been abolished for the duration of the war, many
peace-time officers still wore it in October 1939—stiff shirts,
wing collars, bow ties, bum freezers, trousers with broad gold
braid down each leg, last-war medals. I sat near the foot of the
table, humble in my best everyday uniform with only stiff shirt,
wing collar, and bow tie. Georgian candelabra glowed, glinting off
heavy, ornate silver-ware. After the traditional toast to the King,
the Mess President called for the toast of the day: it was a Thursday. The Vice-President rose and lifted his glass: "Gentlemen, a
bloody war and a sickly season."

The junior officers roared out the echo: "A bloody war and a
sickly season!"

This was a toast made for junior officers. Presumably, a
bloody war would kill only those senior to us, thus opening the
way for promotion; a sickly season was expected to do the same.
But that night we looked forward to the bloody-war part. The port
decanters went around again. I lit a cigar.

Still, it was true that, as I settled into duties in *Acadia*, I was
almost nineteen and hadn't yet seen a shot fired in anger. While I
struggled through basic training and bobbed up and down in potty
little tugs, yachts, patrol-vessels, and oceanographic-survey
ships, great events were passing me by.

When the war started in September 1939, Admiral Karl
Dönitz had fifty-seven U-boats, only twenty-two of which were
ocean-going units and ready for operations. New boats were expected at the rate of one or two a month, the output to be increased to between twenty and thirty a month. The German fleet
consisted of two small battleships, *Scharnhorst* and *Gneisenau*;
three "pocket battleships", *Deutschland, Admiral Scheer*, and
Admiral Graf Spee; two heavy cruisers, *Admiral Hipper* and
Blücher; six light cruisers; and thirty-four destroyers and
torpedo-boats.

Against these the British navy had fifteen battleships and

battle-cruisers, six aircraft carriers, and fifty-nine light and heavy cruisers. The French fleet (soon to be lost to us through the capitulation of France) consisted of eleven battleships and battle-cruisers, two aircraft carriers, and nineteen light and heavy cruisers.

A week before the official declaration of war, German merchant ships were given orders to run for home, and almost a hundred of them, totalling 500,000 tons, reached Germany safely, many with cargoes of war material. Three hundred remained in neutral harbours.

On September 3, Admiralty sent two messages around the world. One was a rather pedestrian announcement that hostilities with Germany were to commence. The other said, "Winston is back."

On September 4, Kapitänleutnant Fritz-Ludwig Lemp in U-30 torpedoed the passenger liner *Athenia*, and one hundred and twenty men, women, and children plunged with her into the Atlantic deeps. Three days later Kapitänleutnant Otto Schuhardt in U-29 sank the aircraft carrier HMS *Courageous* and 518 men, including the captain, died.

The tide of battle ebbed and flowed. In the South Atlantic, Kapitän zur See Hans Langsdorff in *Graf Spee* was driven into Montevideo harbour by determined and incessant attacks by Commodore Harwood's cruiser squadron, HMS *Exeter*, *Ajax*, and *Achilles*. Langsdorff's 11-inch guns should have been able to outfight the 8-inch of *Exeter* and the 6-inch of *Achilles* and *Ajax*, but they could not. Langsdorff scuttled *Graf Spee* and then shot himself. Harwood was promoted rear-admiral and knighted.

Graf Spee's supply ship, *Altmark*, running for home, was boarded in Norwegian waters from Captain Philip Vian's *Cossack*. The boarding-party leaped to *Altmark*'s deck. In the melee that followed seven German sailors were killed and two hundred and ninety-nine prisoners were released to the cry "The Navy's here!"

If new wars add new epics to a navy's tradition they also add new folk-tales. Captain Vian was a proper bastard to work under, a martinet: demanding, austere, ruthless. It is probably safe to say he was hated; certainly he was feared. The glowing legend of his dashing capture of the *Altmark* properly ends on the triumphant note "The Navy's here", and Winston Churchill made much of it. But there's a sequel. As British merchant-service prisoners, after months of incarceration, started to board *Cossack*, Vian's sailors spoke to them earnestly, "Go back, go back. You're better off where you are!"

Hitler wanted Atlantic bases, but his generals assured him that the capture of the Dutch coast would be a long and costly effort and that the French coast might be won after two years of hard fighting. How delighted Hitler must have been when France fell into his lap after only feeble resistance. What about Norway? The British were thinking the same thing, what about Norway? Both Germany and Britain made plans to invade; the German landings were scheduled one day in advance of the British. There were series of both hit-and-run and slug-it-out battles.

The German forces sailed: two battleships, *Scharnhorst* and *Gneisenau*, one cruiser, *Hipper*, and fourteen destroyers. They were to land two thousand soldiers at Narvik and seventeen hundred at Trondheim. The pocket-battleship *Lützow*, the heavy cruiser *Blücher*, light cruisers, and several smaller craft sailed for Norwegian and Danish ports. Off Trondheim HMS *Glowworm* intercepted *Hipper* and was damaged by her destroyer screen, but she closed in on the heavy cruiser. It was 8-inch guns against 4-inch in gale-force winds. *Glowworm* was soon a wreck, fires fore and aft, guns and superstructure largely shot away, holed several times, and sinking. She made a last effort. She rammed, tearing a 120-foot gash in *Hipper*'s side letting in tons of water. *Glowworm* sank; *Hipper* picked up what survivors she could and proceeded with her Trondheim operation. *Scharnhorst* and *Gneisenau* were sighted by the battle-cruiser *Renown* off Narvik: eighteen German 11-inch guns against six British 15-inch. In a ten-minute engagement, between snow squalls, *Gneisenau* suffered three hits, withdrew, and lured *Renown* off to the west—away from the German landings. Trondheim fell, and Narvik, Bergen, Kristiansand, and Egersund. At Oslo, *Blücher* was sunk. King Haakon and his government escaped aboard HMS *Devonshire*. The country's gold reserves went with them.

Everywhere the Kriegsmarine had scored brilliant successes. Their problem was to get out of these narrow fiords before an enraged British navy bottled them up. The Battle of Narvik began. Ofot Fiord is the approach to Narvik—twenty miles of narrow waters leading from Vest Fiord, and a thousand miles from Germany. Captain Warburton-Lee led three British destroyers toward Narvik and in a daring gun and torpedo attack engaged five of the German destroyers. Kommodore Paul Friedrich Bonte was killed and two of his destroyers were sunk, three damaged. Warburton-Lee retired then, but returned with two more destroyers and sank six merchantmen. He retired again down Ofot Fiord, threading his way between the high cliffs to Vest Fiord, twenty miles distant. Suddenly, three German destroyers dashed out from a side fiord, two more out of another fiord ahead. In a fierce running battle at point-blank range two British destroyers were sunk and one was badly damaged. Warburton-Lee was killed.

With the subjugation of Norway and the capitulation of France, Germany had seaports stretching from the Bay of Biscay to North Cape above the Arctic Circle—eight thousand miles of coastline. The news was received in Halifax with dismay and some yearning.

Finally there occurred an incident that convinced me that any further time in patrol-vessels was wasted. We were bobbing outside the net one winter night. The net swung open and four destroyers nosed out, increased speed, and were soon out of sight except for their luminous, boiling wakes. The battleship came next, black and implacable as she butted aside waves that rolled us; then the big transports: *Aquitania, Empress of Britain, Duchess of Bedford, Monarch of Bermuda, Empress of Australia.* Seven thousand more Canadian soldiers were off to war and I was still in Halifax. Next time in harbour I would do something about it.

I had now been long enough in the navy to know who controlled officers' appointments and I went to see him: it was the pale-eyed, red-faced Manning Lieutenant-Commander. I had not been in long enough to be deterred by such things as "the chain of command" or "the proper service channels of communication". I presented my case with a cogency and candour that took the Commander flat aback, and when he recovered he threw me out of his office. "Do you have the temerity to dream I've nothing better to do than listen to the whining importunities of every miserable snotty?"

A week later I left coastal patrols.

two

An Escort to the Convoy

My new ship was an armed merchant cruiser of the Royal Navy, HMS *Alaunia*. She had been a Cunard passenger ship, but the addition of eight 6-inch and four 3-inch guns transformed her into a warship. Nothing else was changed. The tapestries still hung in the lounges and the deep carpets received the same loving care by the same stewards who had tended them in peacetime. A library of perhaps five thousand books was a solace in quiet moments and a gymnasium catered to more energetic moods. The officers lived in the first-class accommodation, the chief and petty officers in the second, and the men in the third. The peacetime crew's accommodation was empty. Although the facilities seemed inappropriate to war, I settled gratefully into my double first-class cabin with adjoining bath.

The Commanding Officer, Captain Hugh Woodward, RN, had been retired from the Royal Navy many years before; the war had brought him back like an old war-horse scenting cannon smoke, or perhaps an old sea-horse scenting spume. He was tall, and heavily built, his face brown and deeply wrinkled, his hair long and sticking out in odd places from under his cap; at sea he wore blue corduroy trousers. He would sit for hours in his chair on the bridge with only an occasional snarl about the station-keeping. Nobody else ever sat in "Father's Chair", even when he was below.

This formidable creature had a habit of inviting midshipmen to breakfast, where the only conversation was a reluctant "Good morning" when you came in and a grunt when you thanked him and asked to be excused. The invitation came regularly every three months.

He had brought to the ship with him a retired colonel who, because of a maimed hand from fox-hunting, had been unable to get back in the army. This colonel had entered with the rank of sub-lieutenant, RNVR; his main function was Captain's Companion

(*above*) HMCS *Andrée Dupré*: an inglorious beginning. (*PAC*)
(*below*) HMCS *Acadia*: a dignified old lady from the First World
War. (*PAC*)

Ships in Bedford Basin await convoy orders. (PAC)

The gate at Halifax Harbour opens, allowing HMS *Revenge* to pass through. (*PAC*)

(*top left*) Returning to Halifax Dockyard from a winter convoy. (*PAC*)
(*bottom left*) Ice was a frequent menace when leaving St. John's,
Newfoundland. (*PAC*)
(*above*) A corvette in moderate seas. (*PAC*)

A typical convoy sails sedately to its destination. (PAC)

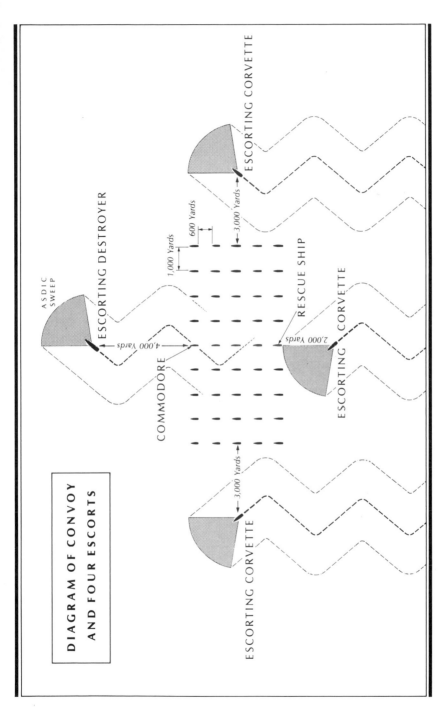

The formation of a convoy, and its four escorts.

Hauling survivors up the scrambling-net. (*PAC*)

or Father's Friend, for he had been a friend of the Captain since youth and they had settled near each other on retiring. He played cards with the Captain at sea and went on walks with him ashore. It was a peculiar sight—these two men, both tall, both about six‑ty, swinging their silver-knobbed canes, one wearing the four broad straight bands of the RN and the other, one thin wavy band of the RNVR.

We were the ocean escort of slow convoys from Halifax to the United Kingdom. After about three days out, *Skeena*, *St. Laurent*, and *Saguenay* would return to Halifax, and we were the sole guardian of some thirty merchantmen against surface attack. Considering that our opponents in any gunnery duel would be *Deutschland* or *Scheer*, there was a certain quiet desperation in the lookout we kept: these pocket battleships had a speed of thirty knots to our twenty, their 11-inch guns outranged our 6-inch by ten thousand yards, and the only advantage we had was that our holds were filled with empty oil drums and ping-pong balls so we would be hard to sink. At least, that was the theory.

An armed merchant cruiser like ourselves, HMS *Rawalpindi*, had made contact. Under the 11-inch gunfire of *Scharnhorst* and *Gneisenau* she scored one hit, was hit repeatedly herself, and turned into a flaming furnace—in fourteen minutes. Konterad-miral Marschall stopped the German ships for nearly two hours to rescue survivors; but when the shadow of the British light cruiser *Newcastle* hove into sight, the German ships made off into the dark.

The years 1940 and 1941 were the golden years for German surface raiders, just as 1942 was to be the golden year for the submarines. The German surface forces we in *Alaunia* could ex-pect to meet were many and formidable. Germany's largest and newest battleship, *Bismarck*, was to sortie for the first time in 1941 with the newest heavy cruiser, *Prinz Eugen*. *Bismarck's* 15-inch and *Prinz Eugen's* 8-inch guns were a match for anything we had. Although *Graf Spee* was a hulk in the mud off Montevideo, her sister ships, *Scheer* and *Lützow*, ranged the Atlantic. (*Deutschland* had been re-named *Lützow*: Hitler feared it would be a serious blow to German national pride if a ship named "Deutschland" was sunk.)

The land war had been disastrous. We had evacuated our soldiers from Norway in April, and from the beaches of Dunkirk in May. Later, the navy would evacuate soldiers from Crete after twelve thousand men had been lost in the defence of Greece. The

Royal Air Force had fought Goering's Luftwaffe to a standstill in the Battle of Britain, but was now exhausted. Both air forces were licking their wounds and regrouping for fresh attacks. Neither the army nor the air force would be capable of much offensive for nearly a year.

Only at sea did we retain the initiative.

Hundreds of millions of tons of vital equipment of every sort was needed in the United Kingdom, in Africa, in Malta. It all had to be convoyed in merchant ships and these had to be protected. Grossadmiral Erich Raeder, Commander-in-Chief of Kriegsmarine, intended to destroy these lifelines.

Herein lay an anomaly. Although we controlled the high seas we fought a defensive war around the convoys. At the same time we fought an offensive war against any break-out of German surface forces. A cordon was thrown between the Orkney Islands, which harboured the Home Fleet, and the Shetland Islands—100 miles; between the Shetland Islands and the Faeroes—250 miles; between the Faeroes and Iceland—250 miles; between Iceland and Greenland—60 miles. Radar had not yet been perfected for us at sea; in maximum visibility one could see only thirty miles foretop to foretop. At that range ships would still be hull-down below the horizon. Not a small-mesh net. Once through, a German ship had about twenty million square miles in which to operate. Elsewhere we had other scouting-forces at sea—the West Indies Squadron and the South Atlantic Squadron. The fall of France gave Germany a shorter escape route through the Bay of Biscay—from Brest, for instance.

The anomaly was compounded by Raeder's orders to his surface forces to avoid engaging superior or equal forces, or even, on occasion, inferior forces: witness *Scharnhorst* and *Gneisenau's* retreat from *Newcastle*. Admiral Marschall, of course, didn't know what was astern of *Newcastle* (nothing, as it happened), but he did know that if there was anything it would be unfriendly. When later he sighted a convoy, how he must have shuddered in sheer delight. But then *Revenge* steamed out to meet him and he withdrew. He didn't even draw *Revenge* with one ship while the other went after the convoy. What a shark among the herrings that would have been! No, Raeder couldn't afford the slightest damage to his ships.

A small pawn in momentous naval battles, I learned the duties of midshipman in large ships. *Alaunia's* officers were mostly from the Cunard White Star, the Pacific and Orient, and other posh

shipping lines. Correct, impeccable, strict, and formal, many of
them were master mariners, and all had been RNR for years
before the war. The bridge watch-keeping officers were
lieutenants in their thirties. One was a lieutenant-commander.
The navigator was a commander. I was Midshipman of the Watch
and as the hours I spent on watch at sea climbed slowly to the
two-thousand mark, I absorbed the sea-sense that is essential to
all who would survive. I learned station-keeping for the first time,
along with other duties vital to a midshipman serving with the
Royal Navy.

One is to make a good cup of ki. Every night the cook left bubbling on his stove a thick paste of what civilians call cocoa. This,
however, cannot be called cocoa because it isn't. It is ki, and to
add milk, hot water, and sugar in the correct proportions to suit
the taste of the particular officer who sent you for it is an art. The
preparation of the ki is also a means of squaring accounts with a
particularly tyrannous officer of the watch. We had one acerbic
watch-keeping officer who was universally disliked. As a cadet he
had attended *Conway*, and then served in one of the spit-and-
polish liners that run to the Orient. He knew how to train snotties;
he'd teach them what's for. Chivvy the little bastards and teach
them to obey orders, chop-chop.

One morning about 0330, when I was coming on watch, the
midshipman of the previous watch was mixing some ki for this
monster, the last cup before he was relieved. I watched, waking
up slowly and acquiring my night vision in the red glow. My fellow
midshipman spoke.

"Want a cup, Lawrence?"

"Yes, thanks."

He set another cup beside that of the Officer of the Watch.
The thick paste was spooned in, lots of sugar added, condensed
milk, boiling water. He stirred carefully, sipped both speculatively, added another half-teaspoon of sugar to each and another
dash of milk. He sipped again, nodded in approval, and pushed
mine toward me.

Then he turned his attention to the cup destined for the OOW:
he pulled back his heavy duffle coat and unbuttoned his fly.

"What on earth are you doing?" I asked.

"Pissing in it."

"Pissing in it?"

"Just a drop or two. Can't spoil the flavour. We all do it to *his*
ki. Don't you?"

"Ah, yes, of course."

I followed him to the bridge. It was a dirty, blustery, cold morning with snow flurries. I watched the OOW as, with obvious gratification, he gulped the hot ki. I felt some gratification too.

Another duty a midshipman must learn is to relay properly rude messages from one senior officer to another.

"Snotty, tell the Gunnery Officer that when I pipe 'Hands to quarters, clean guns', I mean to have them clean. That guns-crew on the fo'c's'le is more interested in keeping warm."

"Aye aye, sir."

"Gunnery Officer, sir, the Commander sends his compliments and wishes to have the fo'c's'le guns-crews more closely supervised."

"The devil he does. What does he think I am anyway, a miracle worker? I didn't want 'Quarters, clean guns' in this weather anyway. He only gives me the hands when he can't use them himself."

"Aye aye, sir."

"Commander, sir. The Gunnery Officer sends his respects and he'll see to it immediately."

Invaluable lesson, really.

More lessons were learned on cipher watch in decoding the messages sent to us from Bermuda, Halifax, or Whitehall. Even more interesting was the wireless room. We never transmitted at sea, for to do so would have caused our position to be plotted by every German raider in our vicinity. We kept a listening watch only. The voices of Bermuda and Halifax boomed in strong, but there were also weak, short messages of ships in distress, and muttered, muted conversations from around the world. Under circumstances of anoprop (anomalous propagation, connected with atmospheric conditions and the Heaviside layer), we picked up transmissions from the South Atlantic, the frantic bleat of , SSS—"Am being attacked by submarine"—followed by latitude and longitude. Or the cry RRR—"Am being attacked by surface raider"—followed by the latitude but no longitude. The transmissions were shortly cut off. Had a shell crashed into the ship's wireless room? Was the hand that had pulsed those dots and dashes so firmly now stilled? I felt a shiver: the war was closer.

The German raiders would not allow us to relax. Besides the big fellows, battleships and cruisers, there were the merchant ships. Where *Alaunia* had a displacement tonnage of about eighteen thousand, they would be between three thousand and eight thousand and better armed. Where the German raiders had modern guns, ours were old. The dates on the breeches of the two aftermost 6-inch guns were 1898 and 1903. Also, the German ships had from two to six torpedoes: we had none. Some Germans had a light aeroplane; two had small motor torpedo-boats.

The first of the German armed merchant cruisers, *Atlantis*, sailed from Germany in March 1940. Her objectives were, first, to sink Allied shipping by gun, torpedo, mine, or scuttling charge; second, to man valuable ships with prize crews and sail them to France. By carrying out these first two objectives, a third would be achieved: she would keep our heavy units hunting the vast reaches of the oceans of the world. And the German raiders disrupted convoy schedules; war and industrial material essential to fortress Britain arrived late—or not at all. Then *Komet* sailed from Germany and hugged the Norwegian coast to North Cape, where she turned east and steamed through the Barents Sea, the Kara Sea, the Laptevykh Sea, and the East Siberian Sea. She turned south through the Bering Strait, and into the Pacific. Russian ice-breakers cleared a channel for her. *Orion* sailed, and *Widder, Pinguin, Michel, Thor, Kormoran,* and *Stier.* It was to be over a year before the menace of German surface raiders was removed. In the month I joined *Alaunia* most of the Germans' victories were ahead of them.

Enemy intelligence was good and seemed to know even our single-ship sailings. German operations kept meshed the complex movements of surface warships, armed merchant cruisers, submarines, supply ships, blockade-runners, and prizes, all operating under the constantly changing conditions of maritime warfare. At one point, five German ships made a rendezvous in the Indian Ocean: *Scheer, Atlantis,* one blockade-runner, and two prizes. That year Germany had at sea, at various times, *Bismarck, Scharnhorst, Gneisenau, Lützow, Scheer, Hipper, Blücher, Prinz Eugen, Atlantis, Komet, Orion, Widder, Pinguin, Michel, Thor, Kormoran, Stier,* twenty-two prizes, thirty submarines, and thirty-six supply ships. Add it up: 105 ships. There was no "phoney war" for the navy.

Gunnery engagements between German merchant cruisers and ours were not infrequent. In July 1940 a sister ship of *Alaunia,* HMS *Alcantara,* sighted *Thor* and gave chase. *Thor's* four-gun broadsides hit *Alcantara* early; her speed dropped as she was hit repeatedly, but she scored two hits. Under cover of a smoke-screen and with *Alcantara* dead in the water but still firing, Thor drew off with four dead and three wounded. In November, Thor encountered another of our armed cruisers, HMS Carnarvon Castle. Thor fired torpedoes and missed, but in devastating broadsides, during a one-hour battle, hit Carnarvon Castle again and again until she was on fire and listing. Five months later Thor encountered HMS Voltaire. The battle lasted an hour, although Voltaire was ablaze after the first three minutes. Voltaire sank and Thor picked up 197 survivors.

Details of these gunnery duels reached Alaunia, plucked out of the ether by our radio receivers, beamed to us by Halifax when an action might draw us into its orbit, mailed to us in Weekly Intelligence Reports issued by Admiralty. We discussed them in the wardrooms of other armed merchant cruisers, HMS Jervis Bay, Ausonia, Rajputana.

Just as I and three other Canadian officers had been sent to Alaunia for training, Canadians served in other armed merchant cruisers.

Most of us had our action station as Officer of the Quarters of the 6-inch guns. How I yearned for my guns to be the best in Alaunia! How I worked my guns-crew—or tried to. The crew of Alaunia were mostly Royal Fleet Reserve sailors, having been retired from the RN or RNR for many years. (We had one steward who was sixty-three.) Most of the guns-crew were over twice my age; most wore First World War medal ribbons and had been at sea for twenty or thirty years. They just didn't take me seriously; and I didn't blame them. A two-week gunnery course and a year in coastal patrol. Faugh!

The guns-crew moved slowly and unwillingly to my uncertain commands. It wasn't that I didn't know the drill book, but rather that I lacked the confidence to drill these forty-year-olds. I noticed with what alacrity they jumped when the Gunnery Officer appeared, responding to his knowledge, his authority, his years at sea, his master mariner's certificate, perhaps. And I noticed something else, too: they feared him. It was not a fawning or an abject fear, for they were seasoned seamen and knew their job. But he represented Higher Authority. I did not. I wrestled with the problem for weeks, and finally made a great resolve, one of the most momentous of my naval career. I would run in the Captain of the Gun, a three-badge leading seaman, grown grizzled in the Service. I would lay a formal charge against him. I might not be old or experienced, but I would not be ignored.

"Guns-crew, close up."

They ambled to their positions.

"Guns-crew, fall out."

They slouched back. I adopted a weary, school-masterish tone ill-befitting my youth, but one I had observed in the Gunnery Officer.

"Captain of the Gun, you really must take charge of your guns-crew. They are far too slow. Drill them."

With a tolerant half-smile he stood back and drilled the crew and with tolerant half-smiles they obeyed him, though not much faster than they had obeyed me.

"That is really not good enough, Captain of the Gun. You do not seem able to take charge of your men. When this watch is relieved you will report to the bridge. I will see you there."

He stared, incredulous. This could mean only one thing: I was treating this as a disciplinary offence. The guns-crew fidgeted and looked away.

The Gunnery Officer was on watch when the Master-at-Arms read the charge.

". . . was derelict in the performance of his duties as Captain of the Gun in that he did not drill #7 guns-crew to the satisfaction of the Officer of the Quarters, Midshipman Lawrence."

The Gunnery Officer looked stunned.

"Good God! I can't believe it! Lawrence?"

"I ordered the Captain of the Gun to drill the crew, sir. There was no snap, no speed. The guns-crew were listless. I warned him, sir. The guns-crew continued listless."

The Gunnery Officer turned to the Captain of the Gun, who was standing with his cap doffed, grey hair blowing, and bracing himself against the roll of the ship. The Captain, in his chair about fifteen feet away, peered at us from beneath bushy brows. The tableau was plain to him: the young midshipman; the old leading seaman; the inscrutable Master-at-Arms; the stern Gunnery Officer talking to the defaulter.

"Can this be so?" asked the GO.

"No, sir. Yessir. Well, sort of."

"What precisely do you mean? No sir, yes sir, sort of. Were your crew drilling properly? Yes or no."

"Well, sir, the ship was rolling and we was taking white water inboard. . . ."

"Of course we were. This is often the case in a ship at sea. Were your crew moving as fast as they could? The OOQ says that they were not."

My nervousness subsided when I saw the position in which the GO had put the Gun Captain. A leading seaman could not argue against an officer's opinion—my opinion.

"Perhaps not. Perhaps they wasn't moving as fast as they could, sir."

"I won't read you a lecture on this," said the GO. "I won't point out that we are liable to go into action at any minute and the serious consequences of a slack guns-crew. Commander's Report."

"Commander's Report," echoed the Master-at-Arms. "On cap, right turn, double march, carry on with your work, report to my office at 0800 tomorrow."

The following day, the Commander was dumbfounded by the charge.

"He what?"

The Master-at-Arms repeated the charge. I felt a glow of pride at the sensation I was causing.

The Commander went to work. He could not understand it, yet the Gun Captain did not deny it. After all these years' service! Previously one of the best guns-crews in the ship. Always good scores at battle-practice targets. Slackness, at sea, in wartime! He need hardly point out to such an experienced leading seaman what the Naval Discipline Act provided as punishment for offences such as this. Previously an unblemished conduct sheet, too. . . .

The Gun Captain stood relaxed, cap doffed again. Ever since the Commander started his tirade, the Gun Captain was more at ease. He was getting his punishment now, he knew. No formal recorded punishment would follow a harangue of this magnitude. The Commander had a part; so had he. He looked appropriately contrite. The Commander ended his peroration.

"I shall not allow one mistake to blemish an otherwise blameless record," he said. "Cautioned. Not to be recorded."

"Cautioned," repeated the Master-at-Arms.

"On cap, right turn, double march, carry on with your work."

Cautioned, not to be recorded. Not recorded on paper, perhaps. But it was recorded in the minds of every officer and man in *Alaunia*. And all knew that another charge of the same nature would be fatal to this Gun Captain. The GO, in his wisdom, had given my first cry for authority the dignity of the Commander's attention when he could have read the same lesson and administered the same caution himself. The Commander, in his wisdom, had merely pointed out to the Gun Captain that he was a bit fed up having to remind a leading seaman that *all* officers are to be obeyed at *all* times, in every way. And I gained a little wisdom. I learned that statutes only talk about authority. If you want it, you've got to take it.

But there was more; namely, that there are unwritten but well-defined limits to authority.

Flushed with my first disciplinary success, I became a gimlet-eyed martinet. I reread Ship's Standing Orders. Good heavens! It seemed the ship was in the midst of a minor crime-wave, and I reacted accordingly. Sailors moved silently out of my path as I walked through the ship, their eyes wary and heads averted. I found the experience gratifying: power is a heady wine. It was not long before I had my second defaulter in front of the OOW, another leading seaman.

"... an act in contravention to Ship's Standing Orders in that he was leaning out the midship passenger hatch while ship was entering harbour."

"Anything to say?" asked the Master-at-Arms.

"No, sir."

"Two hours' extra work."

"You mean one day's number 16, sir?" asked the Master-at-Arms.

"No, I don't. Just extra work."

"Not to be recorded, I expect, sir," said the Master-at-Arms.

"That's right."

"On caps, right turn, double march, report to your part ship."

This was a different kind of "not recorded". In punishment it was the absolute minimum, and within the hour every officer and man in the ship would know that, although my authority had been publicly upheld, I had also been publicly rebuked.

"That was a damn-fool charge, Lawrence," said the OOW.

The Master-at-Arms slid away discreetly.

"But he was breaking ship's orders, sir; he ..."

"And you are acting in a manner unbecoming a miserable and wretched snotty by talking to me with your hands shoved in your duffle-coat pockets. Take them out. Stand to attention when you address me. Square your cap. Who do you think you are? Lord Beatty? Get off the bridge now and in future use your bloody loaf."

There seemed to be fine points about shipboard discipline that I'd missed. I sulked in my cabin for about an hour, then had dinner and turned in. I went on watch at midnight.

"You're adrift, snotty," said the OOW when I reached the bridge. "If I can get up here at 2350, so can you. Stand your watch in the crows-nest."

I started up the rigging. It was not cold but the wind tore at my clothes and the roll was accentuated as I climbed higher and higher. A roll to starboard and I was walking on all fours up a slight slope; the subsequent roll to port had me climbing hand over hand with my back dipping toward the water. I looked down at the foreshortened hull, then kept my eyes resolutely on the shrouds in front of my nose. An astonished able seaman clambered out of the crows-nest and turned the binoculars over to me.

"What's up, mate—sir?" he asked.

"Battleships," I said, "three."

Normally the crows-nest lookout is relieved every half-hour, but it was four hours before I felt the trembling of the rigging as my relief clambered aloft.

Next day I had the afternoon watch. The OOW was working on the chart.

"Snotty. Sharpen this pencil."

"Aye aye, sir," I muttered, and set off for the chart-room one deck below.

I heard the staccato of quick steps behind me, and out of the corner of my eye I saw the OOW doing that particular one-step that precedes the kick-off at a football game. Like a flushed rabbit I sprang for the ladder; but in the heaving of the ship from a half-gale and the wet of spume on the ladder-rungs, I missed my footing and bumped down on my tail-bone. I lay on the deck at the bottom, in considerable pain. The OOW glared down from the top.

"When I give an order, snotty, I want it obeyed with alacrity. I want snap. I want speed. You're listless."

There was a lesson here somewhere.

My turn came up again to breakfast with the Captain. This made the third time and I was beginning to feel more at home in his quarters, not that we ever spoke. He had a private stock of very good marmalade. I was munching toast, ruminating about the spaciousness and luxury of his living space. I wondered if I would ever live in such quarters. I sipped my tea. Then the Captain startled me by speaking.

"What do you think is the most important quality in an officer, snotty?"

Ah, here was a chance to shine. I leaped to the occasion. Summoning my best oratorical powers, I gave a brief discourse on officer-like qualities. Knowledge of your job: this above all. Courage, both physical and moral. Integrity. Endurance. Impartiality.

He listened morosely.

"I suppose so," he said. "Then, of course, there is the ability to leave well enough alone."

In an unprecedented burst of loquacity he went on,

"I sometimes wonder how we live with any comfort at all within the web of rules, regulations, orders, instructions, directives, and memoranda that may entangle us. You might add to your list an officer's ability to turn a blind eye to minor faults."

His point was sinking in when the duty cypher-officer knocked on the door-frame, stepped in, and handed the Captain a message.

"Looks as though we might get some action," said the Captain, and he left for the bridge plotting-room.

The *Scheer* had broken out through the Denmark Strait and was attacking one of our Halifax-U.K. convoys. In the late afternoon of that November day Kapitän zur See Theodor Krancke sighted the masts of the thirty-seven ships. Cautiously he and his officers studied the silhouettes as they rose above the horizon. Was there a battleship escort? No!

One large merchant ship pulled out ahead of the convoy and made for *Scheer*, firing guns, laying a smoke-screen, and firing red rockets. The convoy began to scatter. Krancke would have to deal with the sheep-dog before he could get among the flock. His adversary was an armed merchant cruiser, HMS *Jervis Bay*. Like us, she had 6-inch guns. *Scheer*'s 11-inch opened fire at ten miles—far outside the effective range of *Jervis Bay*. Krancke's tactics were sound. His broadsides soon wrecked the bridge and superstructure of *Jervis Bay*; Captain Fogarty Fegen had one leg torn off and an arm smashed. The stump was bound by the surgeon and Captain Fegen continued to keep *Jervis Bay* between *Scheer* and the convoy; he dragged himself aft and continued the fight from there with his remaining guns. As long as he had steerage-way he would block *Scheer*. At the cost of his own life and the lives of two hundred of his crew he gave the convoy twenty-two minutes of escape time.

The nightmare of operations-room watch-keepers in Halifax

became a reality: there was a battleship amongst the convoy. In the gathering gloom *Scheer* hunted, searching out victims by radar and searchlight. The thunder of the 11-inch and the 5.9-inch batteries was continuous. Tracer from the lighter guns swept the decks of merchantmen. Some fought back gallantly with their single 4-inch. They were overwhelmed. But the convoy had a twenty-two-minute head start and sweating engineers were coaxing every knot out of straining engines as the ships fled into the northern dusk away from *Scheer*. Five merchant ships out of thirty-seven were sunk. *Scheer*, with the help of a smoothly functioning supply system (she had a radar spare-part sent to her in the South Atlantic), went on to a 161-day cruise.

We in *Alaunia* were straddling one of *Scheer*'s anticipated escape routes. With thumping hearts and dry mouths we scrambled to our action stations whenever a mast showed over the horizon. My guns-crew were transformed—alert, eager, snappy—and looking to me as the officer who would direct their fire when the Gunnery Officer's central control was wrecked, which would be sooner, we knew, not later. With what intense relief and with what pious gratitude did we see the "enemy" masts turn out to be an independently routed merchantman. And I learned something else: if a German warship was our greatest enemy and the sea our second, monotony was the third.

Hipper broke out through the Denmark Strait and sailed across *Alaunia*'s Halifax-U.K. convoy route. Mercifully, she missed us. *Scharnhorst* and *Gneisenau* broke out through the Iceland-Faeroes passage and sighted an eastbound convoy. An R-class battleship (*Renown*, who had damaged *Gneisenau* off Norway) pulled out to intercept. Admiral Lütjens remembered and hauled off. Later, farther west, Lütjens found a Halifax-bound convoy and sank five ships. *Scharnhorst*, *Gneisenau*, and two supply ships now formed a 120-mile screen across the east-west convoy route, sank thirteen more ships, and sent three home to Germany as prizes. Total score: nearly 116,000 tons of shipping. Lütjens sailed home to Germany and honours.

And so for months we plodded our way across the bleak Atlantic at eight knots, sometimes reduced to four knots by gales and stragglers. We midshipmen always hoped for stragglers, for then the Captain would get in a fury, and, muttering uncharitable remarks about the delinquents in particular and the Merchant Navy in general, he would swing out of our station between the centre columns and thrash back at a glorious eighteen knots, cutting log-lines with lordly indifference. Stragglers are much like small boys caught in a minor misdemeanour and believe that to keep an impenetrable silence is the safest course, for we rarely got them to answer our lamp. Then the Captain, his face flushed, would pull alongside to hail them by megaphone. Several times the merchant captains must have thought he was going to lean over and pass them a note, so close did he come. And on one occasion, when adjuring a forlorn Greek ship to make less smoke or "every damn U-boat in the Atlantic would see us", a broad Scots voice replied that he "had been trying for seven years to stop this bastard smoking." We all held our breath. Father remained draped over the wing of the bridge, his face hidden by the big parka hood of his duffle coat, his shoulders shaking. He turned and went to his chair as the wallowing Greek dropped astern.

Within four hundred miles of England we were met by RN destroyers. Two more days' steaming would put the convoy safe in harbour; but once the rendezvous was effected and the flock handed over, *Alaunia* would swing about and head west to Halifax. Quite a few of the hands would come on deck for these junctions, for the bombings of Portsmouth had started and we were a Portsmouth crew. Only two days from wives and children they had not seen for over a year, they stoically watched the departing convoy, then went below.

A brighter side of our run was the visit to Bermuda. These clear, blue waters and white-and-pink houses set in lush foliage were heavenly after the drab browns and greys of a Canadian winter.

My station for entering harbour was on the flying bridge aft. As we steamed along the north coast of Bermuda toward Hamilton, I marvelled at the pellucid waters and at the beauty of the coral reefs. Those reefs could be quite dangerous, I thought idly. We tied up at the quay right alongside the main street. Across the road were shops and clubs, the Twenty-One and the Ace-of-Clubs.

We were in a fever to get ashore, but the Navigating Commander, with a perversity rare in him, insisted that I complete some chart corrections which he reckoned I should have finished a month ago. Thus, I was about six hours astern of my mess-mates when finally I got ashore. Flushed with five sherries (midshipmen were not allowed spirits), and feeling very nautical and ship-ahoy sailor-boy in my white uniform, I headed across the street for the Twenty-One. I ordered another sherry with an aplomb that only five previous sherries and twenty dollars in your pocket can give you. But where to go? I left.

"Take me to Admiralty House," I commanded. Respectfully touching his whip to his forehead the driver of the gharry shook his reins and we clip-clopped off. It was just dusk and the scent of jasmin and oleander was heavy. We wound through narrow roads and lanes, occasionally passing a cyclist bobbing along with his lamp burning softly. Admiralty House. That was the place to start the evening and meet some good convivial types. Admiralty House in Halifax would be just working up to tempo about now. The dice would be rolling, drinks would be ordered, girls would be phoned, and plans laid for the evening. I longed for a cigar. I would have one! Also a whisky: what the Commander didn't know wouldn't hurt him. We stopped for both. Under way again, I leaned back and put my feet up. What a life!

As we entered the gates of Admiralty House the salute of the Royal Marine sentry brought me to a more erect posture and we stopped before the door. Asking the driver to wait, I entered, cigar held high.

A dull scene greeted me—a dim light burning in the hall, and in the large living room off it, only one elderly gentleman reading a paper. A radio played quietly. A steward appeared, seemed surprised to see me, and approached uncertainly. The elderly gentleman looked up, puzzled.

There developed an itch at the back of my neck. Something was wrong. I felt a heavy weight in my stomach. The steward was standing before me. The elderly gentleman was on his feet, paper in one hand, pipe in the other. Good God! Admiralty House!

The Admiral!

The Commander-in-Chief, America and West Indies Squadron!

Vice-Admiral Sir Richard Kennedy-Purvis, KCB, MBE, DSO, DSC, RN! Not an officers' mess, but the Admiral's private residence.

I turned and fled, running out the front door and throwing my cigar in the bushes.

The home of one of the RCNVR sub-lieutenants was in Hamilton, and there his parents made us welcome. We met girls, hired bicycles, and toured the island. We swam on quiet beaches and danced at the Castle Harbour Hotel. Tourist prices still prevailed and soon our money was gone. In part because of the high prices, the sailors hated Bermuda. One restaurant posted a sign "Dogs and Sailors Prohibited". It was an unnecessary warning, for the sailors earned only about ten pounds a month and couldn't possibly have afforded to go in. I heard the sight-setter of my guns-crew grumble, "It might be wine, women, and song for the officers. But for us it's rum, bum, and records."

We received word that the Commander-in-Chief would be returning the Captain's call. I was Midshipman of the Watch that forenoon. The Officer of the Watch was on deck also, of course, and the Commander, and the Captain. We had a side party of three quartermasters, two bosun's-mates, a messenger, and a bugler. At the appointed hour the bugle brayed the "Alert", the bosuns' calls wailed in chorus, and the Commander-in-Chief stepped over the side. The Captain greeted him.

"Good morning, sir. Welcome aboard."

"Good morning, Woodward!"

How absolutely extraordinary to hear the Captain addressed by his surname only.

"May I introduce my officers, sir."

I had my hat jammed over my eyes and my telescope rigid under my arm in the rather foolish hope that this might prove an effective disguise.

"Haven't we met before?" asked the Admiral.

"I'm afraid that's not possible," the Captain said before I had time to reply. "Lawrence is a Canadian midshipman who joined in Halifax. This is his first time here."

"Oh, I see," said the Commander-in-Chief, "I see." And he gravely extended his hand.

"To turn a blind eye to minor faults . . ."

We sailed back to Halifax. The mail came on board. Naval Service Headquarters were pleased to inform me that I had been promoted to acting sub-lieutenant. I shipped my new stripe without delay. I never, even in rainy weather, wore the Burberry that obscured it. When driving a car, I carelessly rode with one arm resting nonchalantly along the window-edge. I stared fixedly at approaching sailors, and to my intense satisfaction garnered a richer harvest of salutes than previously.

There was a price to pay for the added glory. With increased rank goes added responsibility. I was told that after our next rendezvous I would stand a bridge watch on my own. Not Midshipman of the Watch, nor Second Officer of the Watch, but Officer of the Watch. It was not to be until we had delivered the convoy to the rendezvous off the south coast of Ireland, not until we were steaming back to Halifax with no convoy to complicate matters. And it was to be a daylight watch only; at night things happen too quickly. And during the forenoon—0800 to noon—when everybody was up and around. Never mind the strictures: I was to get a watch of my own.

Before this first sea-watch, however, came a watch of my own in harbour, 0800 to noon. As I took over the telescope, the officer I was relieving said, "Watch out for the Commander, he's liverish this morning. Watch out for Father, too. His steward tells me he's got his dark glasses on."

For an OOW in harbour, liaison with the Commander's doggie—a midshipman—and the Captain's steward and the Captain's coxswain was absolutely essential. The news that the Commander was liverish and the Captain hung-over, for instance, filled me with a sense of foreboding. It was up to me to supervise the ship's routine and any foul-up would bring as yet unknown retribution.

"Permission to carry on ashore for the mail, sir, please."

"Yes please, Postman."

An unending stream of ordinary and extraordinary matters arose. The Chief Engineer wanted to turn the starboard screw over slowly. Would I check the mooring lines? Yes, I would, and please let me know when you're finished. The Surgeon-Commander wanted several men piped for short-arm inspection; apparently any clap caught in the last port had run its incubation period. The Bosun wanted ten more men over the side to paint, Commander's orders. Would I get them? Yes, I would. The petty officer of the foretop reported he had lowered a lifeboat to the water's edge. I said thank you, wondering if I should do more. The Chief Yeoman of Signals wanted to dry bunting, the Chief Telegraphist wanted to send a hand up the foremast to splice a new antenna and produced the "transmission-broken" board into my safe-keeping until the work was finished. The loading numbers of the 6-inch-guns crews mustered for loading drill and were doubled away.

The Paymaster Commander said that provisioning had started through the midship hatches and he would be finished by noon if he could also use the quarter-deck gangway. I said I'd rather he didn't, the Captain was expecting guests, the captains of *Ausonia* and *Aurania*. The Paymaster said he'd see how it went. The Captain's guest popped, without warning, out of the dockside buildings and started up the gangway. The Corporal of the

Gangway phoned the Commander and the Midshipman of the Watch phoned the Captain's steward. The Commander puffed up just a minute too late, gave me a dirty look, and ducked below again. The Midshipman led the Captain's guests for'ard. Their eyes flicked everywhere, I noticed, like two housewives furtively examining the living-room of a third. Let them look: *Alaunia* would bear inspection. She was a little salt-streaked but the hands were washing down now with fresh water, the hands themselves in clean working rig, hats square on their heads.

For another hour the normal activities of the community bustled along, adjusted by the Commander, the First Lieutenant-Commander, the Mate of the Upper Deck, and a multitude of other heads of departments, to fit this day's current needs. Seven bells struck; in a half-hour I would have survived my first forenoon as OOW without disaster. The Paymaster Commander hurried up with the Butcher and the Chief Victualling Petty Officer in tow.

"Victualling Depot have sent the meat. It's arriving alongside in five minutes. It was loaded first thing this morning and it's thawing. It'll have to be brought inboard immediately and struck down."

"Yes, sir, I'll get extra hands. Can't you embark it amidship?"

"No, Sub, I can't. The passages are jammed with dry provisions. It'll have to come inboard over the quarter-deck."

"I can't do that, sir; the Captain has guests."

"Damn the Captain's guests. I have a hundred and forty-two carcasses of beef, fifty-eight pigs . . ."

"Just a minute, sir."

I phoned the Captain's steward. "Can you predict the Captain's movements, Petty Officer Rothery?"

"I think he'll be another hour, sir. They're just settling in, so to speak."

"What about lunch?"

"He didn't tell me to set up."

"All right. Don't let him get away without telling me first."

"Of course, sir," said Rothery reproachfully.

I phoned the Commander's office. "He's just gone to the wardroom for his morning gin." I phoned the wardroom. Line busy.

The Paymaster Commander stamped impatiently. Three trucks pulled onto the jetty, each piled high with bloody, steaming carcasses. From somewhere I remembered "the main quality of an officer is initiative and his main duty is to make decisions".

"All right, sir," I said to the Paymaster Commander, "get the trucks alongside this after gangway, please."

The Chief Victualler offered, "If your hands get it to here, sir, my hands will strike it down." The Butcher said, "I'll go stand by the fridges."

The sun, which had been playing hide-and-seek all morning, beamed now with full strength. Flies buzzed and circled above the truck. Embarkation commenced. "Up spirits" was piped. My hands went to work with a will, for it was clear that the sooner they got this finished the sooner they'd get their rum. My hands outnumbered the Pay Commander's. The pile of carcasses rose, the black cloud of flies transferred, a hundred or two at a time, from the truck to the quarter-deck. The sun shone warm and a faint aroma tickled the nostrils. The Paymaster saw the problem and sent for more of his hands. The only way to carry a 130-pound carcass is on your head. The hands had taken off their caps but their faces were soon smudged with blood. The mound of dead grew higher. Little rivulets of blood trickled across the white teak deck, running into the scuppers. (My God! I'm seeing the scuppers run red with blood. And I don't want to.)

The comic aspect struck the sailors forcibly. They started to chiyak: " 'Ere, Knobby, 'ere's yer Aunt Nellie, done in by Jack the Ripper."

"Cut the comedy," I rapped, but helplessly.

"Aye aye, sir," they replied cheerfully—but it was out of control. The gangway was slippery with blood and they slid and stumbled, cursing good-naturedly.

The telephone yipped. I answered, "Officer of the Watch."

"The Captain's going ashore."

"Hold him!"

"I can't, sir."

Rothery must have phoned the Commander as well. He materialized suddenly and gazed as though awestruck at the carnage around him: mounds of bodies, swarms of flies, decks running red, gory sailors hurling friendly insults at each other, grinning petty officers. His nose wrinkled in distaste at the stench of nearly rotten flesh. He gazed at me with an expression on his face I'd never seen before, but hatred was one ingredient. I opened my mouth to explain, but the Commander's stare was directed above my head. I turned and looked up.

The Captain and his two brother captains stood at the head of the ladder with expressions much like the Commander's as they looked at the abattoir below. Then their faces became impassive as they stepped down gingerly and picked their way between carcasses and sailors. The Captain lingered an instant behind his guests, and grated in a low voice, "Commander, please see me the instant I return aboard."

He and his guests disappeared into the dockside shed. The commander glared at me for a moment, then pointed his index finger at me, and crooked it slowly. I walked over carefully and saluted.

"Lawrence," said the Commander, slowly, deliberately, "you are an *incompetent!*"

He said much more, of course, and it was long before I got ashore again. But I learned how to run the ship's routine in harbour. I stood every forenoon watch and every afternoon watch, had the dog-watches off, then went on watch again until midnight. Thereafter I was free to seek my bunk unless, in the normal rotation of watches, I had the middle or the morning watch. The other OOWs were delighted.

We sailed again four days later. On this trip I would stand my first sea-watch as officer of the watch. Young officers were expected to make mistakes; it was just that my mistakes were a trifle too spectacular. And I didn't want my first sea-watch to be spectacular. Collisions were spectacular and completely undesirable. The next convoy would tell.

That eastbound convoy was the slowest I ever sailed with. For three days out of Halifax we steamed in fog. Father never left the bridge; he sat in his chair or slept on a raised grating on the deck alongside the chair, with a tarpaulin thrown over him to keep off the drips from the rigging.

After three days the fog cleared and gales set in. The convoy slowed from eight knots to six, from six to four. We bucketed about in a grey, cheerless world. The discomforts of gales were by now familiar. My one great fear was that we would be found by *Scheer, Hipper, Scharnhorst,* or *Gneisenau* and I wouldn't get to stand a watch of my own. Imagine going to the sailors' Valhalla and having to confess you never stood a watch of your own. Imagine telling Saint Peter, and him a fisherman. It would be like telling Saint Barbara you never fired a gun.

We missed the rendezvous. The gales cleared, and there was Ireland. Only a smudge on the port bow, but we were within sight of the United Kingdom. If only the RN destroyers didn't show up for another ten hours, it would be sensible for us to continue in to our home port.

They showed. When the green fields of County Kerry were discernible through binoculars, the destroyers steamed frantically over the horizon, formed up ahead of the convoy, and *Alaunia* turned to go back to Halifax. A convulsive shudder of disappointment ran through the ship's company. I was the happiest man on board.

The next morning I was up at six and on the bridge at seven-thirty. I saluted the Officer of the Watch. He was about forty years old, a master mariner, *Conway*-trained, and twenty-two years at sea, of which fifteen had been with the Cunard White Star Line.

"Good morning, Sub. You're up early."

"Good morning, sir."

"You ready to take over the watch?"

"Yes, sir."

"Righto. The base course is 280° gyro. The gyro is one high. North 68° West Magnetic. We're carrying out Zigzag Number Eleven. Here's the diagram. Right now we are on this leg; in six minutes we alter to that leg. Speed, eighteen knots: seventy-eight revolutions. Have you seen the chart?"

"Yes, sir. Latitude 53°11′ north. Longitude 12°20′ west. It's an 0800 run-on from morning stars."

"That's right. Guns-crews: number 3 and number 4 6-inch are closed up and both after 3-inch. We should be out of range of Boche aircraft by noon. You've seen the surface-raider report? The U-boat dispositions?"

"Yes, sir. The raiders all seem to the south'ard of us. U-boats, who knows?"

"That's right. We're at Damage Control State B. The meteorological charts show high-pressure areas practically all the way to Halifax. That's everything, I think."

"I think so, sir."

"Have you got the weight?"

"I have the weight, sir."

The watch was mine.

The officer lingered.

"Big day, eh?"

"Yessir," I said, impatient for him to be off.

"I remember my first watch. Seems so long ago now. Between Yokohama and Auckland, it was."

"Yessir." Would he never go?

"Well, I'm off."

"Yessir."

Tucking his lifebelt under his arm and picking up his binoculars, he clambered down the after ladder.

Now I really had the weight.

I was startled by the first report I received.

"Midshipman of the Watch relieved, sir."

I hadn't really thought about this; now I had a midshipman under me. A *Worcester* boy, RNR, a year younger than me. We drank together and went ashore together; he owed me ten shillings. Did I dare call him "snotty"? Perish the thought!

With a tact and dignity beyond his seventeen years, he acted as though we'd never met before this morning. He saluted.

"Do you want me to look after the zigzag, sir?"

"Yes, please."

The Yeoman of Signals silently handed me the signal log. The Petty Officer of the Watch reported "Blue Watch closed up". The lookouts reported themselves relieved, and went below. The lifebuoy sentry and the depth-charge sentry phoned in that they were closed up. The Quartermaster reported himself at the helm. The 6-inch- and the 3-inch-guns crews tested communications. The forenoon watch existed, it was mine, and I don't think I'll ever forget a moment of it.

Below my feet was a multi-million-dollar ship of eighteen thousand tons, three hundred souls on board. I was in charge and I was not yet twenty. I exalted in the privilege of belonging to an organization that would place such trust in one so young. About 0830 the Captain came up and sipped a cup of tea. About 0930 the Commander came up and drank his cup of tea. When he went below the Navigating Commander came up for a forenoon sunsight. Then the Gunnery Officer came up and drilled the 6-inch-guns crews for a half-hour. About 1130 I had the bridge to myself again. I noticed the Captain taking morning exercise, walking the breadth of the ship, one deck below, back and forth, back and forth. "Funny," I thought, "I've never seen him do that before. Must be the fine weather." And it was a fine day, a perfectly glorious day. I'd never leave the sea, I vowed.

Some days later I sat down to yet another breakfast with the

Captain. After his fourth cup of tea he said, "Sub, under what circumstances should a naval officer submit his resignation?"

I was caught flat aback. "Never, sir," I said. (Say something, even if it's wrong.) "Or rather, well, perhaps if his conduct has brought disgrace upon the Service."

"If his conduct has brought disgrace upon the Service, a court martial will take whatever action is necessary. Take the case of Admiral Matthews in 1744. The government neglected, starved, and impoverished the navy for years after the Treaty of Utrecht; Matthews engaged the Spanish and French with an ill-trained squadron, we must admit it, but he did quite well. The government needed a scapegoat to cover its neglect. Matthews was dismissed with ignominy from the service of king and country."

It seemed that sub-lieutenants enjoyed more erudite breakfast conversation than midshipmen.

"Or take the case of Admiral John Byng in 1757. A court martial orderd him shot. And he was."

I resolved to abandon Agatha Christie and read more naval history.

"No, Sub," the Captain continued, "the only time you have the initiative and should resign is either when you have been ordered to do something morally repugnant to you or when you think your resignation will call public attention to something that is degrading the Service."

"Yessir. I'll remember that, sir."

"And, Sub. Write me a two-thousand-word essay on Admiral Byng. Tell me if, in your opinion, he should have been shot. You are excused."

It was during these days that two great ships sailed from Germany, between the Danish Islands, through the Kattegat, through the Skagerrak, past the Jutland Peninsula, to a fiord near Bergen to fuel, then off again into the Arctic darkness. A supply train of eight ships was already heading to its stations, and six submarines were to form an ambush through which the German ships could lead pursuers. The electrifying news flashed around the Atlantic: *Bismarck* and *Prinz Eugen* were out, Konteradmiral Lütjens in command.

North they sailed into the Arctic Ocean, then west towards Greenland, then south through the Denmark Strait. *Suffolk* and *Norfolk* patrolled the ice-free passage between Iceland and Greenland at its narrowest point, a distance of sixty miles. They sighted Admiral Lütjens and his force. The alarm flashed to Admiralty and the chase was on.

The Commander-in-Chief, Home Fleet, Sir John Tovey, sailed his battleships, battle-cruisers, and carriers. *Suffolk* and *Norfolk* shadowed *Bismarck* and *Prinz Eugen*. Admiral Holland in *Hood*, the world's largest battle-cruiser, steamed to intercept; *Prince of Wales* was in company. The battle started at a range of twelve miles and within five minutes *Hood* blew up and carried all but three of her 1419-man crew to the bottom. *Prince of Wales* slugged it out, 14-inch against 15-inch, 5.25-inch against 5.9 inch. But she was newly commissioned with civilian workmen aboard; her main turrets were firing broadsides of three shells instead of ten. By the time the range was down to seven miles *Prince of Wales* was hit a seventh time. She turned away, making smoke. Elapsed time: twenty minutes.

The Deutscher Rundfunk was not slow in rebroadcasting the good news radioed in by *Bismarck*. Germany went wild at this great victory. But the seeds of *Bismarck*'s ruin had been sown. *Prince of Wales* had scored two 14-inch hits on *Bismarck*, causing her speed to drop from thirty-one knots to twenty-eight, and, more important, causing her to lose fuel oil. Days later she was caught, battered to a wreck, and sunk with her flag still flying. Lütjens died with her.

Convoys ahead of us were attacked and convoys astern of us, but we delivered our charges safely to the United Kingdom. On one eastbound convoy we heard the prolonged rumble of gunfire to the south'ard. The Commodore of the convoy prudently ordered an emergency turn of forty-five degrees to port to open the range. "The safe and timely arrival of the convoy" was our main concern. *Alaunia* beat to quarters and we steamed out to a position five miles to starboard of the convoy, between the convoy and the sound of the guns. For a freezing afternoon we stood to, but the horizon remained empty and as the dusk deepened we quietly rejoined the convoy and took up our usual station.

To the north of us, another armed merchant cruiser similar to us in every respect, the *Rajputana*, was patrolling the Denmark Strait looking for blockade-runners. She was torpedoed and sank with a loss of forty-two. On board was a Canadian midshipman, Dan Hanington, who was saved in what he described as an almost leisurely "Abandon ship". In fact, he went back to his cabin to pick up a few things he thought he might need in the lifeboat. God bless the Admiralty for filling our holds with empty oil-barrels and ping-pong balls! But his girl friend Margo was a friend of Alma's. The war was reaching our women in Halifax, and the Saturday night supper-dances at the Nova Scotian Hotel and the early-morning partings on the parents' doorsteps took on an added poignancy.

The long convoys were not too long to me. I was piling up watch-keeping time. No night watches by myself, but these would come. On one particularly tedious westbound convoy we laboured into gale after gale, practically hove-to. Day after day the Captain sat gloomily in his chair and surveyed the tumbling seas. He turned to me one day and surprised me by striking up a conversation.

"Do you know, Sub, that in 1534 Jacques Cartier sailed from France to Newfoundland in *twenty* days."

I murmured a non-committal "Aye aye, sir" and digested this bit of erudition.

After the death of *Bismarck* the remaining German raiders were hunted down one by one and so were their supply ships. The day of the long-range German sorties was over, but they had done good work. By December 1941, over fourteen million tons of our shipping had been sunk.

The day of the U-boats was at hand. Dönitz had built up his fleet to three hundred and ten.

With a perspicacity that I had not suspected, my red-faced Manning Commander in Halifax had appreciated the significance of the shift from surface to submarine forces. He appointed me to the anti-submarine forces. I was to join a corvette, HMCS *Moose Jaw*.

I left *Alaunia* with no regrets; there was more to learn in a different kind of navy. I had a quiet dinner at Admiralty House in Halifax, needing time to sort out my impressions. From time to time I took a flimsy out of the inner pocket of my monkey jacket. On it Captain Hugh Woodward, Royal Navy, had written that I had served to his "entire satisfaction", that I was "a promising young officer and fit for watchkeeping duties at sea". Now alongside my name in the Navy List would appear the navy's imprimatur on a qualified sea-going officer: Watch-Keeping Officer. I was an Acting Sub-Lieutenant, WK. Within the year—if I didn't blot my copybook—the "Acting" would be removed. Dönitz's U-boat-building program—forty a month—would do him little good now.

three

Safe and Timely Arrival

On a louring night in September 1941 two Canadian corvettes, HMCS *Moose Jaw* and *Chambly*, butted through a threatening sea off Greenland's bleak eastern coast. Our senior officer, Commander Prentice, RCN, in *Chambly*, was convinced from a study of U-boat dispositions that an attack was forming on Convoy SC-42. He was correct.

SC-42 had departed Sydney, Nova Scotia, eleven days earlier. Sixty-four deep-laden merchantmen covered twenty-five square miles of sea and carried nearly a million tons of vital cargo: fuel, grain, phosphate, lumber, ammunition, and iron ore. The voyage started quietly, except that the surly North Atlantic was whipping itself up to its months-long winter fury.

The first day found the convoy in the Gulf of St. Lawrence. Slowly, clumsily, the ships formed up on Commodore MacKenzie in the leading ship of the centre column. The sea was choppy, the wind had an edge, the sky was clear. Night fell. HMCS *Napanee*, *Matapedia*, and *Chicoutimi*, the local escort, were grateful for the good weather and for the brilliant moon that illuminated an ever-present danger at this season. Two large icebergs towered skyward, taller than the largest ship. SC-42 sailed between them. Three hours later fog closed in. Were there still bergs around? We had no radar to detect them. The submarine-detection set, called "asdic", might give an echo, but more often one had to rely on the feel of a sudden chill, or hear waves breaking against the base of a nearby berg. The second day passed.

On the morning of the third day the fog lifted, luckily; a few hours later a berg passed through the centre of the convoy, and a lone polar bear gazed at us forlornly. There was the mid-ocean escort ahead: the destroyer *Skeena*, and the corvettes *Kenogami*, *Alberni*, and *Orillia*. They would shepherd the valuable flock from now on. Here, off St. John's, Newfoundland, the Commodore

47

shaped a northeasterly course to Iceland. The latitude grew higher, the days grew shorter, the weather grew vile.

On the fourth day easterly gales set in, and so did the misery. Convoy speed slowed, seven knots to six, six to five. These wallowing, ponderous merchantmen have little steerage-way at low speed and they straggle. Escorts race to the rear, ordering them to "keep closed up", then adjuring them, then imploring them, all to no effect.

In the navy, we were taught to manoeuvre at high speed in close formation, about twenty-six knots and just three hundred yards apart. I remember Captain Woodward cutting obliquely through the convoy, ahead of one merchantman, astern of the next. The merchant-service captain finds this a nightmare. He is used to chugging quietly around the world with a whole ocean to himself; if another ship should climb the rim of his horizon, she will pass courteously about five miles off. But in wartime convoys, a merchant captain is surrounded by lunging ships just a half-mile off; the course must be constantly adjusted, now a little to port, now a little to starboard. The engine speed is always changing, now a little faster because his ship drops astern, now a little slower because she forges ahead. Some ships will take sudden unaccountable sheers and everyone scrambles out of the way. At night the ships are blacked out. Instinctively a merchant captain will try to give himself a little more sea-room, a little further astern of his proper station in the orderly ranks of the convoy. Oh yes, merchant ships straggle. And then a corvette comes yapping around their arses. Ignore the bastard!

On the fifth day the gale increased slightly. The sixth day was about the same. The convoy slowed to two knots. The seventh day it hove to, the ships barely keeping steerage-way. By the eighth day the discomfort was acute.

Under such conditions it is impossible to keep food on the galley stove. The bread grows green mould. The cockroaches pit-pat around the decks and bulkheads energetically. The rats grow bolder as they become hungrier. Dry clothes are forgotten. In the foetid, crowded messdecks exhausted men sleep where they can—in their hammocks if they are lucky enough to have a slinging billet, on the lockers, on the deck. Wretchedly sick men—landsmen just a few months before—lie in their vomit until the bosun's-mate hauls them up to push them on watch again.

It is fatiguing to be always grasping a stanchion, a table edge, a door-jamb, and to make progress only by short, lurching steps from object to object. On the other hand, most of our sailors were around twenty, and at this age physical discomfort is lightly borne. Many were not seasick. There was pride, exhilaration even, in seeing a small ship beating a powerful adversary. The sea is neither cruel nor kind—it is indifferent. When you are young, much of life can seem so dreadfully mundane. But a North Atlantic gale—that is something to pit your strength against. You could discern a sort of rueful happiness in the crew, and they drew closer together.

On the ninth day the weather let up a little and the slow crawl to Iceland resumed. The tenth day found SC-42 southeast of Cape Farewell, Greenland. We would traverse the Denmark Strait. This is where *Rajputana* was sunk, I thought; Dan Hanington went to *Orillia* after that.

Here the Commodore altered course to the north, up the Greenland coast. Plots showed an ominous concentration of U-boats across our intended track, but the diversion was in vain. On the eleventh day we were sighted by a patient U-boat captain.

A sighting-signal flashed to Dönitz; back came terse orders to U-boats forming the Greenland-to-Iceland barrier. One by one they slipped in silently for the kill. Some had many miles to steam but eight had the convoy in sight that night.

Towards the rear of the convoy SS *Jedmor* was straggling. She spotted a periscope, saw two torpedo tracks pass close ahead of her, and bleated the alarm. *Orillia* (Lieutenant Ted Briggs, RCNR) swept back and, although she gained no contact, kept the U-boat submerged. It would be many tedious hours before this U-boat could overhaul the convoy and threaten again.

Midnight and the start of the twelfth day marked the beginning of our travail. The blessed moon that revealed icebergs was now a cursed moon that illuminated ships like sitting ducks in a shooting-gallery. This day was forty-six minutes old when a dull "whump" told of a torpedo striking home. SS *Muneric* had time to sound the tocsin on her wireless and then plunged to the bottom, dragged down by her cargo of iron ore. There were no survivors.

Battle was joined.

Kenogami (Lieutenant "Cowboy" Jackson, RCNVR) wheeled and sighted the U-boat making off to the west. She gave chase, firing as she went; the U-boat dived, no asdic contact was gained, and *Kenogami* shaped course to rejoin the convoy.

The object of the escorting ships was not to sink submarines; rather, it was "the safe and timely arrival of the convoy".

Revenge was not sought, but protection for those ships that remained. A U-boat driven away and forced under was, temporarily at least, impotent, and would remain so for perhaps twelve hours. When you were outnumbered two to one, this respite was priceless. But if you stayed too long to hunt one U-boat, another could slip through the gap left in the screen.

Kenogami rejoined. Commodore MacKenzie sighted another U-boat ahead of the convoy. A few minutes later two merchant ships sighted a fourth. Slowly sinking flares threw a ghostly radiance over the packed ships; lurid tracer from machine-guns pointed a fiery finger to a fifth U-boat entering the columns of ships from ahead. This one *Skeena* (Lieutenant-Commander Jimmy Hibbard, RCN) pursued. As *Skeena* flashed by the merchant ships, their skippers bawled through megaphones the whereabouts of the submarine.

Commodore MacKenzie executed an emergency turn of all convoy ships of forty-five degrees to port. What had been an open lane for *Skeena* suddenly became an impenetrable wall of towering ships' sides. Impenetrable? Well, nearly so. By wrenching the helm over, by using full-astern power, then full-ahead, then full-astern, Hibbard squirmed through—sometimes by only a few yards. Though under fire from four convoy ships, the U-boats were doing their damage. SS *Winterswijk* blew up; a few minutes later SS *Tahchee,* then SS *Baron Pentland* burst into flames. *Skeena* swung around the stern of a merchant ship at full speed, firing star shell and attempting to ram the U-boat; it dived. With the water churned up by a score of wakes, asdic contact was impossible. *Skeena*'s depth charges arched out on the approximate position and exploded masthead high. No result.

Alberni chased a sixth U-boat on the starboard beam. *Kenogami* searched the port beam. *Orillia* took the damaged *Tahchee* in tow. There was a lull. *Kenogami* and *Alberni* dropped back to pick up survivors. Time: 0400.

At 0510 another torpedo struck. Star shell sought out the enemy. Thirty minutes later the familiar "whump" came again. A ship on the starboard side sighted a seventh submarine. Torpedo after torpedo tore into ships' vitals. Despairing rockets begged for help, but little could be given. Burning ships glowed red and star shell drifting down cast an eerie white light. Fiery tracer stabbed out, now here, now there; some seconds later the angry chatter of a gun was heard. Constantly came the rumble of depth charges exploding and, periodically, the thud of German torpedoes as the dogs of war harried the near-helpless flock. Wreckage littered the water: boats, floats, rafts, some with wildly waving men clinging to them, others empty. It's hard to say how many men were in the water, but the dull red flicker of the lights on their lifebelts seemed everywhere. Some men lolled limply, heads flopping. Some shouted weakly, hopefully, as an escort approached, and they yelled despairingly as she swept by. "The safe and timely arrival of the convoy" was the overriding consideration and an attack could not be broken off to rescue survivors.

On the convoy front, six miles across and on flanks of three miles each, the escorts fought on as best they could. By dawn, SS *Empire, Springbuck, Stargaard, Sally Maesrk,* and *Empire Hudson* had plunged to the bottom.

The forenoon was filled with alarms, periscope-sightings, torpedo tracks, attack, and counter-attack. At 1445, SS *Thistleglen* was hit; *Skeena, Kenogami,* and *Alberni* searched the area. The rattle of machine-gun fire drew them astern.

A periscope! *Skeena* lunged for a pounce attack. The periscope coolly surveyed the situation for twenty seconds and then quietly slid down. Charge after charge rained down on the U-boat, held now by asdic. A large bubble of air rose to the surface, along with some oil. Asdic contact faded. A probable hit? A possible, anyway. No time to wait, though; the convoy was unguarded. The three escorts bucked head seas back to their flock. There were no stragglers now. Dusk fell.

My captain in *Moose Jaw* was Lieutenant Frederick Grubb, RCN, the only pre-war officer on board. He regarded his officers with gloom, but also with the enthusiasm of a dedicated teacher who hoped to get his backward boys out of the primary grades.

The night before, I had had to call him because I lost contact with *Chambly*; she was guide and we were to keep station on her. I flogged around the ocean for thirty minutes before I told the Captain. That made it worse, and it was an hour before he got me back on station. The night before that, it was the opposite. I was too close, close enough to make his experienced eye stare in horror while mine was tranquil with the ignorance of one who has never heard the grinding, tearing, and shrieking of metal in the agony of collision.

The twelfth day had not yet ended. About 2130 the Captain said, "I'm going to get my head down." (He never slept; he either got his head down or put his feet up.) "Aye aye, sir," I replied.

"About one-two-oh revolutions should hold her."

"Aye aye, sir."

"You shouldn't need to alter more than five degrees to keep station."

"No, sir."

"Zigzag Eleven we're doing. You're familiar with that one?"

"Aye, sir."

"You've read my night orders?"

"Yessir."

He paused. Was there anything else? There was so much else, but my training would take years. There was nothing he could do tonight. He sighed and went below. The rigging creaked rhythmically. The bow wave hissed. All serene.

We jogged along comfortably enough for ten minutes, then the radio telephone (RT) blurted a message from *Chambly*: "Have good contact; am attacking". She veered to port. I followed. I heard a dull thud, and felt a tremor run through the ship. Two white rockets streaked up ahead. *Chambly* said "Submarine". I rang "Action stations". Four more white rockets to port. Star shell blossomed ahead in a sector search. Fireworks galore! A tanker was hit: the flame mounted. *Chambly* said "Firing now", and "thuck thuck" went her depth-charge throwers. Snowflake flares were everywhere, bright as day. The RT was a babble of messages; the ocean surface boiled white and soapy. A black metal snout reared out—U-501!

Just then the Captain arrived and in a tone of honest exasperation demanded, "Lawrence, what *are* you doing?"

Water streaming from her sides, U-501 set off in the general direction of Germany. We gave chase, the Captain manoeuvring to ram. With our primitive weapons this was the surest way for a kill; a corvette in exchange for a U-boat was a bargain. A white light blinked from the U-boat bridge; could it be the night identification signal? Could she be friendly? Impossible! What was the correct identification? Where was the signalman? The Captain was altering around now. Where was the bloody signalman? He arrived with a damp and grubby bit of paper and we peered at it in a dim light. Was the submarine one of ours? No!

The Captain roared, "Stand by to ram." U-501 altered away and we were staring up her stern tubes. The Captain eased over to her quarter, but she pointed her stern at us again. We eased back. Spinney's gun made a hit just for'ard of the conning tower. The Captain edged out again to U-501's port beam. U-501 swung violently to port and suddenly she and *Moose Jaw* were side by side about thirty feet apart, on a parallel course and at the same speed. Germans were on their deck, but our guns wouldn't depress enough to fire. For a few eerie seconds we regarded each other in silence. More Germans erupted out of various hatches; a long swell lifted us within fifteen feet.

"Stand by to repel boarders," sang out the Captain.

Now, there was a thought. U-501 was bigger than us, and probably had more men. A bit theatrical on the Captain's part, though.

The navigator was at my side. "Hal, have you the key to the rifle rack?"

"No. I gave it to Spinney."

"Oh, well, Father wants . . ."

"I know what Father wants but I haven't got it."

"Oh, all right, I'll ask Spinney, but he's pretty busy; his gun's stuck, I think."

I decided to do something myself about the Germans massing on the U-boat's bridge and deck.

"Lewis gunner," I shouted, "knock those Germans off."

No Lewis gunner.

I grabbed the strip Lewis gun from its rack, smacked on an ammunition pan, rotated it anti-clockwise (as taught by CPO Bingham, bless him), cocked it, hooked my arm around a stay to steady myself against the lurching of the ship, and fired.

Click.

No tension on the spring? Recocked. Pulled the trigger.

Click.

Still no tension on the spring.

The Captain swung slowly to port to open the range. U-501's bridge was crowded with Germans. Both ships were rolling about twenty degrees in a beam sea. On opposite sides of a trough the superstructures were close now, although the hulls were thirty feet apart. One German climbed the edge of his bridge, balanced precariously for a few moments, then hurtled through the air in an astonishing standing broad-jump. He landed in the break of the fo'c's'le.

"See what he wants," said the Captain, putting on more port helm to open the range more quickly. At the break of the fo'c's'le I was met by a groggy figure struggling to his feet.

"We are not fighting. Let me speak to your captain," he said.

I led the way up the ladder, thinking half-way up that turning my back on an enemy at the height of an action was unwise. The

Captain had manoeuvred into the position he sought, and was bearing in to ram. We hit, rocked over, metal screaming on metal. I arrived on the bridge with our guest.

"I am the Captain of the submarine. We surrender. Do not fire on my men, please. Do not fire any more."

There was no need. U-501's speed was reduced to about three knots, and beaten men crowded her decks. They jumped in the water and swam toward us. *Chambly* pulled up to U-501. Prentice shouted, "Stop your engines or I'll open fire."

Chambly's boarding-party pulled over in a skiff. The boarding officer, Ted Simmons, grabbed a German who was speaking English.

"Take me below," he ordered.

"No, no. It is not safe. We will sink. We have opened sea-cocks."

Thrusting him aside, Simmons grabbed two more and, jabbing their backs with his .45 and kicking their behinds, propelled them to the conning tower. On the conning tower the Germans refused to go below.

The swell was pounding the skiff badly; two seamen jumped in and lay off. A Lewis gunner covered the prisoners. U-501 was sinking by the stern; there was not much time. Simmons clambered down the hatch. If it were too late to salvage her, he might at least find code-books. The lights were out. By a dim torch he saw water gurgling up; then it flooded in with a rush. The stern sank further. Too late!

Pulling himself out, Simmons gestured the prisoners and his men over the side. Only the conning tower and the bow were awash now. With everyone off, Simmons jumped in the water. The bow reared and U-501 plunged down, sucking Simmons with her. He fought his way to the surface and struck out for the skiff. Hauling himself over the gunwale, he mustered his men. Stoker Brown was missing. Calling his name, they searched. No reply.

We in *Moose Jaw* had been circling the stopped *Chambly* and U-501. When we could we picked up prisoners. The U-boat captain, Hugo Förster, was uneasy about the lights we showed to do this. Twenty-nine Germans were plucked out of the water, frightened and exhausted. Two were dead and were dropped back in. Gunfire was continuous. And always there was the keening of the wind through the rigging and the rush of water down the scuppers.

The stunning fury of battle confuses inexperienced men. The

Cook blotted out the din and retreated in his mind to the safe, warm hash-house where he had been serving hamburgers only a few months before. In the white light of descending star shells and the orange glare of an exploding tanker, I spotted him. His action station was ammunition supply at the break of the fo'c's'le, but at the height of the action, 4-inch shells failed to arrive at the gun. Cookie was crouched in a corner under the gunwale, crying, head buried between his knees and arms over his head. A 4-inch shell splashed off the starboard beam.

I yelled, "Come on, Cookie, get on that goddam ammunition whip!"

I tried to pry his arms off his head but they were set like steel. He was a heavy man, about two hundred pounds, forearms as big around as my thigh. I kicked him in the ribs. No response. I kicked him on the knee. He gasped, raised his head, stood up slowly, and limped to the whip. Probably didn't get enough parade training, I thought; probably didn't get any. The supply of 4-inch to our forward gun resumed. Later the Cook went mad. It was only temporary—an hour or so—but it was a real enough example of shell-shock.

On orders to take up station on the starboard bow of the convoy, we got under way. Men left in the water shouted for rescue. But there was no choice; the safety of the convoy was paramount. We closed our new position. Guns flashed and shells from the convoy whistled over our bridge; the merchantmen were thoroughly and understandably rattled by now. We flicked our navigation lights—high-up, far-apart navigation lights that could not possibly belong to a U-boat. Fire ceased. It was midnight.

At 0145 of the thirteenth day, we sighted the torpedoed *Brerury*, sinking by the head. There were several boats near her and many men in the water. Those in the lifeboats were embarked; one thrust up the ship's cat ahead of him. I was dropped in the skiff to aid those in the water.

Many were dead. You haul a limp man in. Is he dead or only unconscious? You can't tell. Anyway, that man over there isn't dead, he's shouting. So haul him in and push the first out; there's not room for everyone. Fend off that German with your oar. Buggered if we'll pick him up when we can't get all of our own. Those we pulled in were packed between the thwarts, one on top of another; a skiff is small but we jammed in twelve. Others clung to the gunwales. Rowing was difficult; our freeboard was reduced to a few inches and high waves threatened to swamp us. "Back

port", "Give way starboard", "Harder!" Our bow rose reluctantly. Water splashed in. To bail was impossible. Star shell searched
ahead. A ship blew up. Flares revealed the squat silhouettes of
the merchantmen receding. *Moose Jaw* was called away.

"I hope she can find us again!" I thought.

The sea temperature was about fifty degrees, the air
temperature about forty degrees, and some of the survivors we
picked up must have been in the water an hour. They shook as
with the ague. We covered them with our duffle coats but it did little good. One cried softly.

A corvette at speed was passing about a mile away. I flashed
her. She altered, and, as her menacing bow bore down on us, I
prayed that we didn't look like the conning tower of a submarine.

With a flurry of boiling water she put her engines astern and
wallowed a few feet off. It was *Kenogami*. Unloading was tricky in
that sea. One moment we would be level with her gunwale, frantically hanging on to a bow and a stern line thrown us; in the next
instant we would drop dizzily and *Kenogami* would tower above
us as we desperately bore off to prevent being tipped by her bilge-
keel. The survivors had no strength to climb inboard. With lines
secured around their knees and shoulders, they were hauled up. I
found out, a year later, that only two of the twelve lived.

"Who's that," asked an interested voice on deck.

"Lawrence, *Moose Jaw*."

"This is Peter Cock. How are things?"

"A bit bloody."

"These chaps of yours are in bad shape."

"Yes," I said. "Where are you heading?"

"Reykjavik, to fuel."

"See you, maybe."

"Sure. I'll buy you dinner at the Börg Hotel."

The last body was swayed up.

"Can you tell *Moose Jaw* I'm here?" I asked.

"Sure, we'll ask her to come back. You'd better bear off
before we swamp you."

In a few minutes *Kenogami*'s captain, "Cowboy" Jackson,
shouted from the bridge,

"*Moose Jaw*'s coming. I'm off. Good luck."

Kenogami churned away.

In fifty minutes, willing hands in *Moose Jaw* hoisted the skiff inboard. We were wet, cold, tired. From the after end of the bridge,
the Captain viewed the hoisting with distaste.

"No! No!" he rapped. "When you belay a boat's falls, the first turn is taken *inside* the cleat."

At the time, the niceties of RCN procedure were far from our minds.

The fight around the convoy was still going on but lessening in intensity now. Survivors and prisoners crammed the upper deck and the Coxswain was trying to get them separated. The fore-upper mess was packed full also, as prisoners and merchant sailors shivered and stripped their sodden clothes. The Coxswain threw dry blankets at them.

The unconscious were stripped, bundled in blankets, and laid out on the lockers, and a teaspoon of rum was forced between their teeth. Some coughed and struggled up. Others didn't. We had no doctor, no sick-berth attendants, no medical personnel of any sort.

I climbed to the bridge. The convoy had closed the gaps in its ranks. The wind was freshening and the temperature had dropped. We went from action stations to defence stations. Eight hours had passed since we first sighted U-501.

After some twenty-five hours without sleep, I sought my bunk in the after cabin-flat. An armed sentry barred the hatch. "German prisoners down there, sir. Whole bloody flat's full of 'em."

These and thirty-eight merchant-service survivors put sleeping space at a premium. I lay on the wardroom deck; a bed at the Royal York Hotel couldn't have been more comfortable.

A few moments later, it seemed, the crash of our forward gun woke me. The wardroom was deserted. The gun spoke again and again. In a panic I rushed on deck. Another round; the acrid bite of burnt cordite stung my nostrils. About a hundred survivors and sailors were gazing intently off to port. They seemed strangely calm for a ship in action.

Of course, we weren't in action. The SS *Brerury*, loaded with lumber, had not sunk. The secret books had not been destroyed and it was too rough to put a boarding-party aboard. Round after round hit until she was ablaze. Her skipper, Captain Morgan, his officers and his crew, watched impassively as their erstwhile home was destroyed. We rejoined the convoy.

The murky dawn gained strength. We counted the night's losses. Seven more ships sunk. This brought the total to fifteen. Fifteen merchantmen for one U-boat certain and one possible. Not a good score.

There were reasons why it was not better. The simple fact

was that, even after two years of war, our ships were mainly manned by landsmen, some only a few months off prairie farms or city streets. In these two years the Royal Canadian Navy had grown from eighteen hundred to thirty-six thousand; the proportion of properly trained sailors to landsmen was one in two thousand. In *Moose Jaw* we were lucky to have two pre-war men on board, the Captain and Leading Seaman Nanteau. The Captain was twenty-six; the average age of the crew was twenty. That one can't make sailors overnight was proved presently. To me it was the most frightening aspect of the whole operation.

We ran out of feed-water for the boilers. In the excitement of the previous night the engine-room crew simply forgot to distil some. The heartbeat of the engine died away, the roar of the fans dropped, and we lay rolling heavily and silent. The survivors trickled up on deck and our sailors followed. From the upper deck they climbed to the fiddley one deck higher. Captain Morgan and some of his officers filtered to the bridge one deck above the fiddley.

That left only the Germans and the engine-room crew below deck. The engineers wouldn't come up until their honour was regained. The Germans couldn't because of the sentry. A merchant-service able seaman who's been torpedoed makes an excellent sentry; he's just trembling to jab that bayonet.

We fidget; conversation is jerky. The whine of the wind through the rigging and the rush of water as waves pass beneath us fill our ears. Never was there a better lookout kept; conscientiously our binoculars swept back and forth, back and forth.

"I presume that hands are standing by the boats and floats," said the Captain.

"Yessir," said the First Lieutenant, and slid below to make sure.

The Captain leaned on the bridge dodger and stared moodily at the receding convoy. There was a nasty set to his mouth. Thirty minutes passed. From the engine-room voice-pipe came a shout.

"Bridge?"

"Bridge."

"We're ready to go ahead."

The Captain nodded.

"Obey telegraphs," I said. They jangled. As the life-giving steam pumped through her veins, *Moose Jaw*'s heart throbbed again.

"Get back to station," said the Captain; "I'll be in my cabin.

Give the Chief Engineer my compliments and tell him I'd like to speak to him."

Things were looking up. Four more escorts joined—*Gladiolus* and *Buttermere* (British), *Mimosa* (Free French), and *Wetaskiwin* (Canadian; her ship's badge, painted on the gunshield, showed a shapely queen sitting in a puddle of water—the wet-ass queen). In the afternoon the 2nd Escort Group joined from Iceland—HMS *Douglas, Veteran, Saladin, Skate,* and *Leamington. Skeena, Chambly, Alberni,* and *Kenogami* detached to fuel in Iceland. We stayed. Peter owes me a dinner, I thought.

Regular watches resumed—four hours on, four hours off. The destroyers *Douglas, Veteran,* and *Leamington* formed a forward screen. Inside were the corvettes. *Moose Jaw* was on the starboard bow of the convoy.

"Do you know your station?" *Douglas* flashed at me one afternoon.

"Affirmative," *Moose Jaw* flashed back.

"What is it?"

"Green six-oh degrees, two to three miles, leading ship, starboard column."

"Then go back there; stay there."

It appeared I'd wandered. It must be the radar in *Douglas* that tells when we are out of station. The clack of the signal projector had brought the Captain to the bridge. He looked ghastly, having had no sleep, or just fitful dozes.

"What was that about?" he asked pettishly.

"*Douglas* asked what our station was, sir."

"Doesn't *Douglas* know? He's Senior Officer."

"Apparently not, sir."

Watch on, watch off. And following us everywhere was the ping of the asdic set as our sound-wave searched below the water for submarines. Ping, and the reverberations came back over the loudspeaker; reverberations and tiny echoes from seaweed, small fish, debris, fainter and fainter as the pulse of sound energy went out from the ship. Then, ping, again. Hour after hour, watch after watch. The asdic set had been going since sailing and wouldn't stop until we reached safe haven. Then it came.

Ping . . . beep. Ping . . . beep.

"Echo bearing Green three five" sang out the asdic operator, Gaudyk. I rang for the Captain but he appeared as I pushed the bell. I went to the asdic hut only a few paces away and put on my earphones.

"Extent of target?" I asked.

"Wait a minute. Right cut-on oh-three-oh." Gaudyk cut across the target, one step of two degrees for every transmission. Ping . . . beep. Ping . . . beep. Ping . . .

"Go back," I said; "you've lost her."

Ping . . . beep.

"Left cut-on oh-two-two. Extent of target eight degrees."

That could be a submarine with an extent of target of eight degrees. If it's too big it's not a submarine, nor is it if it's too small, unless it's a submarine bows or stern on. In that case one hears closing or opening Doppler, depending on changes in sound-wave frequency. This Doppler was slight high; that meant the target was approaching—a good solid, metallic echo, not fuzzy like a whale.

"Right cut-on oh-two-five. Left cut-on oh-two-oh. Target moving left," said the operator. "Range eighteen hundred yards."

The Captain had hoisted the large black pennant signifying a hunting escort. He stuck his head through the window.

"Well, what is it?"

"Just a minute, sir."

The operator pointed. Although the beeps were coming back to our earphones, there was no trace on the range-recorder. The stylus moving across the chemically treated paper seemed to be loose, too slack. Metal fatigue? Ping . . . beep. Ping . . . beep. The echo was getting stronger, the range closing.

"Sounds good to me," said the Captain. "How do you classify it?"

I looked at the operator. The picture was clear—extent of target, Doppler, range, movement, hardness of echo. He nodded.

"Submarine, sir."

About a minute had passed since the first beep.

"I am going in for a counter-attack," said the Captain. He rang full speed and *Moose Jaw* surged forward.

We started the sing-song chant of orders and information we had learned at the Asdic School back in Halifax.

"Centre bearing oh-one-six degrees. Moving left. Doppler slight high."

"Range?" said the Captain.

"Can't tell. The range-recorder's busted."

"Use your bloody stop-watch." I did.

"Range twelve hundred yards."

Moose Jaw was pounding at full speed, and bucketing about in the head sea. The resultant masking and quenching around the asdic oscillator, which protruded from the bottom of the ship, blotted out the echoes somewhat.

"I'm going to throw off ahead of the submarine now," said the Captain. "Fire when we cross over."

"Can't fire without a range-recorder," I said.

"Then fire when you get instant-echoes."

Ping . . . beep. Ping . . . beep. Ping, beep. Ping, beep. Ping beep. Pingbeep. Pingbeep.

"Fire!" I pressed my buzzers to the depth-charge throwers port and starboard, and to the rails aft.

Thunk, thunk, went the throwers and, turning quickly, I saw the charges arch out, port and starboard.

"Get me a piece of string," I shouted to the signalman.

"Carrying out stern sweep," said Gaudyk.

The repeated crashes of the depth-charges assailed our ears. *Moose Jaw* bucked and surged. Relocating an echo through the noise of your own propellers and the turmoil of exploded depth-charges is difficult. The Captain swung around to give us a clearer arc of search.

"There she is," said Gaudyk as the beep reappeared through the noise.

"This what you want?" asked the signalman, holding up a four-inch length of unravelled hemp.

"It'll do."

I stopped the range-recorder, knowing we had no spare stylus. This present one, loose or not, would have to work. My hands were cold. The wind blew in the open window in front of me and out the open door behind. The Captain leaned in the window. He seemed to be enjoying himself. Nothing like a bit of adrenalin to perk up a man. With clumsy fingers I looped the string over the fragile copper stylus to the solid metal. Gaudyk kept his oscillator pinging back and forth across the fuzzy echo.

If there was a submarine down there, and one cannot be sure until it is blown to the surface, the U-boat crew would be hearing a crackling noise across their hull as the probing asdic finger of sound poked at them. The U-boat captain would know when I cut off and when on again, just as I knew. He would be measuring my range as I measured his. As I was listening for the whirring of his electric motors, he was listening for a speed-up in our thumping reciprocating engines. His hydrophone operator would be passing the same stream of information to him that Gaudyk and I were passing to Captain Grubb. His torpedo crews would be poised the way my depth-charge crews were. His heart would be pounding like mine.

"Range fifteen hundred yards," said Gaudyk.

"I'm altering around and reducing speed," said the Captain. "This'll be a deliberate attack."

As I bent over the range-recorder, my head was near the wheel-house voice-pipe.

"What's going on?" I heard a voice ask.

"Lawrence is fixing the fuckin' range-recorder with string."

"He's what?"

"Christ! What a navy!"

Clearer came the beep. And strong and true the stylus marked the paper. As the paper rotated, the successive range-marks formed a slant to put the firing-bar on. This attack would be more scientific than firing on instant-echoes.

Our black pennant had brought a consort racing up to assist us. She angled out at ninety degrees from our line of attack. After we dropped the next ten-charge pattern, two asdics should be holding the submarine. The convoy had done an emergency turn of forty-five degrees away from us. The submarine was still heading in toward them. The U-boat captain should have a fairly clear picture. He knew we were two corvettes from the sound of our screws. He would therefore make his alteration of course and speed later rather than sooner, for we had a smaller turning circle than destroyers. He would know from the receding and slower thump of the merchant-ship screws, as well as from their slower rate-of-change-of-bearing, that the convoy had altered away from him. If our counter-attack had shaken him up, he could seek sanctuary in the boiling water of the wakes of some thirty large ships. All our asdic would get back from the wakes would be confused noise. Probably it was the best thing he could do, now that he had lost the element of surprise.

The Captain studied the slope of the range-recorder trace through the window. In a conversational tone we fed him information on centre-bearings, Doppler, range, movement.

"I'll throw off twenty degrees," said the Captain. "Fire when you're ready. We're getting into the wakes of the convoy. Looks like this will be your last chance. If your submarine alters away it means he's going up under the convoy. What's the Doppler now?"

"Slight high. He's still closing."

Again the ping beep. Ping beep. The range-recorder trace crept under the firing-bar.

"Doppler same," said Gaudyk. "Slight low. He's altering away. Doppler marked low. Range four hundred yards."

Now we could hear the pulse of very rapid engines. The U-boat was making his move. Increasing speed and altering away, across the track of the boiling convoy wakes. I held fire until the range trace was lost in the transmission trace. "Hydrophone effect," said Gaudyk.

Again we heaved and shuddered as the ten depth-charges exploded. What must it be like below?

"Carrying out stern sweep," said Gaudyk.

But there was nothing. Or, rather, there was everything except a submarine echo. We nosed around for a half-hour and then took up our former station. Too many contacts ended that way. No escort saw this U-boat get out from under the convoy, if ever it did.

Our infinitely slow crawl across the Atlantic had finally brought us within range of aircraft from Iceland. One droned overhead now and disappeared in a search ahead of the convoy. It soon proved its worth. Back flashed a message—a submarine on the surface fifteen miles ahead. *Veteran* and *Leamington* creamed out. By dusk they were back and laconically reported the kill of U-207. Fifteen merchant ships for two U-boats certain and one possible. A better score.

The night was quiet and the fourteenth day dawned with no further losses, as did the fifteenth. On the sixteenth day three United States Navy destroyers patrolled about ten miles to the south'ard. Their role was ambiguous: the United States had not yet declared war.

This day the German captain and two of his officers were aired for an hour. HMS *Veteran* steamed across our bows on some little errand or other. Hugo Förster nudged his Executive Officer, Werner Olbring, and pointed. They talked excitedly.

"Speak English please," I said.

"I was just saying," the Captain said apologetically, "that there is *Veteran*."

"Come on," I said; "anyone with a book of warship silhouettes knows it's a V-class. How do you know it's *Veteran*?"

"You see the galley funnel? How it crooks aft and then up again? None of the others is like that. Oh yes, that's *Veteran*. We've seen her often."

It made you think.

On the seventeenth day low fog set in. Above the fog it was glaringly bright; the sun was high in a cloudless sky and the mist lay just on the surface, perhaps to a depth of a hundred feet. Five U-boats still shadowed. That forenoon we spotted one. It dived. We creamed in with a counter-attack and dropped depth-charges on the swirl, but it took us over a minute to get there. In that time a U-boat could drop to a two-hundred-foot depth and make a speed of nine knots—in any direction. The search was fruitless. After dark a merchantman was sunk, but it was to be the last. As we laboriously climbed our great-circle course toward Scotland, the U-boats drew off, some to Germany to refuel and replenish torpedoes, some to re-form the Iceland-to-Greenland patrol.

At 0100 on the eighteenth day the dimmed lighthouse at the Butt of Lewis flashed out a welcome; one flash every twenty seconds. It was good to be "home". We thought of sleep—and food.

Owing to our hurried sailing, fresh provisions had not been embarked, and ten days previously we had broached the emergency rations. Merchant-service cooks had vied with our cooks to prepare tasty meals, but their talents were tested with only bully beef and ship's biscuits. Even those were scarce, since we were feeding a hundred and forty-nine instead of the usual eighty.

The Commodore ordered his ships into a narrower formation. We wheeled to starboard around the Butt of Lewis, and steamed south through the Minches. To have land on both sides was comforting. To see men walking across fields was amazing. A gentle east wind blew off-shore, moist and earthy.

The convoy dispersed under local escort, some for Londonderry, some for Liverpool, some for Southampton. In fives and tens they broke off. A few bore gaping holes in their sides, a few listed to starboard or down by the head, but they had made it. Skippers came to the wings of their bridges.

"Thank you for your escort," they bawled. We waved.

On the nineteenth day our anchor rattled down in Loch Ewe.

Captain Grubb was taken off to the hospital ship. He had been sick prior to joining *Moose Jaw*, but the doctors had pronounced him "fit for sea". Now, foul weather, bad food, and days of snatched sleep had taken their toll. Later that day we weighed anchor and proceeded on the last short lap.

On the afternoon of the twentieth day we secured at Princes Pier, Greenock. Armed soldiers waited for our prisoners; for them the war was over.

The U-boat captain stood by the gangway as his men went ashore. He offered his hand to the first, but the man brushed by him, as did the next. With heads averted, the U-boat's crew filed swiftly into the waiting vans. Their captain stood smiling fixedly until the last one was ashore and then, thanking us courteously, he followed. Can a captain ever be the first to leave his sinking ship? Even to prevent further deaths among his men? Years later we heard that in his prisoner-of-war camp he was arraigned for court martial by his brother officers. If found guilty of cowardice he would have been executed. Others were. But the prison authorities found out about it, and he was transferred.

Our survivors left with fervent thanks. One oiler hung behind the rest. He was a small man, with a scraggly beard. His pale eyes peered out of the hood of a borrowed duffle coat too large for him. He fumbled in his pocket and pressed something into my hand.

"Thanks for fishing me out. I'd like you to take this," he said; "I havena much. *Brerury* is the second ship I've lost."

I looked at the small pistol he had given me, a thirty-two. "Yes," I said, "I'd like that, thank you." We shook hands and looked at each other, uncertainly.

"What will you do now?" I asked.

"Dinna fash yoursel'. I'll pick up another ship. They're short-handed and it's ma trade."

He jumped up the gangway and clumsily saluted the quarter-deck, a bit embarrassed, I think, at his momentary weakness to navy folderol. He trotted after the rest, turned, and waved.

"Goodbye," he called.

Goodbye.

four

The Wolf-Packs Gather

The hands set to cleaning ship. In the afternoon *Moose Jaw* was towed into dry-dock to have her bow repaired. In the evening I went to the Bay Hotel for a decent meal. It was run by a woman called Jeannie and she made a great fuss over Canadians. Jostling for the available tables were the usual crowds of Poles, Free French, Norwegians, Danes, British, Aussies, and New Zealanders, and about ten Canadians I knew. We were mostly officers of the Reserve, but there were a few straight-stripers from the Home Fleet cruisers, carriers, and battleships.

A girl from the Women's Royal Naval Service was at every man's side. "Wrens" they were called. The whisky went down and the hilarity went up, but after about an hour I was struck by a gloomy streak. I ordered eggs and bacon and another double whisky, found a corner by myself, and allowed my thoughts to drift.

It was September 1941. I had been in the navy over two years. How placid had been those months in coastal patrols. How orderly and civilized had been my year in *Alaunia*. We'd even had a Surgeon-Commander there. Then I'd been made an Acting Sub-Lieutenant; the "Acting" had been removed and now I was Sub-Lieutenant, WK.

I remembered how the word "corvette" had thrilled me and conjured up visions of the days of sail. We'd got to work quickly enough building corvettes in Canada, and a good thing too. When the U-boats outnumbered the escorts you had a sad night ahead of you. *Moose Jaw* was about the twentieth to be finished; she was built in Collingwood.

The war in the Atlantic had attained quite a Canadian flavour in the early months of 1941. The corvette HMCS *Collingwood* had been commissioned in 1940; then came *Wetaskiwin*, *Cobalt*, and *Chambly*. This year we had commissioned *Levis*, *Agassiz*, *Orillia*, *Kamloops*, *Chilliwack*, *Nanaimo*, *Rimouski*, *Pictou*, and *Trail*.

66

Thirty-five more corvettes would follow in 1942, we were told.

How many years of convoys lay ahead? The Allies had lost nearly five hundred ships, two million tons. The tactics of counter-attack, stalk, and deliberate attack were sometimes successful, mostly not. We kept the convoy closed up and screened it as best we could. And we picked up survivors—when we could. *Skeena* once took 220 from *Cheshire, St. Laurent* over 800 from *Arandora Star. Saguenay* was torpedoed but made harbour with 21 dead. *Fraser* was rammed and sunk with 47 dead. *Margaree* was rammed and sunk, 142 dead.

We welcomed replacements: the lend-lease destroyers *Annapolis, Columbia, Niagara, Hamilton, St. Clair, St. Croix,* and *St. Francis.* Built by the USN in the 1920s, they were slim-beamed and shallow-draft. They rolled—how they rolled—and they were cranky. But we were in no position to be particular. Three merchant ships were being sunk for every one replaced by the combined efforts of the Canadian, U.S., and U.K. shipyards. For every U-boat sunk, eight were being launched.

I had left Halifax in June of 1941 with orders to join *Moose Jaw* at Collingwood. Saying goodbye to Alma, I boarded the westbound train from Halifax. A critical rereading of my orders revealed that they were open to a different interpretation; namely that I was to join *Moose Jaw* in Montreal as she passed through on her way down the St. Lawrence River. Interpreted thus, they would give me several frivolous days in Montreal. It was a long time since I'd trod the dance floor of the Normandie Roof at the Mount Royal Hotel. Victor, the *maître d',* would wonder what had become of me. The war could go on without me, while I cavorted around the Normandie Roof and sundry other night-clubs and blind pigs. At Chez Maurice a show girl joined me at my table after the show, drank my champagne, and allowed me to take her home—to a women-only hotel. Eleanor was her name.

When I caught up with *Moose Jaw* at last, the ship's company numbered about sixty and the officers four. On the morning of my arrival the Captain was pointing out to the Navigator that "Colours" was a ceremony that had been honoured for several hundred years, and, although attended in large ships by guards, bands, and buglers, in small ships should be attended at least by a signalman to hoist the ensign (our ensign staff was still bare, while the ensigns of other ships fluttered in the morning sun), and a bosun's-mate to pipe the "Still". The Officer of the Watch should be there also to salute as the ensign rose. The Captain received only a surly grunt from the recently awakened Navigator, who was now, having being sent for, standing unshaven and hung-over on the quarter-deck. Social amenities deteriorated as the discussion progressed. The Captain spoke of naval customs, traditions, discipline, and setting a good example. The Navigator stared at the deck and grumbled. Finally the Captain roared,

"The trouble with you, Pilot, is you've got too much of a mind of your own."

"Yes," replied the Navigator, "and I'm bloody well going to hang on to it!"

The Captain then rose to heights of biting invective and cutting obloquy. I realized I was watching the performance of a master—quite the best I had seen since the Commander of *Alaunia* saw my first defaulter. The Navigator realized it, too, and respect dawned in his rheumy eyes. He murmured, "Aye aye, sir; sorry, sir; won't happen again, sir," and shuffled aft.

I watched this scene from the jetty. After a prudent pause of about ten minutes, I reported aboard. A now impeccably dressed Pilot greeted me at the brow and conducted me to the Captain's cabin. The wisdom of waiting for the ship in Montreal seemed questionable now that Captain Grubb sat before me. But he didn't raise the subject and neither did I. During a chilly interview, the Captain assessed my potential, and concluded that I was as much as he'd a right to expect. After all, his second-in-command had been a tobacco salesman in Vancouver just eight months before and this was the man's first trip to sea. Ruddle-Brown, the Navigator, had a merchant-service mate's certificate and hadn't been to sea for twenty years. Spinney was just six months out of McGill with no sea experience. The Captain released me to the wardroom.

I was greeted enthusiastically by the other officers, who informed me I was duty. Fatigued from the exertions of the past few days I didn't demur but sank gratefully into the familiar routine. The rest of the officers rushed ashore in the late afternoon, and with the patient smile of the satiated I watched them go. Let them gambol. I had work to do.

My jobs were Asdic Officer and Gunnery Officer, which presumably meant that I detected submarines under the water, tracked them with my asdic set, blew them to the surface with my depth-charges, and then nipped smartly onto the bridge to finish them off with my guns. Filled with dreams of coming glory I set out to learn something about the equipment, and the next two days passed pleasantly.

We sailed for Halifax on a bright June morning. Our bow swung out from the pier and caught a brisk three-knot current, and we set off at a spanking pace down the channel. Navigating down the St. Lawrence from Montreal to Quebec is easy. There are buoys every mile or so and all you have to do is stay between them. Since, however, this is one of the busiest waterways in the world, traffic is heavy and ranges from small bateaux to large liners. Passing the large ships on curves in the channel is tricky. However, with confident ease I swept along and attributed the rather strained expression on the Captain's face to gas.

After Quebec the river widens and it is here the navigator owes so much to the churches whose shining spires make such good fixing-points: St. Pacôme, Rivière du Loup, Trois Pistoles, Rimouski, Mont Joli. By Cap Chat the northern shore dipped out of view and we swung south around the Gaspé Peninsula and headed for Nova Scotia. Between Cape Breton and the mainland is the Gut of Canso, a twenty-mile-long strip of water about a half a mile wide. We swept through with a good tide behind us; without regret I passed the lights of the patient examination vessel in which I'd spent so many months.

After Isle Madame is the Atlantic, and *Moose Jaw* made her first gentle curtsy to the ocean that was to be her battleground for the next three years. Then she made a deeper obeisance; and another. A crash of dishes below told of unsecured gear. A signalman bolted for the leeward side and Bernatchez, the Yeoman, regarded him wryly.

"Nous arrivons," he murmured.

The next morning was warm and calm as we threaded our way up the familiar Halifax Harbour. A handkerchief fluttering in the City Hall window marked my special homecoming, for, although censorship regulations were vehement on this point, I'd made my arrival known to Alma in my last letter by allusions so vague and circuitous that Admiral Canaris himself could not have known that *Moose Jaw* had arrived to swing the tide of battle in favour of the Allies.

Truly we were needed. Every ship was.

Dönitz had by now two types of operational U-boats, the five-hundred-ton with a cruising radius of eleven thousand miles and the seven-hundred-tonners with a cruising radius of fifteen thousand miles. They carried up to twenty-one torpedoes, which could be fired from as far away as fifteen thousand yards, from a depth of two hundred feet, and which drove in at a speed of forty knots. On the surface the U-boats could go faster than a corvette; submerged, for short periods they could make nine knots. And they could remain at sea for as many as four months.

The German submariners were the finest a good navy had to offer. Günther Prien in U-47 had carried out the skilful penetration of the anchorage of the Home Fleet base at Scapa Flow and had sunk *Royal Oak*. By March of 1941 he had sunk 245,000 tons of Allied shipping. In the same month he died under the depth-charges of HMS *Wolverine*. Joachim Schepke in U-100 had over 230,000 tons on his tally when he was rammed and sunk, also in March, by HMS *Vanoc*. A third ace, Otto Kretschmer in U-99, had sunk over 200,000 tons before U-99 was destroyed by HMS *Walker*. Kretschmer lived to become an admiral in the post-war navy. Endrass and Frauenheim were not far behind these three great commanders. U-boats ranged from North Cape in Norway to Cape Town, South Africa. They probed also far into the Atlantic. Wolf packs of perhaps six or eight U-boats were homed onto convoys by long-range aircraft, and, just a year before, had sunk shipping within eight hundred miles of Halifax.

At Halifax, *Moose Jaw* was fuelled and provisioned. Then the staff officers took us to sea and gave us a rudimentary working up. One day doing search turns with *Chambly* and basic anti-submarine tactics, the next day gun trials and the firing of a few depth-charges. Then off to war. What a pitiably inadequate preparation!

The convoy route from Halifax to the United Kingdom was four thousand miles, a distance that imposed impossible demands on our short-legged escorts with their small fuel capacity. Closer to the convoys' destination by five hundred miles was Newfoundland, and we had based an escort force there. Newfoundland was to be *Moose Jaw*'s operational base.

The oldest of Britain's colonies is a bleak rock. Granite cliffs plunge into the sea and little green can be seen. The cold Labrador Current mixes with the fringes of the warm Gulf Stream and in the summer produces almost incessant fog. In the winter it is lashed by gales. By contrast there is the unfailing warmness of the Newfoundlander's heart.

The entrance to St. John's is a crevice in the granite cliff, and the Atlantic swell surges constantly, making it difficult to pass through. We were picked up by a long swell (*Moose Jaw* was only 290 feet long) and swept forward. A violent helm order to port, another to starboard, slow the engines, and we were steaming placidly up this almost land-locked harbour, the water as calm as a goldfish pond. There were a few huts clinging to the base of the cliff just inside and a fish-packing plant clamouring for the attention of our noses.

We had now been in commission about two months and had not yet practised more than a few basic exercises in Halifax. Our senior officer in *Chambly*, "Chummy" Prentice, was a monocled, bushy-eyebrowed, hard-driving type with a career in the Royal Navy behind him. Not the sort of man to lie in harbour when his group needed working up. It would be several days before the convoy departed; we would spend them at sea.

We sailed. It was blowing hard outside and in less than sixty seconds we went from the calm of the harbour to the writhing motion of a corvette in a half-gale. There was no sound of breaking dishes below, for the lesson of the Gut of Canso had been well learned—stores were in short supply and most messdecks had about one plate to every five men. The signalman made his first-of-the-voyage rush to the leeward side. Bernatchez compassionately took over the signal lamp again.

Chambly liked to keep his ships in company close astern. Even so we got in too close and for a minute or so when we were sitting on top of a swell we were looking right down on *Chambly*'s quarter-deck. And when we plunged into the trough she had just vacated, her stern was at eye level, as, with a flick of her backside, she pitched over the next one. The Captain was wedged behind the binnacle watching intently.

"It is virtually impossible to hit another ship from astern," he said casually. "All you have to do to avoid is put your helm over."

The training had begun, and it went on without end. If you were sick you carried your bucket with you. It was while we were on this training cruise that we had been sent to the aid of SC-42. Well, we had aided SC-42, I suppose; and we had delivered it to U.K. ports—or what was left of it. I could not dispel the memory of my effort to pull a gasping survivor into *Moose Jaw*'s lifeboat. His arm had come off in my hands.

"You like another whisky, eh?"

I looked up. It was a Polish lieutenant.

"Yes, sure, thank you," I replied.

"No good to sit here and think," he said. "Come with me to the
bar and not think. Better to come back from the past and live in
the present, eh?"

So we did.

The laughing mob opened to receive us back in. A Wren was
sitting on the bar, singing:

> If I were a marrying girl,
> Which thank the Lord I'm not, sir,
> The sort of man that I would wed
> Would be a rugby scrum-half.

The chorus roared out:

> Oh, he'd push hard
> And I'd push hard
> And we'd push hard together;
> We'd be all right in the middle of the night
> Pushing hard together.

My Polish friend jumped up alongside her.

> If I were a marrying girl,
> Which thank the Lord I'm not, sir,
> The sort of man that I would wed
> Would be a rugby quarter.

> Oh, he'd put it in
> And I'd put it in
> And we'd put it in together;
> We'd be all right in the middle of the night
> Putting it in together.

Some senior types, mostly Escort Group Commanders, were
drinking more quietly at the end of the bar. With them was the
Commander-in-Chief Western Approaches, Admiral Sir Percy Noble. He apparently liked to get his information at first hand, and
frequently came up from his HQ at Liverpool. The words of one of
the Escort Commanders could be overheard: "If only we could get
some ships, sir, that were especially constructed to pick up survivors. That would be their only function. It's hard to leave your
own men in the water. And you shouldn't really stop to pick them
up. . . ."

In a fortnight or so *Moose Jaw*'s bow was repaired, Captain
Grubb had returned from hospital, and we set sail for Tobermory,
a work-up base on the Isle of Mull. Tobermory was a peaceful
fishing village with grey stone cottages ringing the harbour and

green fields behind. At least, it was peaceful for the inhabitants, if not for the ships sent there to work up. The Reigning Deity, Admiral Stevans, saw to that.

I don't know what "Monkey" Stevans' age was at that time— middle sixties, I would guess—but he was tireless. We had barely dropped anchor when he and his staff bustled aboard. He inspected the ship's company in their working rig, then the messdecks, storerooms, magazines, shell-rooms, cable locker, paint locker, the upper deck, boats, floats, standing and running rigging, depth-charge throwers and rails, 4-inch gun, .5-inch machine guns, Lewis gun, wheel-house, and bridge. Then he sent us to action stations. Dummy-runs in surface fire and AA fire; tow for'ard, tow aft; dummy depth-charge runs; flag-hoisting exercises (bridge knee-deep in bunting); rig collision mat (for'ard fore and after for'ard, after fore and after aft. God bless Budge). In thirty minutes we had ground to a standstill in indescribable chaos. After our ineptitude had been cogently displayed, the Admiral mustered us aft.

"Moose Jaws," he said, "you are a very brave group of men."

We nudged each other, winking. This was better. After all, we had sunk a submarine.

He repeated, emphasizing each word, "a very brave group of men."

The Admiral swept his eyes slowly over us, over each one of us, lowered his voice, and said, slowly, distinctly, earnestly, "To have sailed this ship, in the condition she is in, from one side of the Atlantic to the other."

We had no rest from that moment. We slaved from sunrise to sunset, and at any hour of the night, action stations might ring and we'd pour on deck to find an enraged Admiral bellowing for more speed.

We left Tobermory in late November, exhausted. Apart from church service, the weekends were working days like any other. As we steamed out into Loch Sunart we saw the Admiral boarding an inward-bound corvette. We had profited: there was a new spirit of professionalism in *Moose Jaw*.

A convoy had sailed north from Liverpool and picked up some ships at the Solway Firth, more at the Firth of Clyde, and the last at Loch Ewe. We steamed north up the broadening Minches, wheeled to the west around the Butt of Lewis, and headed back to Newfoundland. As we left the Minches, another convoy, SC-44, was arriving in the Outer Hebrides. The first Canadian corvette had been sunk in SC-44—*Levis. Mayflower* and *Agassiz* picked up forty of her sixty-man crew.

The escorts of that winter's convoys rushed from emergency to emergency, from sinking to sinking, outnumbered by U-boats, with inadequate equipment, through survivors howling for help, chasing a precious asdic contact that might give them a kill. Rescue ships, specially fitted for taking on survivors, were not yet with us. And it didn't matter that much. Five minutes in the freezing water was the most a man could last.

Death was practically painless, the doctors assured us; the victim just drifted off. Of course, if there was fuel oil in the water, he tended to choke and retch, and dying was not so simple. And if depth-charges were exploding near by, the end was definitely painful. Not to worry, though; a grateful government was aware of our plight and we would soon be issued with a new design in lifebelts. The Mae West we wore at the time simply tied around the chest and was blown up by mouth. The new, improved lifebelt fitted like a jacket and fastened down the front. It had a buoyant flap that stood up behind a man's head. The better to lie back and rest? A yellow hat made him easily visible. By night, a little red lamp on the top of this hat blinked on and off. And that was not all: it featured a large, triangular padded section to protect his balls from exploding depth-charges.

Sleet, snow, rain, ice a foot thick on the forward superstructure; four hours on watch, two hours chipping ice, sleep and eat in between. It was a macabre and desolate winter. When we were not under attack, monotony and a numbing fatigue took their toll. In a December fog *Windflower* was rammed by a ship in the convoy and one of her boilers blew up. *Moose Jaw* was in the station just ahead of her. I heard *Windflower* go, but couldn't see anything, of course. *Nasturtium* picked up forty-seven of the crew of about sixty, but three later died. Gale followed gale that extraordinary winter, which was just as well, as it kept the U-boats under. We envied those U-boat crews—warm and dry a hundred feet down. I spent my third Christmas at sea.

The first Christmas, 1939, we had rolled our guts out in *Ulna;* the second, in *Alaunia,* forty officers had dined together with sherry, port, and cigars; this third Christmas of 1941, we passed in a gale, a hurricane really, just south of Iceland. About one in the afternoon of Christmas Eve the wind gusted to one hundred and twenty knots. There were no big waves; the tops were blown off them and spindrift covered the surface so we couldn't see the water. Occasionally a black wave would poke up through the white spume. We couldn't keep a lookout: the force of the wind pressed our eyelids closed. About two in the afternoon hail fell and drove the bridge watch inside the asdic hut. Stones a bit smaller than marbles, driven at nearly a hundred miles an hour, broke the window of the asdic hut at the forward end and on the port side before we got up the wooden black-out screens. After twenty minutes they ceased. I went on watch again at midnight. It was black and the convoy was scattered, so there wasn't anything to do but steer the mean course and keep steerage-way on. And keep a lookout for merchantmen: *Windflower* was fresh in our minds.

The submarines would be at one hundred feet tonight. Probably the enemy had had a carol service earlier in the evening, certain in the knowledge that tonight's rest would be undisturbed. They would have a special Christmas dinner tomorrow and the Captain would lead them in prayers for the boat and for their loved ones at home. I wrapped my own warm memories around me like a cloak. All in all, it was a good watch.

The wind moderated about mid-morning of Christmas day, but the sea rose again. We hadn't eaten hot food for some days, as the cook couldn't keep anything on the stove. That was really an academic point anyway, because we were again down to canned bully-beef, hardtack, and cheese. But we shouted "Merry Christmas" to each other as the watches were relieved and I don't remember that we were particularly down-hearted.

We had Christmas dinner a few days later in Reykjavik after we tied up. Then we slept all afternoon and went for another dinner at the Börg Hotel.

With its northern coast touching the Arctic Circle, Iceland is desolate, as you may imagine. Less than half of one per cent is wooded. The rest is covered by glaciers, tundra, and ash from over a hundred volcanoes. The population is less than that of Ottawa. Since the ninth century the world's crises had pretty much passed Icelanders by, but now they had been occupied by foreign powers. Make no mistake about that: the Allies occupied Iceland much as Germany occupied Norway—as a matter of military necessity. The invasion was bloodless and the occupation benign, but the Icelanders were resentful at being flooded with sailors— and even worse, soldiers. I don't know of any who ever had a hospitable word said to him by an Icelandic man or woman.

But the *girls* thronged to the Börg Hotel and sat in groups of three or four. Most were truly beautiful: lissom, blonde, blue-eyed. They would dance with us, but we circled the floor in silence. Then they returned to their tables. Their brothers and other menfolk watched, hard-eyed. I danced with a girl called Eva; when the music ended I returned to my table to sip weak Icelandic beer fortified with dollops of navy rum I carried on my hip. As the music started again, Eva glanced over, we danced again, and again returned to our separate tables. Five times.

"Her brothers are the inhibitors," I thought. She had pointed them out, two of them and big. "If I could get her out of here, rum might melt my Icelandic iceberg."

"Couldn't I meet you somewhere afterwards?" I asked.

"There is nowhere else."

"Would you like to visit my ship tomorrow?"

She shook her head.

"For church service," I added desperately.

"I am sorry, that is not possible," Eva said. Was there a ghost of a smile at the corners of her lovely mouth?

We sailed and flogged westward to Newfoundland. The Labrador Current was sweeping pack-ice south, and the convoy and escort ceased zigzagging and ground through it. The ice was perhaps one to three feet thick and some of the chunks were maybe twenty feet across. It wasn't dangerous if you went slowly; although, of course, there was always the risk that one would be a berg that went down not three feet but fifty. Then *Moose Jaw* would come up all standing. The sailors in the fore-upper and the fore-lower messdecks tended to sleep in the after end. The noise was worrisome, though. My bunk was against the ship's side and just below the water-line. I would turn in and look at the bulkhead and listen to the bumping and grinding and tearing, thinking of the ice on the other side of that thin steel plate.

We detached from the convoy at the western rendezvous—the Western Ocean Meeting Point (WESTOMP)—and the local escort took over to shepherd the merchant ships south to Sydney, Halifax, Boston, and New York. Yet another escort group took over there: to Norfolk, Charleston, the Gulf of Mexico, Panama, Curaçao, Aruba, and Trinidad. Then onward to Georgetown, Paramaribo, Cayenne, Pernambuco, Rio de Janeiro, and Buenos Aires. Some corvettes went on to Tierra del Fuego and around Cape Horn.

But we headed for dear old Newfie, to Captain D's weekly

cocktail (drinking) parties at the Newfoundland Hotel, to nightly dances at the Colony Club, where the girls spoke to you, and to the Crow's Nest.

Every home in St. John's was open to sailors; the home I went to was the Duckworths', and every time I found a house brimming with fun and crowded with people. Mrs. Duckworth spent most of the war baking for us: as one escort group left, another arrived. Her daughters must have logged a million miles of dancing, for they were always escorted by two of us, sometimes three.

Captain Rollo Mainguy and his gracious wife held parties every Friday for seagoing officers. The parties were just for our entertainment, but I suppose Captain Mainguy was like Sir Percy at the other end of our run. He liked to know what really went on as opposed to what would be written in Reports of Proceedings. Anyway, he seemed to spend more time talking to sub-lieutenants than to escort group commanders. Then, on to the fifty-nine wooden steps that led up to the garret converted to the Seagoing Officers' Club—the Crow's Nest. A distinguished local citizen was sometimes there—Sir Leonard Outerbridge. It was his warehouse, I think.

Here was warmth and friendship and good companionship, and excitedly told stories of recent battles. If it came out that someone we knew had gone down in this ship or that, there was a momentary pause while we digested the fact that we would not see him again. We made brief murmurs of mutual commiseration, and then the present flowed on into the future.

"I've been invited fishing tomorrow. Want to come? Leave at noon, be back by dark."

"Never mind tomorrow. What about tonight?"

"Let's force on to the Colony."

"You got a crock?"

"Yeah. You?"

"Yeah. You got a popsie?"

"No. You?"

"No. The hell with it. We got two crocks."

After three days we sailed again for WESTOMP, took over the convoy, and plodded eastward yet again. The U-boat wolf-pack tactics were proving effective. Some convoys would be attacked by twenty U-boats or more. In one convoy we lost more ships in two days than I'd previously seen go down in a week. Survivors were everywhere in the water, amidst wreckage, burning ships, overloaded lifeboats, and surfacing submarines. To go on was suicide and the whole convoy—what was left—retreated to St. John's.

I went below to spread the good news. Bill Spinney was sitting morosely in the wardroom flicking over the pages of *Liberty* magazine. He was prone to seasickness and had his bucket on the deck beside him.

"We're going back," I said; "be in Newfie day after tomorrow."

"That means I've got to get my Confidential Books mustered," he said, and, taking his bucket, he went out into the wardroom flats and opened the CB vault.

It is worthy of note that, during the whole of the fighting war, the paper war was waged relentlessly. Indeed, I sometimes thought it was the lesser crime to carry out a poor attack on a submarine than to submit a late report. I reluctantly concluded I'd better follow Spinney's fine example and get the Wardroom Wine Account up to date. ("Wine" is a naval euphemism for booze of all sorts.)

This was a particularly onerous job, as I had to keep three sets of books. The first set was produced for the inspection of shore authorities and showed every officer drinking a steady but moderate ration every day, though none at sea, of course. The second set was for the inspection of the Captain, who wouldn't have believed the first set anyway, but had to be shielded from the true state of affairs. The third set I kept locked under my bunk, and this showed what *really* went on. Accounting difficulties were compounded by the fact that, since no one drank anything at sea, the officers' wine bills had to be made out on the basis of *actual* drinking, except for one officer who had grown used to a nip now and then during the day. He kept a bottle in his cabin and his method of accounting was to tally the empties (which, by agreement, he kept in the drawer with his socks—each wrapped in a woollen stocking to prevent clinking). This I did weekly. Bill drank very little at any time, so I could load him (in the first and second books) with some of that drunk by the rest. It never came out even, even counting and recounting all the chits filled out by the stewards. I would have to go from officer to officer, chit-book in hand, trying to persuade them to sign for more. When this source of added income was exhausted, there was the overproof rum. This was forty per cent over proof, came in fifteen-gallon kegs, and could take quite a bit of watering before being noticably weaker. After some hours' work I had a reasonable relationship between booze consumed and booze remaining.

A delightful thing happened after we docked at St. John's: a fifty-foot-high iceberg drifted in and blocked the narrow entrance to the harbour. We couldn't get out. For the first time in over a year I looked forward to more than three days in harbour. I took long walks in the bush and fields surrounding the city. I went to movies instead of to the Crow's Nest or the Colony Club, and got back to the ship at about eleven instead of at two or three. It was with a great deal of regret that we saw that iceberg drift off on its southward course. We sailed to Halifax.

Here the First Lieutenant was replaced. The Captain, after a long and gallant battle, finally had to admit his sickness and was hospitalized. The Cook was drafted to a shore base. A seaman torpedoman was finally forced ashore by the doctors; Gaynor was his name.

His trouble was chronic seasickness and constipation. He was always sick at sea—twenty-four hours a day, and some of the voyages were fifteen, sixteen, seventeen days; one was twenty-one. He couldn't keep anything down, and so lost several pounds each trip. But in harbour he'd stuff himself and gain some back. He refused to admit his condition and he never missed a watch; he was always there with his tool-kit when some electrical fitting went phffft. The doctor said that chronic constipation was serious, but this ST would point out with some heat that "if you don't eat you don't shit." In our circumscribed world, Gaynor's bowels were a source of interest and conversation. But it was the second day in harbour that was crucial—after Gaynor had a day's food in him. As we went in to breakfast, Smith, the senior steward, would give us the good news.

"Gaynor had his Morning George an hour ago."

About this time Prime Minister Churchill steamed west in *Prince of Wales* to meet President Roosevelt in USS *Augusta* at Placentia Bay, Newfoundland. History records the signing of the Atlantic Charter, the decision of two great English-speaking democracies to oppose Nazism and Fascism. To us it meant that the United States Navy would take over some of the convoys as far as Iceland, and maybe we would get more time in harbour. I didn't fancy USN ensigns hanging around the Börg Hotel, though.

After a year at sea we were much the same crew that had assembled at Montreal. It seemed sometimes I'd known them all my life. Discipline in fact was not at all what I had envisaged in *Alaunia* as a callow midshipman. I remembered Captain Woodward's words about turning a blind eye to minor faults.

St. John's to Glasgow: Glasgow to St. John's. Sometimes St. John's to Lough Foyle and a brief leave in Londonderry. Sometimes when we got to the Mid-Ocean Meeting Point (MOMP) we would sail right through, but sometimes we were detached and we put in at Reykjavik. Again I circled the dance floor with Eva, grown more talkative now. But I never saw her outside that room. Twice *Moose Jaw* went to Hvalfjord.

The base-ship *Hecla* was moored there and her acres of machine-shops were a blessing to engine-room artificers who had been trying to keep their engines running with baling wire and string. *Hecla's* bakeries turned out an ample supply of delicious brown bread. Movies were shown nightly, but the vile weather usually made it impossible to row across. Outside of the fact that you were in no danger from submarines, Hvalfjord was a bust. The high hills shut out what little winter daylight we got: it became grey about 1100 and was dark again by 1400. This produced an unorthodox routine. Although the Royal Canadian Navy as a corporate body would not have approved, we didn't call the hands until 0730. The isolation of our anchorage gave us a feeling of immunity. The Officer of the Day slept in the wheel-house, where he could keep an eye on the weather and check anchor-bearings. Aft, by the jumping ladder, was the Quartermaster. A couple of hands in the boiler room and two more in the engine room completed the anchor watch. One morning I woke in the wheel-house, saw the clock on the bulkhead reading 0905, noticed the ship was silent as a tomb, and drifted off to sleep again.

I had a dream. Why was the ship so quiet at 0905?

My eyes flew open. 0906. Why was the ship silent? Why hadn't I been called? I leaped up and raced aft. The Quartermaster was wedged comfortably against a depth-charge thrower, duffle-coat hood over his eyes. He snored; and so did all the remainder of the crew. A motorboat was approaching: a bearded gentleman was resting his arms on the after canopy, arms with the two and a half stripes of a lieutenant-commander. Two and a half *straight* stripes. My God! Must be the CO of one of our destroyers. RCN officers were still held in awe by sub-lieutenants RCNVR like me. Our new captain was a lieutenant RCNR. A junior lieutenant. And if I didn't get him up chop-chop he was likely to remain so. I kicked the QM in the ankle.

"Call the Captain. Call the Captain *first*. Tell him the Escort Commander is coming alongside. Then call the hands. I want every mother's son moving about in five minutes."

My bearded gentleman was coming over the side. His eyes were freezing blue.

"Good morning, sir."

He nodded.

"Won't you come this way, sir? The Captain is seeing Requestmen. He'll be along directly."

The Quartermaster, flashing past me from the Captain's cabin on his way to the fo'c's'le, picked up his cue.

"Captain's Requestmen secure," he piped. Then, showing himself to be a born improviser, he disappeared into the messdecks, crying, "Fall out messdeck sweepers. Hands to quarters, clean guns."

I led our visitor, Lieutenant-Commander Herbert Sharples Rayner, DSC, RCN, Commanding Officer, HMCS *St. Laurent*, to the wardroom.

Leading Steward Smith appeared, looking sleepy and ruffled. He opened his mouth to explain why he was adrift. The wardroom clock said 0915. I cut Smith off.

"Now that you've finished clearing up the breakfast things, Smith, I wonder if you'd be good enough to make us a pot of tea?"

The QM was now warmed up to his act and he clattered down the ladder.

"The Coxswain wants to know if he can keep the quarter-deckmen from quarters clean guns, sir. He wants to re-stow the tiller flat."

"Yes."

The QM bellowed up the hatch to an imaginary messenger, "Tell the Coxswain okay." Then he disappeared, and, through the forward bulkhead, you could hear thumps as signalmen and tele-graphists were tipped out of their hammocks. 0920.

The Escort Commander sat in bleak silence.

Another clatter of steps down the ladder. If that fool QM overplayed his hand I'd . . .

It was the Captain.

"Good morning, sir," he greeted the Group Commander.

"Good morning."

"I said you were seeing Requestmen," I interjected.

The Captain considered this, then continued to the Group Commander, "Before we go to my cabin, sir, may I show you something on my bridge? This, I think, has a bearing on both sea-keeping and fighting qualities. . . ."

They disappeared up the ladder.

"Smith, never mind that bloody tea. Go and make up the Captain's bunk. Chop-chop."

An hour later Lieutenant-Commander Rayner departed.

I stood Officer of the Day for the three remaining days in harbour; the QM stood watch with me. Watch-on and stop-on— seventy-two hours.

"No marks or initiative in this bloody regiment," I grumbled.

My QM agreed. "Too fucking true." Then he added, spitting judiciously, "but we mightn't be watch-on stop-on if the Group Commander hadn't cottoned on to our play-acting."

"Our play-acting? Your play-acting! And what a bollicking the Old Man gave me!"

Yes, Hvalfjord was a desolate place. In thirty minutes the quiet black waters could be whipped to white foam as a gale roared down between the mountains. Small ships had to up anchor and mill about in confusion until the wind subsided. Hecla was firmly moored fore and aft; besides, she was firmly aground on a shoal of empty gin bottles. The US and RN heavy cruisers seemed immune too. But the little ships had a bad time. Skeena dragged onto the beach and several of her crew were lost; her bones lay on the Iceland rocks for years.

I remembered my father's words in one of his infrequent references to life in the trenches in the First World War. He said you got so that you stood and debated whether you wanted to go up this traverse or that, or whether you would send the sergeant to the left with two sections and take your two to the right, or vice versa. Or, finally, whether you would put on your left boot first, or your right. Soon, I couldn't fall asleep when I turned in, although I was exhausted. I would lie and stare at the ship's side by my bunk and think, "If a U-boat has worked herself up on the bow of the convoy at, say, two miles, and if she is firing a spread of torpedoes, say, now, then it will take the fish three minutes to arrive." And then I would count up to a hundred and eighty seconds. One, two, three, four . . . Then I would say, "Well, I guess she didn't fire. But, if she were firing now. One, two, three, four, five . . . " And in the morning I'd tell myself that it was just another form of counting sheep.

In February of 1942 the Manning Commander at Halifax summoned me again. I was appointed ashore to King's College, Halifax—now HMCS Kings—for a short navigation course. With few regrets and after a boisterous all-afternoon party, I boarded the "Newfie Bullet" for the twenty-four-hour train trip from St. John's to Port aux Basques. Snow or gales could stretch this trip indefinitely. If the wind was blowing too hard going over Topsails, for instance, the train was stopped and buckled down to the tracks. Several yarns grew around this train. Like the one about the station-master at Botwood who said, "Here comes the Bullet. Right on time; Thursday." Or the young lady who asked the conductor when they would arrive in Port aux Basques.

"That's hard to say, ma'am."

"But it's very important that I get there as soon as possible."

"Yes, ma'am."

"You see, my child will be born soon."

"Good heavens, ma'am! You shouldn't have boarded *this* train in *that* condition."

"I didn't."

We made Port aux Basques in thirty-four hours, then took a ferry to Sydney, Nova Scotia, escorted by a corvette. Another train to Halifax, and there was Alma waiting at the station, just as I remembered her, though perhaps a little more finely drawn, a little tauter. We drove to *Kings* that night, happy in the knowledge that we would have a few months together.

One day in May, I found my name in *The London Gazette*. I'd achieved moderate fame:

> THE KING has been graciously pleased to
> approve the following award:

> For good service in HMCS *Moose Jaw* in
> action against Enemy Submarines and in
> rescuing survivors from a Merchantman.

> MENTION IN DESPATCHES

> Sub-Lieutenant Harold Ernest Thomas
> LAWRENCE, R.C.N.V.R.

The First Lord of the Admiralty, A. V. Alexander, sent me a certificate. Vincent Massey, the Canadian High Commissioner in London, wrote me a congratulatory letter.

Well, it had really been a case of floundering around the Atlantic in a skiff, cold and afraid, and tying down the stylus of the asdic with string. But yes, I suppose you could put it the way the *Gazette* did. It certainly sounded much better, neat but not gaudy. And I could now wear an oak-leaf cluster on my medal-ribbon.

five

Heroics in Southern Climes

HMCS *Kings* was located adjacent to the campus of Dalhousie University and a short walk from the Waegwaltic Boat Club. It was there I passed the first few months of 1942, seeing Alma every evening after classes, eating regular meals, and sleeping eight uninterrupted hours every night. The memories of the North Atlantic were just beginning to blur when, in April, I was appointed to another corvette, *Oakville*.

My captain, Jones, was an RCNR lieutenant, and not war-time navy either—he knew the ropes. His Number One was Ken Culley, a Montreal banker, trained in *King Alfred* in the U.K., and with sea-time under his belt. He used to say, "I've wrung more salt water out of my socks than you've sailed over." The other two sub-lieutenants had both been to sea before; one, RCNVR, a little, the other, RCNR, a lot. This last had a penchant for coprology; not to put too fine a point on it, he delighted in talking about shit.

We were on the triangle run, Halifax to Boston to Newfoundland. The weather was milder than on the run from St. John's to Reykjavik to Lough Foyle, but foggier. However, radar had come to sea to ease the watch-keepers' burden. Sir Robert Watson-Watt, a boffin in Admiralty Research, had invented the magnetron. Ten thousand bridge and plot watch-keepers around the world blessed his electronic genius. More than any other single factor, this doomed the U-boats and thwarted Dönitz. More important, it made a watch on the bridge bearable in bad weather.

We had slipped from Halifax in an April snow-storm and felt our way out of harbour by radar and the mournful dirge of the lighthouses and buoys. My local knowledge, hard won in *Andrée Dupré*, quite impressed Captain Jones. That was Mauger Beach off to port, that was Lichfield, that Inner Automatic. Off to starboard was the double blast of Chebucto Head, further to starboard was Sambro Lighthouse, and there, ahead, Sambro Lightship. What old friends they seemed.

Getting in station was not easy, but at last the radar screen looked roughly like the diagrammatic sketch of the convoy. There were the five columns of merchantmen, six in each; there, the three reported straggling; there the one in the starboard column way out of station. And, zigzagging around the convoy, the five ships of our group.

"Bloody well time too," said the Captain, heaving himself out of his chair where he had spent the last nine hours. He stumped below and left the watch to me. It was still snowing heavily, but, as there was no wind, the snow fell gently in large, wet flakes. The sea was smooth and we steamed along serenely, as steady as if we were in harbour. The only sound was the muffled wail of the fog-horns as the leading ships of each column sounded their pendant numbers. Ki arrived on the bridge. I put the ship on the outward leg of the zigzag and, with a contented sigh, eased myself into Father's chair, secure in the knowledge that I had six minutes before the next alteration was due.

The next morning the wind was up and we were pitching a bit. The snow continued and it stayed mild. The evening of the following day in Massachusetts Bay we saw the convoy, on our radar, form into a single line and alter towards Boston. We swung to the south and headed for Cape Cod. Truly, this had been a ghostly convoy. Not once had we seen any of the thirty-odd ships we were escorting, or any of our consorts. The sky cleared. We made passage of the Cape Cod canal and anchored for the night off Martha's Vineyard.

The next day we steamed past the pleasant estates of Long Island. We passed between the Bronx and Queens and saw the spectacular skyline of New York. This has always seemed to me a better entrance than the familiar, much-photographed one.

That night we explored the part of New York City that was to become so familiar to us in the next year. Harry James was playing his golden trumpet at the Taft Hotel; at the Starlight Room of the Waldorf-Astoria we would dance to Xavier Cugat; at other hotels to Jimmy Dorsey, Tommy Dorsey, Glenn Miller, and Benny Goodman. "Chattanooga Choo-Choo", "String of Pearls", "The Jersey Bounce", Brazil", "Tuxedo Junction".

Do some of you remember the girls of 1939? Saddle shoes, bobby sox, flaring skirts just below the knee, "sloppy-joe" sweaters with sleeves pushed up below the elbow, long, loose hair, flashing brown legs, and flushed faces, and bright eyes. They danced to the soaring virtuosity of Goodman's clarinet, the confident authority of James' trumpet, the mellow trombone of Dorsey in "I'm Getting Sentimental Over You", or the sweet nostalgia of Miller's "Moonlight Serenade". And the couples would melt together so you couldn't tell where he ended and she began, and the lights would dim, and the hall would be silent except for the aching beauty of fifty musicians playing their hearts out. Life was unbearably sweet and you dimly perceived it would not always be thus.

The United States at war inspires awe, not only in its production of ships and tanks and guns, but in the social back-up as well. Clubs for officers and men abounded. My headquarters was the Commodore Hotel on 42nd Street. Did we want tickets for a play or a musical? A concert, a ballet, an opera, Radio City Music Hall, nightclubs, restaurants? Our uniforms opened all doors; more, they got us a table near the front. One night at the Stage Door Canteen I was introduced to Lady Hardwicke, whose husband, Sir Cedric, was making a film in Hollywood. The play she was in had closed its doors after a short run; it had failed, in fact. Therefore, she had leisure unbounded; and I took up some of it. Her entourage was large, but transient; its members tended to fly back and forth to Hollywood. Charles Ruggles was the first I met, Robert Benchley the second. C. Aubrey Smith was another. One Sunday afternoon, after their weekly radio broadcast, I met André Kostelanetz and his wife, Lily Pons.

Pixie Hardwicke had open house every weekday at six—cocktails or whatever you wanted. Afterwards, five or six of us would go and see a play that had had better luck than hers. Then, about eleven, we would meet for supper at Sardi's, where all the theatre world congregated after the shows. Here your table served merely as a base; table-hopping was the rule, and usually the only drink you bought was the first one when you sat down. The leading men and leading ladies of established plays ate their first big meal of the day and received the plaudits of all who would tender them. After a first night, the party went on until dawn brought the morning papers and the reviews. *Oklahoma* was SRO every night; the *New Yorker* carried a Helen Hokinson cartoon of an indignant matron expostulating at the box-office, "But I'm *from* Oklahoma!" We got tickets by some back-stage managerial

Merchant-seamen survivors on board a corvette. [PAC]

(*left*) Icing was an irritating feature of convoy life. (*PAC*)
(*above*) A small sea breaks inboard. (*PAC*)
(*below*) U-190 off Newfoundland after its surrender. (*PAC*)

MEN of VALOR
They fight for you

Two-man boarding party from the Canadian corvette 'Oakville' subdues crew of German sub in Caribbean

(*top left*) A damaged U-boat surfaces. (*PAC*)
(*bottom left*) A U-boat survivor plucked from the sea. (*PAC*)
(*above*) Department of Defence artists restore the author's pants in this representation of the boarding of U-94. (*PAC*)

Press coverage of the U-94 affair, November 10, 1942. (*Toronto Star Syndicate*)

HMCS *Sioux* at twelve knots. (*PAC*)

Depth-charges exploding at fifty feet. (PAC)

magic. How inexpressibly pleasant to be on the inside, to belong, to be one of the select few!

My middle-aged friends would begin to yawn about one-thirty or two, half a dozen taxis would be summoned by the doorman, and the evening would be at an end. For them.

I had a standing date at the Hurricane Club every morning at two-thirty. I had found Eleanor again, Eleanor of Chez Maurice, back in Montreal. She didn't expect me to hang around the club all evening, but she liked me to catch her last show at two-thirty. Now, Eleanor arose about 3 p.m. each day and didn't check in to the Hurricane until eight. The first show was at nine, there was another at midnight, and the last was at two-thirty. She got off work at four. Her day's work was finished and she expected to be entertained. I tried. There are clubs just working up to tempo at four in the morning, would you believe it? We examined most of them, together with one or two of her friends from the chorus line and their boy friends—men of unspecified professions but usually associated with the entertainment business. At about seven, Eleanor and I boarded the Lexington Avenue express. I got off at the Staten Island ferry and she continued on to Flatbush. Thirty minutes' sleep on the ferry and I arrived at the ship in Staten Island Navy Yard just before the hands fell in for Colours. The ship's business was just enough to keep me awake until noon, when, after a ten-minute lunch, I got my head down until three. Then it was back to the ferry and the Lexington Avenue express.

After the relative sterility of Halifax, St. John's, Reykjavik, Glasgow, and Londonderry, I sensed the riches of New York and sought to partially assuage the unquenchable thirst that had grown in the past three years. And so, happy and wondering, I took advantage of shore leaves in the city to wander solitary through the Metropolitan Museum or the Brooklyn Museum. The New York Public Library, just down 42nd Street at Fifth Avenue, near the Commodore Hotel, nearly always had some interesting exhibition. Sometimes I caught an earlier ferry and went to the Metropolitan or the New York City Opera. And then, about six, I would head for Pixie Hardwicke's apartment.

After three days in New York, it was usually with some relief that we slipped *Oakville*'s moorings and steamed out with a convoy to the comparative tranquillity of war.

Still, the war in the Atlantic was increasing in magnitude and ferocity. *Scharnhorst, Gneisenau,* and *Prinz Eugen,* under Vice-

Admiral Otto Ciliax, made their daring dash from Brest through the English Channel to the Elbe and Wilhelmshaven. *Scharnhorst* hit a mine and Admiral Ciliax transferred to a destroyer; when she was damaged he transferred to another destroyer. *Gneisenau* struck a mine and *Scharnhorst* a second mine, but they made harbour. *The Times* (London) said: "Vice-Admiral Ciliax has succeeded where the Duke of Medina Sidonia failed . . . nothing more mortifying . . . has happened . . . since the 17th century."

Scientists on both sides were producing. Germany invented a torpedo that homed on a ship's propellers. We responded with "cat" gear—a device towed astern that lured the homing torpedo to it. The Coxswain of *Oakville* summed up that scientific exchange breezily, "Isn't that fuckin' typical. They invent a new torpedo and we tow a bed-spring astern."

Long-range Catalinas had extended the air cover from Canada. The gap in mid-Atlantic—the so-called Black Pit—was six hundred miles wide in 1942, but this was being narrowed. Some merchant ships now carried an aircraft, one that could be catapulted off the deck. Unfortunately, it couldn't get on again, and the pilot had to bail out and hope to be picked up before he froze or drowned. Small escort carriers were sailing with some convoys. These were merchant ships with a flight deck. They still carried a cargo but also about four aircraft permanently ranged on deck. Often the pilots could land on again.

Our scientists provided us with High Frequency Direction Finding sets which could intercept and take a bearing on submarines' sighting and attack radio transmissions. Two bearings gave us a fix. HF/DF—"Huff Duff"—was a great help. We acquired radar; the U-boats likewise. We got a radar search-receiver to find German transmissions; so did they to find ours. We employed airborne radar; the German search-receivers picked up the transmissions and the U-boats dived. We employed very-high-frequency (VHF) radar, especially effective in British anti-submarine aircraft. This the Germans didn't know about and their search-receivers couldn't detect it. The U-boats treated their conning towers with radar-absorbent material, but it never worked well. Our VHF radar could pick it up. The U-boats got *Schnorkel*, a tube which, pushed above the surface, allowed them fresh air to run diesels and recharge batteries without surfacing. We could pick up *Schnorkel*.

The German scientists came up with the *Pillenwerfer*, which could decoy our asdic beam off the U-boat. We learned the characteristics of a *Pillenwerfer* echo. Small balloons with radar reflectors were released by surfaced U-boats: a small sea-anchor allowed them to drift slowly down-wind. Many an escort chased a balloon while a U-boat quietly slid off in another direction. The disadvantage of our depth-charges was that they exploded at a pre-set depth. We invented the "hedgehog", which threw twenty-four mortar shells ahead of the attacking ship and exploded on impact. These would punch a hole in a U-boat hull. Better still, we could fire without crossing over the target and masking the U-boat echo with our wake. We made a bigger mortar and called it "squid". As well as our three-hundred-pound-depth charge, we brought out one that weighed a thousand pounds. Germany brought out a pattern-running torpedo. We superimposed a weave on our zigzag. And so it went.

When severely depth-charged, a U-boat would release a large bubble of air and some fuel oil to give the impression it had broken up; then it would lie silent and deep. The intestines of animals would be shot out to the surface and deceive the hunting surface ships into thinking they had sunk a submarine. This flotsam was gathered and put into refrigerators as evidence, the guts, presumably, of disembowelled Germans. Not so, said the pathologist when this evidence was produced. Pigs, sheep. So we looked for arms and legs. Rumour had it that even these were carried by U-boats, to use as a ruse. It became harder and harder to convince a sceptical Admiralty to award a "kill". Even a "probable" was rare.

Oakville left New York with a few merchant ships and three other Canadian corvettes. Off Boston we picked up more of the convoy. A large section joined from Halifax, off Sable Island. The weather-reporting U-boat informed Dönitz of the juncture: there was always one stationed there. We continued on to WESTOMP and handed over to another Canadian group. The Canadian navy was now responsible for nearly half the convoys between North America and the United Kingdom. The RCNR and the RCNVR formed the majority of the crews of these escorts—from captain down. We had been accepted into the club.

During this period there was a lull in the Iceland area. It was "the happy time" for the U-boats and most were down the U.S. eastern seaboard. Now we had Rescue Ships and a lot of survivors were scooped up. Literally. On one occasion, the *Komet*, despairing of picking up survivors in a gale, opened the cattle doors and survivors were washed in. The crew pounced on the wretched men before they were swept out again.

These Rescue Ships had first gone to sea in 1941 under the aegis of Sir Percy Noble, and now that they were operating we realized how we had yearned for them. Someone to take the responsibility of picking up survivors from the escorts; or, perhaps, allowing us to leave survivors with a better conscience when battle conditions did not permit us to stop. Or picking us up if we bought it. There were over thirty Rescue Ships at sea between 1941 and 1945. Five were sunk: the *Syrian Prince* and *Pinto* whilst picking up survivors; *Zaafaran*, lost with convoy PQ-17 together with twenty-three merchant ships: *Walmer Castle*, bombed and sunk; and *St. Sunniva*, lost with all hands. Over their lifetime, the Rescue Ships saved over four thousand hands. *Rathlin* held the record with 634, *Zamalek* was next with 611. Yes, it was good to have a Rescue Ship along: a total of 797 convoys thought so.

We left the convoy at WESTOMP, mentally wished it good luck in the "Black Pit", and went hooting and hollering into Newfie to see who was at the Crow's Nest, who at the Colony Club. From there it was on to Halifax and the supper dances at the Nova Scotian, and from there to Boston, to the Merry-Go-Round bar at the Copley Plaza or the Terrace Room at the Statler.

The ladies of Boston had decided they could safely entertain commissioned officers, at least for the duration of the war, and officers' clubs abounded. Mansions, most of them were. Eligible young ladies of impeccable breeding took a duty one night each week. I think they were mostly from Radcliffe and Wellesley, and they were very refined.

On one occasion, my shipmates persuaded the principal hostess—her name was Lodge, I think, or Cabot—that I had been a radio actor for the CBC. With regal dignity this grande dame tapped a glass for attention and a respectful silence fell.

"Ladies and gentlemen. Mr. Lawrence, of the Royal Canadian Navy, is going to recite for us."

A patter of polite female applause. Cheers from my flotilla mates and the Brits.

"Up, up, up," cried my mates.

I stood on a chair, all modest confusion.

"I really don't know what to recite."

The pianist was now playing what she considered introductory flourishes.

One of my mates shouted, "Tell the story of the three . . . You know."

I plunged in.

I'm an autocratic figure in these democratic states.
I'm a dandy demonstration of hereditary traits.
My position in the structure of society I owe
To the qualities my parents bequeathed me long ago.

The Principal Hostess nodded grave approval. This she understood. What a *suitable* sentiment!

My father was a gentleman, and musical to boot.

More grave nods from the assembled matriarchy, but a horrified glare from the young lady I had been sitting with. She moved away.

He used to play the fiddle in a house of ill-repute.
The Madam was a lady,
A credit to her cult.
She enjoyed my father's fiddling [lecherous giggle],
And I was the result.
So my mummy and my daddy
Are the ones I have to thank
That I'm the Chairman of the Board
Of a stable Boston bank.

There followed two other verses in which two more bastards described their worldly successes, and then the poor ordinary man spoke up.

I'm an ordinary figure in these democratic states,
A pathetic demonstration of hereditary traits.
My position in the structure of society I owe
To the qualities my parents bequeathed me long ago.
My father was a married man and what is even more,
He was married to my mother—a fact that I abhor.
I was born in holy wedlock, consequently, by and by
I was rooked by every bastard that had plunder in his eye.
I invested, I deposited, I voted every Fall.
I saved up every penny and the bastards took it all.
But now I've learned my lesson
And I'm on the proper track.
I'm a Self-Appointed Bastard
And I'm going to get it back.

Even today, a recitation of "The Three Bastards" is a show-stopper in some circles.

The corvette escorts grew more numerous and the convoys larger as 1942 went on. The largest I ever saw was eighty ships, a vast armada formed up in ten columns with about six or seven ships in each. The convoy front was five miles across and it was about four miles deep. Within a mile around this would be, in a well-screened convoy, perhaps eight escorts: destroyers ahead, frigates or corvettes on the beam and astern. Other destroyers might be on a loose weaving screen out ahead at five or six miles. This is a community of between four and five thousand souls, covering an area of nearly one hundred square miles. Tactical considerations apart, there is a lot of administration in a community this size. The convoy route from New York to WESTOMP was about a thousand miles. A northeasterly course could be held for days with only slight variations. Station-keeping was not a major problem, at least in calm weather. The spring and summer of 1942 gave us many fair days, some fog, an iceberg or two, but few gales.

There is some bustle around a convoy on a fine forenoon. The Commodore asks a question of the ships by flag-hoist. Gaily coloured bunting rises to the yards of fifty ships as they reply. Signal-lamps chatter. The Rescue Ship, manned with naval signalmen, acts as a signal-link between one side of the convoy and the other. Some days she might relay sixty or seventy signals. The Senior Officer of the Escort wants to know the percentage of fuel remaining. One ship wants to borrow a spare part from another. They come together, make an exchange, and part. A merchant ship wants medical advice. Either the doctor in the Rescue Ship or the doctor in the destroyer will make a house call and transfer by jack-stay. A line attaches the two ships while they are still under way, and he is swung over.

One day a British merchantman from the Clydeside buried a seaman. He had died of natural causes. The crew mustered aft with bared heads. You could see the captain reading the burial service. A piper played the lament "The Flowers of the Forest".

Every ship has seamen on deck chipping, wire-brushing, applying primer, painting, tarring rigging, stitching canvas, splicing wire or manila—all the daily chores. Cooks in white hats step out on deck for a breath of air. Off-watch stokers smoke or play cards abaft the funnel. It is warm and dry on the bridge and the morning coffee is a welcome break. Nearly everyone who can find a reason comes to the bridge and stays to chat.

At noon all ships hoist flags showing their estimated noon position. Some, at wide variance with the others, excite the scorn of the navigator. Then there's a two-hour lull while everyone off watch zizzes. Who knows, you may be up all night if you're attacked. And if you're not, you're ahead a two-hour kip. And the voyage is two hours shorter. Tea and toast at four. The chess games resume; many captains play each other and the signal-lights flash the moves from ship to ship. Supper, and finally sunset at nine. Then the ships put up their black-out screens. Our community steams into the night, placid, rested, watchful. The asdics probe under the water, the lookouts and the radars sweep the surface, the Huff-Duff searches the wave band for enemy transmissions, and the guns-crews and depth-charge parties hunch behind their weapons.

In July Captain King joined *Oakville* and we were transferred to a more southerly link in the convoy chain, Trinidad to New York. Better and better. Winter was coming on, and if you must fight a war, then fight in warm weather; if you are fated to drown, then drown in warm water.

The convoys came up from Georgetown, British Guiana, the last mustering-point on the eastern seaboard of South America, about 350 miles from Trinidad. They entered the Gulf of Paria through the southern Serpent's Mouth and anchored off Port of Spain. There we joined them, departed through the northern Dragon's Mouth, and set a westerly course for Curaçao, about 470 miles away. Along the way we picked up some ships from La Guaira—the seaport of Caracas, Venezuela—and some from Aruba. We took tankers only, fast tankers. More joined outside Maracaibo. Course was altered to the northwest if the convoy was going through the Windward Passage between Cuba and Haiti; 500 miles to the northeast for the Mona Passage between Puerto Rico and Dominica. All convoys had to pass through these two narrow channels, the most direct routes through the thousand-mile barrier of the Greater Antilles.

Our cargo was oil, the life-blood of war. Dönitz, his U-boat fleet now grown to three hundred, wasted no time in moving to deny Britain this vital commodity.

The code word for the U-boat offensive off the United States eastern seaboard was *Paukenschlag*: literally, a beat on a kettle

drum. Kernaval, headquarters of Flag Officer U-boats, set the
date at January 13, 1942. Hardegen in U-123 warmed the bell a little and on January 12 sank the British freighter *Cyclops*, nine
thousand tons, off New York, and the tanker *Norness*. New
Orleans had a dozen sinkings within twenty miles. Galveston,
Texas, had been remote from the war for three years but now suffered sinkings as well. A dozen ships were sunk off the Panama
Canal and about three dozen off Trinidad.

The U-boat captains were helped a great deal by our lack of
security. Torpedoed ships on the American seaboard and those
assisting them chattered away on the 600-metre wave-band.
U-boats in transit to their war stations tuned in from mid-Atlantic
to eavesdrop on coastal defence stations as they sent out a steady
stream of information on rescue work in progress and the
schedules of vessel and aircraft patrols. The USN was new to war,
and its destroyers patrolled with a predictable and clockwork
regularity that delighted the Teutonic mind.

Hartenstein in U-156 went for the fuel tanks at Aruba, but a
premature explosion blew off the muzzle of his 4-inch gun and
wounded two of the guns-crew. He sawed off the damaged muzzle
and later sank two ships with that gun. Achilles in U-161 got in
through the Dragon's Mouth to the Gulf of Paria and sank two
ships. Poske in U-504 sank ships off Miami and Palm Beach with
torpedo and gunfire. German "milch cows" brought out ammunition, fuel, stores, spare parts, even new personnel. Each could
supply fifty tons of fuel to twelve medium-sized boats. The U-boat
commanders were mostly old hands who had served their appren-
ticeships against Captains Donald MacIntyre and F. J. Walker,
RN, and Captains Hibbard and Prentice, RCN. The successors of
Prien, Kretschmer, and Schepke fought on and fought well. There
was Trupp in U-552, Mutzelburg in U-203, Lassen in U-160,
Schuch in U-105, Gregor in U-85, Mohr in U-124. Mohr sank nine
ships on one patrol and reported to Kernaval:

> *The new-moon night is black as ink.*
> *Off Hatteras the tankers sink,*
> *While sadly Roosevelt counts the score,*
> *Some fifty thousand tons—by*
>
> Mohr

Sinkings by U-boat were to rise to 495 ships—two and a half
million tons. Of these, 143 were the precious tankers we escorted.
Lancasters and Bristol bombers, Spitfires and Hurricane fighters,

waited in vain for these cargoes of aviation gasoline, and thousands of potential sorties were aborted. The total number of the crews of 495 ships sunk would be about twenty-five thousand men, though not all were killed, of course.

On August 25, 1942, *Oakville* departed Port of Spain, Trinidad, with convoy TAW-15, comprising twenty-nine ships. This convoy was guarded by three Canadian corvettes: ourselves, *Snowberry*, and *Halifax*; by the Dutch *Jan Van Brackel*; and by three small patrol craft of the United States Navy, plus the powerful USS *Lea*—a destroyer and senior officer of this escort group. The escorts weaved to and fro around their precious charges. *Oakville* zigzagged on the port quarter.

We steamed a westerly course and were joined by more tankers from Aruba and Curaçao. Then we altered to the northwest and shaped course to pass between Cuba and Haiti through the Windward Passage. By August 27 we were just south of Haiti.

Trinidad to Halifax was the first leg of a perilous voyage for these wallowing, deep-laden tankers whose port-quarters we screened. At Halifax other Canadian corvettes and destroyers would escort them to a rendezvous at WESTOMP off Newfoundland. Thence, Canadian veterans of the North Atlantic— *Fraser*, *Saguenay*, *Rimouski*, and others—would shepherd yet another flock past Greenland's bleak Cape Farewell. This was the "Black Pit". A sighting by one U-boat would bring the remainder slipping silently up for the kill.

Our convoys were hunted by experts. Before being killed or captured Günther Prien, Joachim Schepke, and Otto Kretschmer had, between them, sunk nearly eight hundred thousand tons of our shipping; over one hundred ships. Their spirit, courage, skill, and devotion to the cause lived on in the younger commanders. One such young commander we were shortly to meet—Oberleutnant Otto Ites of U-94.

Ites was twenty-four and had been four years in U-boats. He had sunk over one hundred thousand tons. The previous April Hitler had awarded him the Knights Cross of the Iron Cross. As daring as he was able, Ites was admired by his crew as a fighter and liked too—they called him "Onkel Otto". But by the evening of August 27, his career as a fighter had less than an hour to run.

Ites had spotted TAW-15 and was coming in at dead-slow speed on the convoy's port bow, only his conning tower awash. Gebeschus, his executive officer, was on the bridge with him. Ites squinted at three escorts weaving restlessly across the front of the convoy—those lovely fat tankers he had come four thousand miles to destroy. If he could edge around the leading corvette, *Snowberry*, on the near bow, he would have a better shot. He estimated convoy course at about 340 degrees; speed, ten knots; he was steering 180 degrees at three knots. The range of the nearest ship was four miles. To get into the best position to fire torpedoes was a neat geometry problem in relative velocities— not difficult except for the weaving *Snowberry*. Still, she seemed to stay on one leg of the zigzag for a minimum of three minutes. After her next turn away, then. He must cut as close to *Snowberry* as possible and yet stay out of range of her probing asdic set. Tricky, but certainly not impossible.

Snowberry was turning away. *Oakville* was three miles back. That left a nice-sized gap on the flank. The small USN patrol craft in between he could ignore—a PC didn't pack much punch.

What Ites didn't see was the patrolling USN aircraft, her belly pregnant with twenty-six hundred pounds of depth-bombs. Down she roared. Ites cursed. U-94 dived.

The urgent jangle of the action-station bells in *Oakville* jerked me from sleep. Swarming up the bridge ladder I got a heel in the face—some matelot in an equal hurry to get to *his* action station aft. We struggled past each other.

Three steps brought me to the asdic shack. Leading Seaman Hartman, our best man, shoved the cruising-watch operator out of the seat and, donning the headphones, pointed ahead. Four plumes of water from the aircraft's depth-bombs were subsiding into a misty haze and showing small, ethereal rainbows in the moonlight. Hartman knew his job and was swinging the transmitter around to the bearing of the depth-bombs' splashes. Ping, went the oscillator. The sound-wave searched outwards, reverberations coming back fainter and fainter. Carefully, Hartman trained his transmitter three degrees to the right. Ping, again; the reverberations died away. The aircraft circled in a continuous, tight bank, making S's in Morse code with its signal-light. Its engines were loud and I had to press the earphones against my head. A flare drifted down, its ghostly radiance matching the moon.

"Fire a five-charge pattern when we cross the spot where those depth-bombs landed," rapped the Captain.

Lieutenant-Commander Clarence King had won a Distinguished Service Cross in the First World War for sinking one

U-boat and getting two "probables". His score in this war was zero and he didn't like it.

He was quivering, but his excitement was controlled. *Oakville* trembled under the thrust of her screw at full speed. I pressed the fire-bell; out arched depth-charges, one either side from the throwers; three splashed from the stern. We tensed. Because of our relatively slow speed these things could damage us as well. With a rumble they exploded. Water erupted to mast-head height. *Oakville* bucked, shuddered, and resumed her eager trembling. Poor old girl; there was worse to come.

Hartman was still sweeping his arc; three degrees to the right; ping. Before the reverberations died out, there came a low drumming note in our earphones. Intuitively, Hartman swung the oscillator rapidly right. The low drumming changed to the clamour of fast engines and the unmistakable turbulence of a submarine blowing her ballast-tanks. She was surfacing.

"Submarine hydrophone dead ahead," I reported to the Captain. After a few moments Hartman asked, "Moving left?" I watched the instruments: yes, that submarine was moving left. "Target moving left," I responded. This report, which should have elicited from the Captain a quiet "Very good", was answered by a dozen shouts, "There's the bastard!"

A black snout reared out of the water. The conning tower burst through a swell and she surfaced completely. Water cascaded from her decks, white and foamy in the moonlight.

"Ho-ho," cried the Captain, not very nautically.*

The Captain altered course to ram. Two rockets, the submarine-sighted signal, hissed skyward and burst into white stars.

We had only about three hundred feet to manoeuvre in. The Captain couldn't make it and we missed. U-94 bumped down the

---

* My captains were a constant source of disappointment to me in the matter of public utterances. Just before action was joined at Trafalgar, Admiral Lord Nelson said, "This day England expects that every man shall do his duty." When Captain John Paul Jones in USS *Bonhomme Richard* in 1779 was battered by HMS *Serapis* and asked, "Do you surrender?" he replied, "I have not yet begun to fight." When Commodore Farragut in USS *Hartford*, fighting during the Civil War in the Battle of Mobile Bay in 1864, was warned his line was falling into confusion—one sunk, one stopped, he said, "Damn the torpedoes! Full

port side. The Captain opened the range to get another run-in. This gave the gunners a chance.

Our 4-inch gun roared out again and again. Two splashes we saw and then a satisfying orange flash on the submarine's conning tower. The Oerlikon banged away, the red tracer flowing out and ricocheting at wild angles off the pressure-hull of U-94. Our bow swung on again.

Now the .5-inch machine-guns started their insane chatter. The port gunner, ignoring the Captain's ear just six inches from the muzzle, let go the first burst. Have you ever seen a standing side-jump of twelve feet? Captain King did one that night. Olympic standard, I thought, and him fiftyish too.

We bore in. The 4-inch flashed again and U-94's 88-mm gun rocked over. Four streams of lead spewed from the .5's, and down below I could hear the Lewis gun spitting. With precision and speed the German gunners poured out and made for their weapons. In that murderous fire none made it.

Ites was manoeuvring U-94 with skill and by now at good speed. We hit with only a glancing blow; again U-94 passed down the port side, this time about twenty feet off. Now we unleashed a weapon hitherto untried in modern warfare.

Stationed on the fiddley abaft the funnel were six stokers not needed in the engine-room during action. Their job was to reload the depth-charge throwers. But we weren't firing the throwers and so these stokers had nothing to do. And yet here were German faces on the bridge of a U-boat just a few feet away. U-94 was so close our guns could not depress to fire. Also on the fiddley abaft the funnel, the canteen manager stowed his empty Coke bottles. To the stokers, ignorant engineers uninstructed in the art of war, the connection was obvious.

Imagine, if you can, six stokers pelting the enemy with Coke bottles at twenty feet, crying, "Yah! Yah!" Ducking heads on U-94 testified to their accuracy. If Ites' courage ever forsook him, it must have been then.

---

speed ahead!" Commodore Lawrence in USS *Chesapeake*, after his ship was reduced to a shambles of fallen rigging and when he was being carried below wounded, said, "Don't give up the ship." Captain Grubb in *Moose Jaw* when he joined action with U-501 could do no better than, "Lawrence, what *are* you doing?" Now, Captain King was joining action with U-94 and he said, "Ho-ho." This is not the stuff of which naval legends are made.

Depth-charges were fired again. One exploded directly under her. She bucked, spray obscured her, then she slowed. *Oakville* opened the range. If destroyers are the "greyhounds of the Fleet", corvettes are the tenacious terriers. We opened the range, swung round, and plunged in the third time. The two .5-inch sent a steady stream of fire at U-94. Bullets whinged off at wild angles, red tracer glowing hot. The Captain was getting the hang of it—this time his aim was sure. At right angles we struck U-94, our bow reared up, and U-94 rolled under. Beneath our bottom we felt three distinct shocks and heard rending metal. U-94 wallowed astern, and stopped. But Father was just warming up.

"Away boarding-party," he cried. "Come on, Lawrence! Get cracking!"

Obediently I slid down the ladder to the boarding-party locker, piously hoping I'd brought the list of names up to date and posted it on the notice-board. To my relief all twelve hands were there, struggling into their gear.

This gear requires a word. Obviously you keep on the lifebelt we all wore at sea. You need a pistol. Hand grenades might be handy: I had two. A gas-mask is recommended—"in case of toxic fumes". One fathom of chain bent onto a fathom of rope is mandatory; you tie the rope to something on the U-boat bridge and lower the chain down the hatch so the wily German can't close hatches, submerge, and leave you foolishly treading water. A flashlight is secured around your neck with a lanyard. That makes two lanyards; the other secures the pistol. The signalman has a lamp to signal with. The engineer has a bag of tools for his own mysterious purposes. And so on. A forked stick for carrying messages is about the only thing *not* demanded by the Regulations.

"Never mind lowering the boat," bellowed the Captain from the bridge above; "I'll put you alongside."

I thought sceptically of his two misses. Meanwhile, the guns hammered away.

"Port side," yelled the Captain.

I noted as we mustered on the port side that the 4-inch gun was silent. It had misfired. Was the round truly misfired and completely dead or was the charge smouldering and would it go off in five seconds, say, or ten, or thirty? A ticklish point; but in action there's no time to ponder. Gordon, the Captain of the Gun, tenderly eased the breech open, gently slid the charge into his arms, took five lurching steps to the ship's side, and dropped the smouldering charge over. As you may imagine, the rest of the guns-crew watched this in silence and with interest.

Now with a whoop they loaded again. They were so intent they didn't notice my boarding-party. The muzzle swung. I was leaning over the rail gauging the narrowing distance to U-94 when I heard the reports given:

"Layer on."

"Trainer on."

One startled look over my shoulder and I scuttled for safety. "Fire!"

Only fifteen feet from the muzzle, the blast was stunning and blew us all into an untidy heap in the break of the fo'c's'le—a drop of ten feet. I came to in a few moments with Petty Officer Powell shaking me and slapping my face.

"Come on, sir, we're nearly alongside."

A bump and the grating of metal brought me to my senses, although my nose was bleeding and my ears were buzzing. I sprang up. No time for the rest of the boarding-party, groping about, still confused.

"Well, come on then. Over we go," I said.

Now, I was always a romantic youth, and from age ten onwards, stories of the Spanish Main were a large part of my literary diet. And so, as I dropped the eight-odd feet to U-94's deck I thought incredulously, "Mother of God! I really *am* boarding an enemy ship on the Spanish Main."

A small calamity brought me back to earth. As I hit the deck of U-94 the belt of my tropical shorts snapped on impact. My pants slid down to my ankles. I stumbled, kicked them off, and rose. Clad only in a pistol, two grenades, a gas-mask, a length of chain, a flashlight, and a lifebelt, I lurched up the deck.

"The bridge," I yelled to Powell, just as a wave washed me over the side. Powell helped me back but the chain was on a thousand-fathom journey to the bottom. "The bridge!" We started forward again, swaying up the heaving deck.

The enemy were still below but they wouldn't stay there long. If we could gain the bridge first, we would be in control.

Oakville was stopped a half-mile away. Her after-gun opened up at us. Luckily it started at the other end of the U-94's hull and methodically worked its fire to our end. The bullets ricocheted off with nasty whinging sounds. "There's always *someone* who doesn't get the word!" I thought resentfully. Over the side again; we were safer in the water.

I swam back on board with the next wave, throwing off the gas-mask. A sort of strip-tease had started: first my pants, then the chain, and now the gas-mask. Powell was there again.

"The bridge," I said desperately. "Damn it, this is becoming more like a swimming party than a capture."

Despite casualties, there were still some thirty able-bodied Germans on board. We were two. We reached the forward gun, by now a tangled mess of steel. A German slid from behind it. With my pistol barrel I knocked him over the side. Twenty-nine to two.

Rounding the conning tower we saw two more. We rushed. Both took a long, horrified look at my uniform—or lack of it, and jumped into the water when we were within three feet. They must have been thinking along the lines of "Blimey—he's come to bugger us all."

Powell flushed another and kicked him over. Twenty-six to two.

"The bridge," I urged again; "we can't fight the whole bloody crew one by one. We've got to keep them below."

Too late! As we reached the top of the ladder two were out. A third was emerging.

"Get below," I ordered the leading one. It wasn't in German but a pistol three feet from one's face is international for "stop". He kept coming. I fired and he flipped backwards over the side under the awful power of a .45 slug. Powell fired. The second sagged. Twenty-four to two. The third man, half-out, bobbed down.

A body lay crumpled behind the hatch; another hung by the after-gun, his arm swinging limply as U-94 rolled.

"Now keep them below," I ordered Powell. "Find out if they opened the sea-cocks or if they set scuttling charges. I want to look at that open hatch aft."

I jumped down the ladder, hung on as a wave washed over, then tore for the open hatch. Made it! As the next wave swept the deck I hung onto the hatch with both hands. That's the secret, I thought. The brilliant moon showed the compartment flooded; no one would flank us from here. On a lifting deck I rushed back. Powell was sitting on the rail, his gun dangling casually, his eyes alert. The prisoners below were shouting.

"Better let them out if we're to salvage this boat," Powell said.

I knelt by the hatch. "Sprechen Sie Deutsch?" A clamour told me they all did. "Ja, ja."

"No, no, I mean, sprechen Sie Englisch?" Silence.

"How are you going to get them up?" Powell asked mildly.

Well, we had certainly been definite about their staying below. And, apart from "Auf Wiedersehen", which did not seem to fit the situation, I had exhausted my German vocabulary.

I put the pistol on the deck, shone the flashlight on my face, and spoke in what I hoped was a reassuring voice.

"Come on up. It's all right. See—no gun." I grinned, pleasantly. "See—no gun." I beckoned encouragingly.

A muscular arm shot up. I leaned back, startled. Another arm followed and a body heaved out, and another, and another. Soon I found myself in a veritable mob, my pistol and flashlight trailing around my ankles. The pistol banged my shins painfully and the flashlight lanyard threatened to choke me. Someone was standing on the light. Such was the squeeze I couldn't bend to pick up either of them.

I had certainly lost command of the situation.

Powell hadn't. He shoved and kicked the submariners to the after gun-platform that abutted the bridge. Magically, I was unimpeded.

The bridge was pocked with bullet-holes, one section blown away completely. The forward end of the bridge was crumpled from the ramming and the hatch was stuck open at about fifty degrees. I slid over the body lying there, wriggled underneath the hatch, and dropped down.

Directly below the bridge was the conning tower.

It was black. From repeated wettings my flashlight was burning dull orange. Nothing here. Down the next ladder.

Now I was in the Control Room. Here it was blacker still, the water about chest height. In this compartment were the flooding valves I must close.

Now concentrate! Numbers one, three, and five were main-ballast tanks. Numbers two and four were trimming-tanks and unimportant. Number one was aft, three amidships, and five forward. The pressure gauges were all on the port side.

She rolled heavily. I slipped and went under. Coming up, I trod water. She rolled the other way. With a rush the water receded to my knees and I was standing again. But now, dammit, which side was port? I'd lost my bearings. Tortuously, I pulled myself from instrument to instrument, now floating, now standing, looking for the pressure gauges. The effective range of my flashlight was about a foot and getting dimmer.

A thump and a sudden list told me a water-tight bulkhead had given. Was it forward or aft? I didn't know.

At last I came on the pressure gauges. Before I could recall the correct procedure, there came a thump and a lurch and a particularly long roll to port. She lolled; there was little buoyancy now. Clearly, U-94 was mortally hurt.

"Come up, sir," yelled Powell, "she's going!"

Murmuring a "Hail Mary" I swam for the ladder. Water showered in from above. The sailor who had been slumped around the hatch had slewed around in the rushing water and stared sightlessly skyward.

Powell glanced at me with the question written on his face. The prisoners were huddled near his weaving .45.

"Get them over," I said.

Powell jerked his thumb; the prisoners plunged over the side.

"You too."

Powell stepped off.

Only a few moments left. A cloud obscured the moon. The black waves rolled toward us, white crests hissing gently. The water to leeward was ablaze with green phosphorescence. Off to the north the dark bulk of the convoy receded. Two "whumps" of torpedoes striking home told me other U-boats were attacking. A pillar of flame erupted, mounted, and briefly took the shape of a crooked tree; star shell and flares blossomed. *Oakville* was a black silhouette about a mile away. The rollers crashed over our side. U-94 would never lift above them again; she would never be steamed into harbour flying the white ensign of a captured ship either. It's a sad thing to see a ship die, and to lose a prize of war.

I slid over, swam hard for a minute, and looked back. We hadn't abandoned U-94 too soon; she lifted her bow, and slid under.

Forty-five minutes had passed since first sighting.

Meanwhile, *Oakville* had been a busy corvette. Much of her bottom was torn away, the port and starboard feed-tanks were leaking, as was the port domestic water-tank, the asdic compartment was flooded to the deck-head, and the lights were out in the after boiler-room, itself flooded to water-level. This last injury was serious.

With steam held captive at two hundred and twenty-five pounds per square inch at four hundred degrees Fahrenheit, contact with (comparatively) cold water is fatal. *Windflower* had blown up this way. Stoker Petty Officer Wilson, after getting his men out, swam around the side of the boiler in the dark to the release-valve and vented the steam.

The engine-room hands have a private horror of their own: they never know what's going on. They hear gun-fire, they are rocked by our depth-charges much more severely than those on deck, lights smash, fuses blow, telegraphs jangle orders to them, the revolution indicator clangs out its message. They are below the water-line. The temperature is above one hundred degrees. The smashing and tearing of two rammings must have been appalling. Yet, the revolution pointer must be kept exactly *there*; the steam pressure must be precisely *that*.

The damage-control ratings were shoring up bulging, straining bulkheads with heavy lumber. The sick-bay attendant was dealing with the German wounded, his gentleness a strange contrast to the ferocity of the previous hour.

The Captain sat on the bridge enjoying himself hugely. At the beginning of the action, USS *Lea* had closed us from the opposite side of the convoy.

"What is your target?" asked *Lea*.

"Submarine, rammed twice."

"Do you need assistance?"

"No, thank you."

Some more chit-chat followed, and, as the submarine sank, *Oakville* asked *Lea*, "Will you pick up my boarding-party?"

"Glad to."

I had hoped someone was thinking of me. I was feeling forlorn and tired. Also my strip had gone as far as it could. I had dropped my pistol, grenades, and flashlight and now had on only the lifebelt. There was a lot of blood in the water and the fish were active—shark were here, and barracuda. You have no idea what confidence a pair of cotton shorts can give or how I missed them. I swam on my back with one hand; the other protected vital parts.

The USS *Lea* pulled up in a welter of foam and we all struggled for the ladder. There must have been twenty of us and it was every man for himself.

"Gangway for an officer," I protested. "We can't all be saved."

On deck I was grabbed and hustled aft along with the German prisoners. This was the bitter end!

"I'm a Canadian officer."

"Yeah."

The deck was burning my feet and the gobs were hurting my arms.

"Goddamit, I am!"

"Yeah."

In some Royal Navy gunroom messes, obscenity is an art. *Alaunia* was one of those gunrooms. It stood me in good stead now. A steady and ever-rising stream of vituperation flowed out. I covered the probable profession of their mothers, the probable diseases of their fathers, the certainty of animal ancestors, and more.

They dropped my arms.

"I would like to speak to your captain."

"Yeah," said one, "sir." (The "sir" came hard.) "This way."

I danced up the hot deck. We must have been over a boiler-room; forward, the deck was cooler.

I saluted, self-consciously aware of my dishabille. I briefly told the Captain of the *Lea* what had transpired. These USN officers were kind. They escorted me to the wardroom and offered me coffee. Josephus Daniels! Coffee! The Exec brought in a singlet, pants, and gym shoes.

With slow, provocative gestures I undid the cord of my final garment, my lifebelt; leisurely I slipped it off and flipped it away. The strip was complete.

With handshakes, back-slapping, and see-you-in-Guantanamos, I was sent back to *Oakville*. It was 0100, Friday.

"Well, you're back, eh," said the First Lieutenant. "Good boy. We're still at action stations. The skiff picked up Powell. You'd better get up to the bridge. It's your watch."

In the west the moon sank, wanly. Dawn came redly, reflected off cumulus clouds towering above Haiti. We secured action stations and ate a hilarious breakfast. On the wardroom settee Otto Ites lay silent, one leg broken, the other with bullet-wounds, his face to the bulkhead.

We arrived at Guantanamo, Cuba, that afternoon. The prisoners were landed—twenty-one from *Lea* and five from *Oakville*. Out of U-94's original crew of forty-five, nineteen were dead. The SS *San Faban* and the SS *Rotterdam* had been torpedoed, and fifty-nine of their survivors were landed. I was right in fearing the fish: some survivors were badly chewed. SS *Esso Aruba*, though torpedoed, made port under her own steam.

The Commander-in-Chief, US Atlantic Fleet, sent his congratulations; Admiralty informed us that Their Lordships congratulated us. It was all very pleasant, but we were a bit sombre; a lot of men had died.

But *Oakville* had no casualties, or at least only one: when I wriggled down the U-94's hatch I had cut my elbow on a broken Coke bottle.

Now came a pleasant ten days in Guantanamo whilst temporary repairs were effected on *Oakville* sufficient to get us to Halifax. My first captain in *Oakville*, Jones, was now stationed ashore in Guantanamo as Canadian Liaison Officer. At his house we lazed away the long hot days with long cool rums.

After *Oakville* completed her dickey-refit we departed Guantanamo. Only one boiler-room was serviceable, but we limped back to New York with a convoy. We weren't really in fighting condition, but escorts were short. We formed a physical barrier at least between U-boats and convoy.

New York. Staten Island ferry. Lexington Avenue express uptown. Pixie. Eleanor. Lexington Avenue downtown. Staten Island ferry. Hands fall in. Routine chores. Lunch. Zizz. Staten Island ferry. Lexington Avenue express uptown. . . . We sailed for Halifax with a convoy.

There hadn't been much good news about the naval war in the Canadian press; in fact nearly all of it was bad. But the *Oakville*–U-94 battle had all the ingredients of a newspaper editor's dream: the Spanish Main; a boarding-party; lurking submarines (U-boats always "lurked"; our submarines were "gallant" or "swift and silent"); an American aircraft; an American destroyer; a Dutch tug; gunfire, depth-charging, ramming. I was a "young veteran of the North Atlantic". It was time the Canadian and American public got some good news.

When we got back to Halifax the public-relations types swarmed on board with a battery of photographers. Several of the eastern papers sent their own reporters and photographers. Would I pose over here with my arm around Powell's shoulder? No, I wouldn't. Would I crouch on the rail and hold a revolver? No, that would look silly. I told and retold the story. There is no doubt that initially this sort of attention is pleasant, but it palled and I wanted to go on leave. (Mother was at the family cottage at Lake Couchiching and I hadn't seen her for a year and a half.) I was told I had to go on tour. I demurred. I was sent for. A newspaper was waved under my nose. "The Naval Minister [Angus L. Macdonald] says, 'This incident affords a striking example of the close partnership in which the navies of the United States of America and Canada are working in the Allied cause.' Now go and bloody well talk about that striking example!''

I went to Toronto and played the triumphant home-town boy. The mayor met me on the steps of City Hall before an admiring multitude of lunch-hour shoppers. I was taken to my old school, St. Clare's, at the corner of St. Clair Avenue West and Dufferin Street. Here I was photographed at the desk I used to occupy in Grade 7. Brother Steven, who had taught me then, seemed to have forgotten all the cuffings and strappings, and he pronounced me an ideal pupil. The little fellow who now occupied the desk seemed apprehensive as to what might be expected of him in the future. I went to the town of Oakville, met Mayor Deans, inspected a guard of honour of the local cadets, and spoke at a lunch. I mentioned how much the ship's company of *Oakville* appreciated the scarves, mitts, and balaclavas the ladies of Oakville had been knitting for us. I went to Port Arthur, where *Oakville* was built, met another mayor, and spoke to the shipyard workers. They presented me with a fifty-dollar war bond, which I surreptitiously cashed before leaving town. I went to New York to meet Mayor Fiorello La Guardia, gave radio and newspaper interviews, and finally appeared on a show of the radio-interview type.

This last proved my downfall. I was the last guest on an hour-long program called "We the People"; Miles Bolton was MC. I had been wined very well before the program, and after twenty minutes on stage began to feel quite uncomfortable. If I'd had any brains I'd have either gone to the heads before or tiptoed off then, when I still had thirty minutes. I didn't. With just a few minutes to go to my turn the pain became unbearable, and I had to leave. When I arrived back the band was playing "The Maple Leaf Forever" for the third time and Mr. Bolton was ad-libbing frantically. I slid into my seat in front of the microphone. The script! I had left it in the heads.

"Tonight, ladies and gentlemen, we have with us Sub-Lieutenant Hal Lawrence of the Royal Canadian Navy," began the MC, "and he is going to tell us about one of the . . .''

When it was my turn the script was shoved across to me. I answered and shoved it back. Then came the easy part.

"Now tell us, in your own words, what happened next."

I relaxed, and started. This was a good story and I seemed a natural raconteur. Three million listeners sat transfixed as I went on, my voice rising and falling in measured cadence. I gestured, "and there, off to starboard . . ." A man behind the studio window revolved his hand at frantic speed. I looked at the clock. Good God! Only two minutes and I wasn't even inside the blasted submarine yet. I finished hastily. The commercial came on—just a bald announcement—and we went off the air. Everyone left quickly and I was sent home the next day.

I went to Lake Couchiching. I caught frogs in the marsh again, swam out to the island, and, in the evenings, sat on the veranda and talked of old friends.

We played the old songs on the gramophone: familiar tunes from *The Maid of the Mountains*, which had been playing in Cork in 1912 when Father met Mother there; John McCormack singing "I Met Her in the Garden where the Praties Grow", and "Mother Machree". We played the songs of the First World War: "Take Me Back to Dear Old Blighty", "It's a Long Way to Tipperary".

"Is Father expecting to be sent overseas?"

"I hope not," Mother said. "I spent the whole of the last war reading the casualty lists in the papers. You're quite enough to worry about."

When the twilight faded we would light the oil lamps, make tea and toast, and go to bed.

One Saturday afternoon Mother asked, "How long is it since you've been to confession?"

"Quite a while."

"We'll go tonight."

We drove to Orillia. Mother went to her regular confessor and I to another. When I came out Mother was at the altar rail saying her penance. I knelt beside her.

"What did you get?" I asked.

"Three Hail Marys; what did you get?"

"The rosary."

Mother looked at me with mingled horror and awe.

Oakville's refit was completing, the lazy days of my leave were ending, and I set off for Halifax. I stopped over at Brockville to see Father, who was running the Engineering Wing at the army camp there. Among the courses taught was "Rendering Mines Safe"; another was "Bomb Disposal". I asked how things were going.

"As well as may be expected. We've sent about a hundred bomb-disposal officers overseas to date. But far too many have been killed."

"Do you expect to go over?"

"I'm doing everything I can."

The subalterns were great fun and we spent jovial hours at the bar whilst Father played bridge with the Brigadier. I taught the subalterns fleet manoeuvres over drinks, and, each following afternoon, we practised in eight jeeps in a nearby field. Turns in succession, turns together. Blue nine, alter ninety degrees to starboard together; nine blue, alter ninety degrees to port together. Blue eighteen, reciprocal. I was flagship and stood in the centre jeep.

"Nine blue," I shouted and raised my arm.

"Nine blue," the squadron repeated and raised seven arms.

"Execute." I dropped my arm.

"Blue eighteen." Up arm. Other upraised arms signified they understood.

"Execute." Down arms. Round we went.

"Speed thirty. Execute." The speedometers flicked to thirty.

One night after dinner the Adjutant invited the Brigadier to see our show. The Brigadier assented graciously, but Father's lips were compressed. A fine summer evening—about eight o'clock—and all the officers in the mess followed the CO. The cadets and the troops got the buzz; and, all in all, about a thousand congregated around the field. We had a final double at the bar to fortify ourselves.

In an expectant hush we steamed onto the field in single line ahead. Every jeep carried a walkie-talkie. "Speed ten. Nine blue, execute." We turned to line abreast and steamed slowly toward the Brigadier, who had parked his jeep on a knoll by the western ditch.

"Speed zero."

"Execute."

The flotilla stopped about fifty feet short of the Brigadier. Father sat beside him. I produced a bosun's call and piped the "Still". The sixteen subalterns rose, two in each jeep—one "helmsman" and one "captain". We saluted. Impeccably the Brigadier replied. I piped the "Carry on". The "helmsmen" sat down.

"Nine blue. Speed ten. Execute." We wheeled left and circled the field in line ahead. "Nine red. Execute." Each jeep wheeled in the wake of its next-ahead. Cavalry officers observed critically: this was not new to them. We completed the perimeter. Time to increase the tempo.

"Speed thirty. Standard distance twenty. Execute."

On white turns now one's starboard for'ard fender barely cleared the next-in-line's starboard after fender.

"Speed forty. Execute."

This was a taste of the heady wine of command. Let's give the Brigadier a thrill.

"Blue nine. Execute." We were heading toward him.

"Standard distance ten. Execute." The jeeps closed in.

"Speed sixty. Execute." We thundered toward the jeep on the knoll. The Brigadier stood up. Father got out.

"Division One, nine blue. Division Two, blue nine. Stand by, stand by . . ." Fifty feet to go, forty, thirty, twenty.

"Execute," I screamed. But the walkie-talkie had crapped out.

We missed the Brigadier, but grazed our next-to-port. He grazed his next-to-port, and the next fellow rammed his. The Starboard Division skidded to a stop. Two went in the ditch. When we regained our feet the Brigadier had gone. Casualties were patched up at sick bay. The jeeps were towed off. With some justice mine was the only severe injury—a sprained wrist.

Father said, "I expect your leave is about up."

I agreed and left next morning for Halifax.

Oakville sailed. New York, Guantanamo, Wilhemstadt, Port-of-Spain, New York. Staten Island ferry, Lexington Avenue uptown, Lexington Avenue downtown. Staten Island ferry. We returned to admiring American girls in New York after losing some merchantmen. The U-boat officers returned to admiring French girls in Lorient after sinking those merchantmen.

Now that *Oakville* was doing her fighting in southern latitudes, we sailed in high spirits and with a sense of expectancy. The numbing cold that had been a constant incubus in the north was dissipated by the trade winds.

I think that physical comfort is one of the main preoccupations of men fighting a battle: the luck to find a spot to sling your hammock where the water does not drip on your face; the chance that today you might be given a slice of bread without green mould on it; the possibility that tonight, when you are lookout, you will be on the leeward side and the freezing spray will drench your chum on the other. The knowledge that each day may be your last is pushed to the back of your mind as one of the facts of life that must be accepted, like the coxswain's bad temper and the stink of unwashed bodies, caused by a bloody-minded engineer officer who thinks that water for his boilers is more important than water for washing. And never is there any decent food.

From a culinary point of view, neither Trinidad nor New York was much affected by the war. Ashore, life was filet mignon with mushrooms, eggs and bacon, and apple pie. But on board, with a parsimony learned from generations of grasping pursers, the fare remained meagre and unappetizing. It had been the custom of the century before in the Royal Navy that the more the captain could save on victuals the more went into his own pocket. It seems now a short-sighted way to run a fighting ship, but in the days of fifty lashes for a misdemeanour that would rate thirty days' detention now, perhaps it was not out of place. This abuse slowly died out but was followed by something not much better. The well-fed Lords of the Admiralty decided that a British sailor should be given an allowance with which to buy his food, and this was set at about ten cents a day. Considering that this man's pay was about fifty dollars a month, it is not surprising that he skimped himself, and a breakfast of bread and dripping was usual. This was called canteen messing, and each mess chipped in, bought a month's food, cooked it themselves, and served it themselves.

Some of this had rubbed off on their Canadian descendants, and as late as 1946 Canadian paymasters were trying to make a reputation for thrift by being sparing with food, when, in fact, what they saved in a month did not equal the cost of two hours' high-speed steaming when the navigator was out on his calculations and had to make up time.

But eventually we met up with the United States Navy, where the amount of food was of glorious inconsequence, where polite Filipino mess-boys took a personal pride in filling a plate twice or more. And although ashore we could buy what we wanted, at remote anchorages we could also have our fill; each American destroyer would have a Canadian ship either snugged alongside or anchored close. For we had a commodity that a misguided Secretary of the Navy, Josephus Daniels, had denied the USN thirty years before—whisky.

In the dog-watches our wardroom would be jammed with American officers, and at four cents a tot we could be generous. The conversation would grow heated about the relative advantages of kings and presidents and we invariably found ourselves in that peculiar Canadian position of explaining the English to the Americans. (In the previous three years we had been explaining the Americans to the English.)

After many drinks we would troop happily across to the ship of our gallant allies and examine the menu with satisfaction.

And the weather! A balm to our fog-shrouded souls! Now, the North Atlantic is not as unpleasant as some novelists would have you believe. There were weeks and weeks when the weather was fine and the convoy steamed on unharried because, I suppose, the submarines were taking annual leave. But in the main it was gale, followed by fog-bank, followed by ice-field. Even the finer weather had an air of impermanence about it that the Caribbean does not know.

My promotion to lieutenant came through. I was twenty-two. I was also appointed Executive Officer of *Oakville*, Second in Command. Now I really had something to sink my teeth into. I was responsible to the Captain for the fighting efficiency of the ship, for the morale and well-being of the ship's company, for everything.

I had always hated first lieutenants who seemed unable to slip their ship without a stream of shouted commands from the bridge. I called the petty officers of the tops together. The headline was number one, the fore-spring number two, the after-spring number three, the stern line number four. The Captain nearly always went ahead on number two to spring the stern off; then we could slip numbers one, three, and four. Then the Captain went astern to back off the jetty and we could slip number two. Holding up one, two, three, or four fingers would signify which line I was talking about. Flicking the hands upward meant let go: clenched fists meant hold on. As I saw it, quietness could be equated to efficiency.

There came another of the intense satisfactions of being in charge. I stood in the wing of the bridge as we sailed and watched Skeggs quietly and methodically arming the depth-charges, Gordon checking the ready-use ammunition of his 4-inch gun, Decheyne and Martin loading the 20-mm guns, Shiles with his pom-pom, Drinkwater with his strip Lewis (always tension on the spring). The ordnance artificer made his rounds, the top-men swung the lifeboat out against the griping spar. Lines and fenders were stowed. Lifebuoy sentry and lookouts closed up. Dinner would be ready exactly as the last report, "Secured", came in. The Coxswain was drawing the rum, the mailman sorting the last delivery. Rum and mail would be distributed simultaneously. The chaplain I had borrowed for the trip would be there, sipping a tot, taking advantage of this relaxed time to make contacts. Everything shipshape and Bristol fashion.

The ship's radio played the record "Boogie-Woogie Bugle Boy from Company B". It was a favourite with the crew. (Under Shultz and later under Mohr, U-124 sailed to the music of "Alexander's

Ragtime Band''.) The placid confidence of a good crew is discernible. And, as I saw it, I was the architect and keystone.

Added to the heady wine of promotion was an announcement published in the December issue of the *Canada Gazette*:

> The King has been graciously pleased to approve
> the following awards:—
>
> *Distinguished Service Cross*
> Lieutenant Harold Ernest Thomas Lawrence,
> R.C.N.V.R., H.M.C.S. *Oakville*.
> For gallant and courageous action in close contact with the enemy.

Lieutenant Lawrence was in charge of a boarding party of two which attempted to prevent the scuttling of a U-boat. With complete disregard for his own safety, this Officer, accompanied by a Petty Officer, boarded the U-boat and, having subdued the enemy crew, he took action in an endeavour to prevent the scuttling of the U-boat, notwithstanding the fact that it was then sinking. His spirited and determined conduct was worthy of the highest traditions of the Royal Canadian Navy.

Neat, a trifle gaudy.

The year drew to a close. We spent Christmas of 1942 at sea en route from Curaçao to Haiti. Thank God for His blessings. The weather was good and the leave ports lively. But the war was going against us. That year we lost 1,664 ships—7,790,697 tons; 1,160 were sunk by U-boats. Yet statistics are arid. The loss of over a thousand ships means little to the individual. Instead, he remembers the sight of a lifeboat full of merchant sailors rowing frantically from the side of a burning tanker, and the sound of their screams as the flames engulfed them.

six

A Destroyer in the Home Fleet

It was in February 1944, in Cowes on the Isle of Wight, that I first saw her and knew how fascinating she would be. She carried herself with a graceful arrogance. Although she was slim, there was a toughness about her, a lethality, and also the unmistakable air of the coquette. An aristocrat with the tendencies of a wanton. She exuded primal power; yet, properly handled, she would be obedient, a vestal virgin consecrated to Mars and to a spectacular duty: death to the King's enemies. It was perhaps this knowledge that gave her an aura of vindictiveness. Some fusty man in the dusty recesses of Admiralty had given her an appropriate name—*Vixen*. The Royal Canadian Navy had bought her from the Royal Navy; she was, after all, only a chattel to be bought and sold and used. In some similarly obscure office in Ottawa she had been given a new name which emphasized her latent ferocity. This was His Majesty's Canadian destroyer *Sioux*.

Examination vessels, patrol vessels, armed merchant cruisers, corvettes, were all in the past. In *Sioux* I would join the Home Fleet, whose Commander-in-Chief was Admiral Sir Bruce Fraser. It was the ships of the Home Fleet that had sunk *Bismarck* and were the proper adversaries of *Scharnhorst*, *Tirpitz*, and *Gneisenau*. In 1914-18 this fleet had been called the Grand Fleet, and, under the command of Admirals Lord Beatty and Lord Jellicoe, it had battled the German Imperial High Seas Fleet. The Grand Fleet had won that war. I felt that Sir Bruce would like to know that I was here to help him win this one. I was finally in the "real" navy.

I had left *Oakville* without regret, spending a few days in Halifax to say goodbye to Alma, a difficult goodbye. We tried to pretend that the war was a temporary thing, but a lot of our friends had been killed. Their names kept cropping up in conversation, followed by a short silence, then a babble of trivia, and then another round of drinks. We knew some twenty-year-old widows who still hung around Halifax rather than return to their homes inland. They said there was nothing for them back there, and they were very gay. They were usually escorted by their dead husbands' shipmates.

There was a destroyer building for the Royal Navy at the Hingham shipyards outside Boston. The officers designated for *Sioux* were to help man her on the passage to Londonderry. There, the RN officers would join and we would go on to join *Sioux* at Cowes. I left Brockville for Boston and en route had a stop-over in Montreal. Here I met another officer bound for *Sioux*.

We sat in his room at the Mount Royal Hotel and sipped whisky. He poured a very weak drink. His wife was with him and they were both rather silent. I knew how they felt, for I had just said my own goodbyes. His boy, who had a leg in a cast from a playground accident, whined on the bed. I started to go several times but was asked to wait: "I've got to put my wife on the train home in twenty minutes."

After they had gone I sat and meditated. He seemed a nice chap, a bit dull perhaps and not a person I'd have chosen to be shipmates with for two years. Family responsibilities were weighing a bit heavy, probably.

The door burst open and he thundered in.

"What ho, Lawrence, my newly acquired friend, let us toss off a bumper."

Pouring his glass three-quarters full of whisky and gingerly adding a few drops of water and a lump of ice, he struck a heroic pose.

"Let this drink be the symbol of the metamorphosis. No more do we see Smith the family man. We see Smith the fighter! We see Smith the lover! Soon shall the rumour run around the wardrooms of the German Navy and the drawing-rooms of Mayfair. Some shall whisper it in dread and some shall whisper it in anticipation: 'Smith is coming!'"

He drained his glass. "The Normandie Roof! Phone the good Victor and tell him we require a table at his most excellent club. For nine o'clock. A table for four."

We never looked back.

The rest of *Sioux*'s officers we met in Boston. The ship we were to commission was HMS *Seymore*, and of her permanent crew only the Captain, the First Lieutenant, and the Engineer Officer were there. All the other men on board were destined for *Sioux*. It would not be too much to say that we didn't really have

the best interests of *Seymore* close to our heart. There were about
ten of *Sioux*'s officers aboard and most had been recalled from
leave with unspent money in their pockets. And we were leaving
the bright lights of the land of plenty for the blackout and the rationing of the United Kingdom. We were determined to make the
most of the few days left. We had between us a little over nine
thousand dollars. We took four adjoining double rooms at the
Statler Hotel, where the habitués of the Terrace Room came to
know us well. *Seymore* commissioned, our money ran out, and we
sailed.

Back across the North Atlantic in winter. Nothing had
changed: the U-boats still drained our strength. We steamed up
Loch Foyle to Londonderry. After a winter crossing, the green
fields and cosy cottages looked particularly pleasant. A ferry took
us from Larne to Stranraer, and a jolting, unheated train transported us from there to Portsmouth via every siding on the
way. Another ferry took us across to the Isle of Wight—a blessed
isle in peacetime and a yachtsman's paradise, now a mass of for-
tifications, barbed wire, and suspicious sentries. Passes were
closely scrutinized, for the threat of invasion lingered.

Although my first glimpse of *Sioux* had impressed me deeply,
she was not looking her best. A ship a-building is a drab thing.
Welders' arcs flare, riveting-guns keep up a constant staccato
chatter, burners' torches spray sparks, cables and wandering
leads festoon every compartment, bowler-hatted men consult
ship's drawings and look non-committal when asked about a com-
pletion date. *Sioux* was behind schedule, and so I was sent to the
Gunnery School in Portsmouth, HMS *Excellent*. My knowledge of
gunnery acquired over three years was inadequate for *Sioux*'s
modern control system.

Naval gunnery had been taught at *Excellent* since 1842. The
school is on Whale Island, or "Whaley", as it was known familiar-
ly. The patron saint of *Excellent*—and of gunners generally—is
Saint Barbara. Saint Barbara was a young maiden of the third
century after Christ, daughter of a Greek nobleman and pagan,
Dioscorus. Hagiographers have pieced together her history. She
was a lovely girl, and her father confined her to a high and inaccessible tower so that no man might see her. Nevertheless (it is
not clear how), she was converted to Christianity. She had persuaded her father to build her a bath at the base of the tower to
ease the tedium of her lonely imprisonment. Dioscorus had acced-
ed to this request but with the proviso that the room have only two

windows, and these so high as to be quite inaccessible. During her father's absence Barbara persuaded reluctant workmen to add a third, and great was her father's rage upon his return; more so, when Barbara lectured him upon the mystery of the Holy Trinity, using the three windows symbolically. Dioscorus drew his sword to slay her, but miraculously the rocks opened and she escaped. She took refuge with two shepherds, but one succumbed to avarice and betrayed her. Marcian, the local magistrate, urged her to recant but she steadfastly refused, even after prolonged torture. Marcian therefore ordered her execution by the sword. As she was led to the block she prayed earnestly for help. Her prayer was answered in a rather peculiar way which truly illustrates the inscrutability of God's motives. At the very instant that Dioscorus severed her head, a thunderbolt fell from Heaven, killing both her father and Marcian.

But there is nothing insular about good Saint Barbara. In the director's room at the Nobel powder factory in Sweden hangs a life-size tapestry of her in the traditional attitude, holding a tower in one hand and a palm in the other. A plaque taken from a German artillery headquarters in 1918 bears an invocation to her. She is particularly well known in Bohemia. The Spaniards colloquially call their shell magazines "Santas Barbaras". During the First World War, a war of massive artillery duels, G. K. Chesterton wrote *The Ballad of Saint Barbara*; presumably she decided in favour of British artillerists in that war.

Accommodation was short and a hulk had been run up on the mud-banks near by to take the overflow. It was in this hulk, the old royal yacht, *Victoria and Albert*, that we were billeted. Lying in the still-luxurious and very gingerbready cabins, speculating about the previous occupants, gave me a feeling hard to describe. What a change in England's fortunes since this yacht slid down the ways! Once the greatest manufacturing nation in the world, England was guaranteed her supremacy by her merchant fleet of six hundred ships. But Prince Albert had died eighty years before and his unhappy widow, Queen Victoria, had reigned for forty lonely years after that. The first war had killed three hundred thousand of England's young men, and the depression had disillusioned the generation following. The country's money was now gone, mortgaged in the last two years while she stood alone. Now she was a beleaguered island short of food, and short of fuel, and more Englishmen died nightly under German bombs. She was short of everything except pride and stubbornness, and now, with the help of allies, she was fighting her way back. But the England that *Victoria and Albert* had been born to was gone forever. It saddened me.

That's where the English pubs came in. Plenty of beer was still available, and every evening saw us in the Barley Mow, where it was noisy and smoky and you didn't feel so transitory. In fact, most nights about closing time you felt positively immortal.

To commission a ship for the first time is very different from joining a ship already in commission. When you join a ship in commission you're a stranger joining a family, a family that has been together for months, perhaps years. They have shared experiences and dangers and have family jokes known only to themselves. Like: "What's Archie doing?" "Don't know. Probably writing that Wren in Newfie." A roar of laughter from the rest and a small uncertain grin from you. As time goes on—not very long—you become one of the family.

In commissioning a new ship there is no family, just two hundred and forty strangers. Initially it is little things that draw you together. One morning the Coxswain came to my cabin.

"Able Seaman Farquhar was in choky last night. Held by civil power. I sprung him this morning at eight-thirty. He has to appear in court at eleven."

"What's the charge?"

"Wilfully damaging public property."

"What'd he do?"

"Kicked out all the glass panes in a public telephone booth."

"*Kicked* them out?"

"Yessir" (smiling a little).

"How the hell could he?"

"Said he had to jump a little to reach the top ones." (Smiling broadly now.) "I believe him. The back of his head's a mess from falling over backwards. The doctor's patched him up."

I took the patched-up Farquhar to court to represent him. "How the hell'd you do it?" I asked.

He smiled modestly. "I can jump pretty high," he said.

He pleaded guilty. I testified to his normal sobriety and good behaviour (from his service documents—I didn't know him personally yet). He was fined five pounds and we returned. Rum was being issued on the quarter-deck; as we came over the side, I turned forward to go to the wardroom and he went aft to pick up his tot. His messmates surrounded him.

"What'd you get?" asked one.

"Five quid."

"That's about right," said another judiciously. "How the hell'd you do it?"

"I can jump pretty high," said Farquhar.

We had started to become a family. Old shipmates from other ships still talked about previous commissions in "Bones" or "Sally" (*Assiniboine* and *St. Laurent*), but they grew less frequent as *Sioux* acquired a history of her own.

How a sailor can change his allegiance so often has always perplexed me. Every two years or so he changes ships. For a while there is nothing like the last ship, the last captain, the last cook. And then, in only a few months, comes a pride in the present ship. She is the best ship in the division, the flotilla, the whole goddam fleet.

And now came my debut into real gunnery. No more for me of the ancient 6-inch of *Alaunia*, which were more dangerous at the after end to the guns-crew than at the for'ard end to an enemy; no more of the erratic 4-inch of a corvette manned by enthusiastic but ill-trained sailors. (I still had pain in my left ear from the *Oakville* action.) In *Sioux* we had four beauties; they were 4.7-inch and threw a thirty-pound shell ten miles.

Sioux sailed into the Solent to do her first AA gunnery practice. The Principal Control Officer for this shoot was a specialist from *Excellent*, out with us for the day. We sat in the High-Angle Director—the director layer and the director trainer in front of me, the range-taker, Leading Seaman Baker, beside me. High above everyone else we were; and, below us, joined by telephones, voice-pipes, loudspeakers, and innumerable automatic electrical transmissions, were eighty-two well-trained men waiting my orders to put this beautifully co-ordinated machine to its job of dealing out death. It nearly dealt out death the first time I used it.

A slow aircraft, towing a drogue a mile astern, droned down the starboard side. The air-defence organization of the ship creaked into motion.

"Starboard lookout. Can't you see that aircraft?" I heard the Captain shout.

"Yessir," replied the lookout meekly.

"Well, report it."

"Yessir. Bearing red two-oh. Angle of sight three five. An aircraft."

"It's *not* red two-oh. It's green two-oh."

"Yessir. Bearing green two-oh, an aircraft."

"It's not green two-oh now, you bloody fool," said the Principal Control Officer. "It's moving. It's about green four-five now."

"Yessir. Bearing green . . ."

"Never mind. I've got it."

"Alarm Aircraft Starboard," said the Principal Control Officer. "Follow PCO's sight." The dials in front of my layer and trainer started to whirr. The trainer swung the director to the right and the layer elevated. We all stared intently through our binoculars. As the pointers in the dials clicked to rest and our pointers came to rest over them, the drogue appeared in our field of vision.

"Layer on," said the layer.

"Trainer on," said the trainer.

"Director target," I reported through my telephone.

Working my angle-of-inclination graticules, which automatically transmitted the course of the drogue to the gunnery-control computer, I also gave an estimated speed. "Speed one-three-oh."

"Is the aircraft approaching?" asked the Gunner's Mate from the bowels of the ship. The computer-room was four decks below us.

"Yes, Chief."

"Then you have your graticule the wrong way about."

The range-finder had been clicking beside me. "Cut," said Baker and pressed his foot-push. "Have range-finder," came the report from below and then a moment later, as the radar operator strobed his echo, "have radar."

"Armament target," I reported to the PCO.

"Open fire," he replied.

"Commence. Commence. Commence," I ordered, uncertainly.

There was a heavy sea running and just then *Sioux* slopped into a trough. The drogue disappeared from my binoculars. The layer and the trainer cranked frantically. The fire-bell rang and the broadside roared away. Where the devil was the drogue? Ah, there it was. I waited for the four black bursts in the sky.

"Cease fire!" shrieked the PCO.

I took my eyes out of my binoculars and stared, aghast. The cease-fire bells shrilled all over the ship. My four black bursts were right around the tail of the aircraft, nowhere near the drogue it was towing.

The puce face of the PCO appeared over the front of the Direc-

tor. "What in the name of God are you doing up here?" he asked
in a low, venomous voice. "Didn't you learn anything at Whaley?
There's a mile of wire on that target. A mile! That's to safeguard
innocent pilots against idiots. Ordinary idiots." His voice rose.
"And you," he turned to the director trainer, who had been intently studying his boots. "Call yourself a director trainer. Jesus
Christ! My poor old arthritic father could do better than you. And
he's drunk half the time." He glared at us all. We fidgeted and
looked away. Only Baker sat composed, secure in the knowledge
that line errors and elevation errors could not be attributed to
him. Range errors, yes, but not line or elevation errors.

"We'll try again," said the PCO. "That is, if I can persuade
that pilot to come back. He has, quite properly, pointed out to us
over the RT that he is pulling that target, not pushing it." We did it
again. And again and again. By late that day we were not bad and
the next day a little better. During the next week we carried out
other drills: seamanship exercises, anti-submarine exercises, and
so on. At last it was grudgingly admitted we were as good as we
could be right then; and we sailed to join the Fleet.

And thus was initiated another legend: "Do you remember
Lawrence's first shoot? Jesus sufferin' Christ!"

The base of the Home Fleet was in the Orkney Islands, just off
the north coast of Scotland. Enclosed by the islands of Pomona,
Hoy, South Ronaldshay, and Flotta is Scapa Flow. It was in Scapa
Flow that the ships of the Home Fleet swung at their moorings.
(Flow is a Norse word for enclosed body of water.) The gaps between the islands were blocked by nets and booms with gates,
similar to the one at Halifax. The heavy ships sat in the northern
part of the Flow and went out Hoxa gate; destroyers were moored
further down and went out Switha gate.

It was to Scapa Flow that the Grand Fleet escorted the Imperial High Seas Fleet in 1918 after the surrender of Germany:
sixteen capital ships, eight light cruisers, fifty destroyers. Here,
seven months after that war ended, the Kaiser's fleet scuttled
itself in a magnificent gesture of despair. That fleet had re-
generated itself and was now as great a menace as it ever had
been. In particular, the German heavy ships threatened the convoys we were trying to push through to Russia.

In 1941, Averell Harriman, representing the United States,
concluded an agreement in Moscow to provide arms and
materials to the Soviet Union. There were three routes by which

supplies could reach Russia: through the Persian Gulf to Basra and Hormuz and thence overland; across the Pacific to Vladivostok and thence overland across Siberia; or from the United Kingdom up the Norwegian coast to Murmansk and Archangel. Of the three, the Norwegian route was both the shortest and the most dangerous. The danger was twofold: weather and enemy forces.

The foulest weather in the world prevails in the Arctic Ocean in those bleak stretches bounded by Iceland to the west, Spitzbergen to the north, and Novaya Zemlya—which divides the Kara and Barents seas—to the east. Akureyri, on the north coast of Iceland, is just fifty miles outside the Arctic Circle. *Moose Jaw* had put in there, so I had sailed the Arctic before. Now I would go to the high latitudes—in one convoy only about eight hundred miles from the north pole. This stretch of water between Greenland and Norway is about nine hundred miles wide and is most turbulent. The North Atlantic I knew: gale following gale; rain, sleet, hail, snow. In the Arctic I would be at home, for it was the same Atlantic gales that followed their northeastern course to North Cape and Spitzbergen. Their fury spent, they would die here in the high-pressure area over the polar ice-cap. They were the same gales, but colder. The southern ice boundary is North Cape in the winter, Spitzbergen in the summer. In summer, daylight is continuous, and aircraft and submarines were able to attack around the clock. In winter, once we had steamed north to about Narvik, darkness was continuous. Strong and uncertain currents, no sun sights to check your ship's position, no radio beacons. The air temperature is below freezing. Spray will freeze on a ship and if not chipped off constantly will capsize her. The sea temperature rarely exceeds fifty degrees Fahrenheit and is often forty degrees or lower. A man cast into the water will not live more than two or three minutes and it is impossible to pluck him out in less time. Sailors tend to shed their bulky life-jackets in these latitudes. Might as well be comfortable, they say.

The enemy forces were equally formidable: a battleship, *Tirpitz*; a battle-cruiser, *Scharnhorst*; two pocket battleships, *Scheer* and *Lützow*; two heavy cruisers, *Admiral Hipper* and *Prinz Eugen*; two light cruisers, *Köln* and *Nürnberg*; and sixteen destroyers. Grossadmiral Raeder's strategy was sound. This comparatively small German fleet tied up a disproportionately large fleet of British, American, and Canadian forces. At the maximum, the Home Fleet consisted of seven capital ships—six British and the

USS *Washington*. When *Sioux* joined there were three battleships, *Rodney, Anson,* and *Duke of York*—wearing the flag of the Commander-in-Chief; four large and twelve small aircraft carriers; five heavy and eight light cruisers—including the USS *Tuscaloosa*; and forty destroyers. We had friends from Canada in the destroyers: HMCS *Athabaskan, Haida, Huron, Iroquois,* and *Algonquin*—about sixteen hundred Canadians. Not attached to the Fleet but escorting the convoys were six sloops, thirteen frigates (five of them Canadian), and twelve corvettes.

The Germans could sortie at will and at a time of their own choosing. We had to defend a convoy along a two-thousand-mile route, every mile within range of German aircraft: 103 long-range bombers, 30 dive-bombers, 42 torpedo-bombers, and 72 long-range reconnaissance. Airfields lay all along the route at Trondheim, Narvik, Barderfoss, Tromso, Hammerfest, Banak, Kirkenes, and Petsamo. From these last two it was only about ten minutes' flying time to reach convoys entering Murmansk. As well, there were about twenty U-boats.

The Home Fleet had, then, two tasks: to protect convoys to and from Russia, and to prevent a break-out of units of the German fleet into the Atlantic. With a dozen or so heavy Allied units up north with a convoy, this latter danger was ever present.

The year 1942 marked the nadir of Allied fortunes. Winston Churchill had said, "This is not the end. It is not even the beginning of the end. But it is, perhaps, the end of the beginning."

The Japanese were victorious in the Far East. Singapore had been captured. Canadian soldiers of the garrison at Hong Kong were either dead or held captive. Siam, Indochina, and the Malay States provided practically unlimited oil and rubber for the Japanese. HMS *Prince of Wales* and *Repulse* were sunk. Java and Rangoon were occupied, and the fate of Burma and India hung in the balance.

In the Pacific, the Japanese landed in New Guinea. Australia was menaced. The US Pacific Fleet was building up from the crippling blow at Pearl Harbor. The Philippine Islands were occupied by the Japanese. General MacArthur fumed in Australia.

In the bloody Battle of the Java Sea, the Dutch admiral Karel Doorman led his striking force against the invading Japanese fleet. From four Allied navies he commanded two heavy cruisers, USS *Houston* and HMS *Exeter*; three light cruisers, HMAS *Perth*, HMNS *De Ruyter* (Doorman's flagship), and HMNS *Java*; and nine destroyers, USS *John D. Edwards, Alden, John D. Ford,* and *Paul*

Jones, HMNS *Witte de With* and *Kortenaer,* and HMS *Encounter, Electra,* and *Jupiter.* All five cruisers were sunk along with four destroyers. The Japanese landed unharmed. Admiral Chuichi Nagumo's carrier force was now free to raid the Indian Ocean.

In the Far East Admiral Sir James Somerville awaited him with five old battleships, three small carriers, eight cruisers, and fifteen destroyers. The Japanese struck at Colombo and Trincomalee. In four months Nagumo operated a third of the way around the world and had sunk five battleships, a carrier, two cruisers, and seven destroyers. He had damaged several more capital ships, sunk two hundred thousand tons of allied merchant shipping, and shot down hundreds of allied aircraft. Not one of his ships was damaged.

In the Mediterranean, Admiral Sir Andrew Cunningham was fighting against desperately long odds. Outnumbered by the Italian fleet and with no air cover, his Malta-bound convoys were bombed from dawn until dusk from airfields only twenty minutes' flying time away. One merchant ship out of ten was getting through. To previous evacuations of our soldiers at Dunkirk and Norway was added the evacuation of Crete—Captain Lord Louis Mountbatten sunk in *Kelly.*

In the Atlantic, the U-boats were sinking an average of half a million tons a month.

In the Home Fleet at Scapa Flow we stood outside the wardroom of *Sioux* while she swung her buoy, and looked into the northern darkness. We knew what awaited us there: *Tirpitz, Scharnhorst, Scheer, Lützow, Hipper, Eugen, Köln, Nürnberg,* sixteen destroyers, twenty U-boats, and maybe a hundred shorebased Junkers, Heinkels, and Condors.

But there were no German aircraft carriers. To our advantage the Home Fleet had four large and twelve small carriers. We young officers in *Sioux* gave no thought to such strategic considerations. Maybe the Captain thought on such an elevated plane (after all, he was twenty-five), but we younger officers didn't. We didn't notice that what Admiral Nagumo could do in the Pacific and Indian oceans, Sir Bruce could do in the Arctic. We didn't notice that the main unit of a fleet was no longer the battleship; rather, it was the aircraft carrier.

As Odysseus had lurked in his tent for most of the Trojan war, *Tirpitz* lurked in the gloomy northern fiords of Norway, poised to strike at Russian convoys. Altenfiord was outside the range of the RAF's heavy bombers,and Murmansk and Archangel airfields were too primitive to mount a raid from the north. In September 1943, *Tirpitz* sortied from Altenfiord and bombarded a meteorological station in Spitzbergen. It was the only time her big guns fired in anger, yet how her shadow loomed over us! She tied down heavy units of the Home Fleet, so urgently needed elsewhere.

But that same month RN X-craft penetrated Altenfiord's defences. These were midget submarines of about thirty-five tons with a four-man crew, designed to stick limpet mines on the bottom of a target. They could be regarded as the successors of the fire-ships with which Drake had terrorized the Spanish at Gravelines in 1588. Six specially fitted submarines each towed one X-craft the fifteen hundred miles to Altenfiord. One X-craft sank en route with all hands; another had to be abandoned; a third sank in the fifty miles up Altenfiord; another, in a series of misfortunes, lost both compass and periscope. But two got through and fixed their mines. The crews surfaced and hurriedly surrendered before the resultant explosion lifted *Tirpitz* several feet out of the water. She was temporarily immobilized. *Scharnhorst* remained at large.

In December 1943, Sir Bruce, in *Duke of York*, caught *Scharnhorst* off North Cape. With Sir Bruce was the light cruiser *Jamaica* and four destroyers. Vice-Admiral Burnett covered a southbound convoy with one heavy cruiser and two light cruisers. On Christmas Day, a southwest gale with snow squalls hindered the operation, but on Boxing Day contact was made by Burnett's cruiser squadron. He illuminated *Scharnhorst* with star shell, and, at a range of over ten miles, *Duke of York* opened fire. In a slugging match and a stern-chase, they fought it out. The destroyers HMS *Scorpion* and HMNS *Stord*, through a blazing barrage of shell-fire, closed to three thousand yards and fired torpedoes. *Savage* and *Saumerez* fired from the other side. *Scharnhorst* sank; out of her crew of two thousand, thirty-six petty officers and men were plucked out of the tumultuous Arctic Sea.

The convoy *Scharnhorst* had sought—*Iroquois* and *Haida* were part of its escort—steamed on unmolested. Weapons change, tactics change: the imbuing spirit behind them doesn't. In the *Regulations and Instructions Relating to His Majesty's Service at Sea* of 1806, we find,

> The officer who shall have the charge of a convoy trusted to him
> is to consider the protection of it as his most particular duty, in

the execution of which he is to be very watchful to prevent it being surprised, and very alert in defending it if attacked.

Tirpitz was soon patched up and threatened us again. Sir
Bruce decided to go and get her.

As long as memory persists I shall remember that glorious
March day. When I am an old man huddled by the fire, a rug
over my knees and a shawl over wasted shoulders, great-
grandchildren marched in for the filial-piety ritual of the mandatory once-a-month visit, staring curiously and with some
deference at this relic of a long-forgotten war—as long as my
faculties allow it, I shall remember that brisk, clear, windy day,
March 30, 1944.

The destroyers streamed out of Switha gate with Rear-
Admiral (Destroyers) in the van. Astern of him were three Captains (D) with their flotillas for a total of twenty-four destroyers.
Our Captain (D) was in *Myngs*, leading *Volage, Virago, Venus,
Verulam, Vigilant, Algonquin* (ex-*Valentine*), and *Sioux* (ex-*Vixen*).
The Yeoman of Signals, a three-badge petty officer, stood poised
beside the primary voice-circuit. A leading signalman was on the
secondary. An ordinary signalman (White was his name, aged
eighteen) served as messenger. Below, a three-badge petty officer
telegraphist monitored his wireless circuits: tactical primary and
tactical secondary, the Whitehall listening watch, the ship-air
frequency, the U-boat frequency, the gun-direction net. . . .

Rear-Admiral (D)'s Yeoman crackled out his orders with
bewildering speed. With equal speed the "Rogers" flashed back.
The Yeoman pointed off the port bow and said to the Captain,
"Over there." Following some secret hierarchical pattern that
escaped me, he waited for two more "Rogers", then pressed his
transmitting key, "Poppa Whisky, Roger, out." RA (D) was creaming back at 180 degrees with a bone in his teeth. The Captain
altered thirty degrees to port and increased to thirty knots. *Sioux*
shivered and thrummed and dug her nose into the choppy seas.
Myngs put all the flotilla on his quarter. The Yeoman's "Over
there" and the Captain's immediate alteration had given us a
fifteen-second lead, and we were on station soon after our
"Roger" to *Myngs*. Destroyers seemed to be going every which
way; they slewed, swung, and slowed. Suddenly, with RA (D) in the
centre, we were in an inverted V formation, steaming to cross the
leading battleship. When we turned ninety degrees to port
together we would be on the same course.

On our starboard bow the heavy ships steamed out Hoxa gate:

the Commander-in-Chief in the battleship *Duke of York*; astern of him the second-in-command, Vice-Admiral Sir Henry Moore, in the battleship *Anson*; astern of him the battleship *King George V.* Rear-Admiral Fleet Carriers was in *Victorious*, astern was *Furious*. Then came Rear-Admiral Escort Carriers with *Nairana*, *Puncher*, *Nabob*, and *Fencer*; Sir Roderic McGrigor, Rear-Admiral Light Cruisers; and Sir F. G. H. Dalrymple-Hamilton, Rear-Admiral Heavy Cruisers.

I sat in my cockpit in the Director, high above everyone else in the ship. We were testing communications through the computer-room to the guns. My view was unimpeded throughout three hundred degrees. The battleships butted implacably west, on our starboard bow and drawing aft. The destroyers steamed north on this near-collision course. The cruisers formed on the flagship, then the carriers. I felt a sense of wonder at the force and precision of it all, and dimly perceived the hours, days, weeks, months, even centuries of training behind it. The van battleship was two miles on our starboard bow and steaming so as to cut through the bent lines of destroyers.

I thought, "There's seven admirals and nearly fifteen thousand men out here."

Tactical primary crackled out to all destroyers, "Nine blue, nine blue, stand by, stand by. . . ."

Rear-Admiral (D) in the centre destroyer was just a mile ahead of the flagship and crossing her bows.

"Execute."

The "Rogers" rippled down the line.

All destroyers turned ninety degrees to port together.

And the destroyer screen was exactly in a spearhead formation ahead of the Fleet, steaming in the same direction and at the same speed. The sheer strength of what I was witnessing for the first time left me dumb. The young men shall have visions and the old men shall dream dreams. Well, the dream of that day will never fade; it will be a constant source of aesthetic and sensuous pleasure. That day I was a young man having visions, and the visions were fulfilled three days later.

The weather was unusually favourable and the convoy we were covering (RA-58, a convoy to Russia; JW-58 would be the returning convoy from Russia) was doing well. USS *Milwaukee* was with the convoy; shortly she would be turned over to the Russians. The good weather induced the C-in-C to advance the strike against *Tirpitz* by twenty-four hours. This called for some hard steaming, but we got there.

That morning, April 3, 1944, we closed up at our action stations at 0130. Baker and I hunched against each other and dozed in our eyrie. About 0430 the sun rose over a calm sea. We were a hundred and twenty miles to seaward of Altenfiord. The Fleet altered into the wind, and the fly-off began. The aircraft launched off each carrier in a steady steam, climbed, and circled the Fleet; they formed squadron after squadron of Wildcats, Hellcats, Avengers, and Barracudas. Each of the two fleet carriers had a wing of twenty-one Barracuda bombers. Forty fighters would accompany each wing. One hundred and twenty aircraft circled and formed as the tip of the sun showed over the horizon.

At 0530 the first wave of bombers hit *Tirpitz*. The attack was beautifully co-ordinated; surprise was complete. The fighters sprayed *Tirpitz* and shore AA batteries with machine-gun fire. Nine bombs hit. Smoke and flame poured from *Tirpitz*. At 0630 a second wave hit, but, as was to be expected, a smoke-screen had been laid in the fiord and the defending AA fire was intense. Five more bombs hit, resulting in four hundred casualties aboard *Tirpitz*. The light bombs of carrier-borne aircraft could never sink her, but again she was temporarily immobilized.

Rear-Admiral Dalrymple-Hamilton had with him as escort for this convoy, besides his flagship *Diadem*, twenty destroyers, four corvettes, two small carriers, *Activity* and *Tracker*, and five sloops. From the Western Approaches Command came another group of sloops, commanded by Captain F. J. Walker—"Johnnie" Walker, of course. (Their total bag since they had formed under Captain Walker, in *Starling*, was eighteen U-boats sunk, and they were still going strong.)

On March 30, the homeward-bound JW-58 was detected by enemy reconnaissance aircraft. Wildcat fighters from *Activity* made the job of the shadowing German aircraft hazardous, and managed to shoot down six of them. But the convoy's position, course, and speed were radioed back to Germany and sixteen U-boats had taken up a patrol line three hundred miles southwest of Bear Island. Then Captain Walker sank U-961. Avenger aircraft from *Tracker*, in a co-ordinated attack with the destroyer *Beagle*, sank U-355. The destroyer *Keppel* sank U-360. Then *Activity*'s Swordfish, assisted by an Avenger and a Wildcat, sank U-288. JW-58 evaded the patrol line of ten U-boats, and all thirty-six merchantmen arrived safely in Loch Ewe. The Fleet returned to Scapa Flow.

Scapa Flow is in latitude 60° North, further north than Juneau, Alaska. The islands are wind-swept and rain-driven; there are few trees. Low rolling hills are covered with gorse, heather, and a few bushes. It's about fifteen miles from north to south and about eight miles across. The principal entrance is to the south'ard from Pentland Firth through Hoxa Sound; on the west Hoy Sound leads to the Atlantic, on the east, Holm Sound to the North Sea. Lathering tides of nine to twelve knots rush through here. It has only one advantage: it sits across the routes through which German warships must foray. Strategically beautiful, socially it was not so. The winter is long and cold and wet and dark; in the winter solstice the sun rises about 1030 and sets about 1500. Ashore there was an officers' club where you could get beer and where tea was served daily to prove that this war was only an unpleasant incident in the history of a long and glorious empire. There was a petty officers' canteen and a men's canteen. NAAFI (Navy, Army, Air Force Institute) provided tea and buns at all hours, a radio, and a few books. It was the only place you could take a girl in the winter; in the summer there was the heather.

There was also a Wrennery. In our first weeks in Scapa we did all we could to meet these Wrens, and all officers spent a great deal of time ashore personally drawing stores, clothing, spare parts, anything. So did the chief and petty officers, for that matter. Every last sailor in the ship who was in charge of anything at all suddenly discovered he lacked many vital items, typed out long indents, offered to go ashore and supervise the acquisition personally, and was told by his petty officer, "Never mind. I'm going ashore anyway. I'll look after it."

The Chief Gunner's Mate said to me one day, "I've quite a few stores to get tomorrow, sir. I'll go on the 0900 drifter and be back by noon."

"Never mind, Chief, I'm going ashore anyway. I'll look after it."

"No, sir. I mean, there's some stores I'm particular about, very. I want to see myself what I'm getting."

We looked at each other. I thought, indignantly, that the Chief was supposed to be a happily married man and that I had better protect his family from his impending folly. Then the Chief offered, "It's quite a long list, sir; suppose you get half and I get half."

I had to admit it seemed more efficient.

Next morning, every department head and his chief were in the drifter. Disconsolate leading seamen watched the drifter chug off on its appointed rounds through the destroyer anchorages—there were thirty destroyers swinging around their buoys, one drifter to each flotilla. Contacts were made with various Wren clerks. Flirtations at the issuing counters of stores depots developed to teas in the NAAFI and matured in long walks through the damp hills.

With typical naval pragmatism, the provision of Wrens was co-ordinated by C-in-C in a way that would have looked like wholesale pimping to an outsider. Just before entering harbour, each ship was invited to state its Wren requirements. The first time we put in for seventy—that being the number of ship's company who indicated interest in entertaining a Wren aboard. This number was flashed to the Port War Signal Station, "Sioux, Wrens, seventy". This made its way to the Wrennery notice-board:

> Any girl wishing to be entertained in HMCS Sioux—dancing, tea, and cinema—sign below. Maximum seventy. Drifter leaves at 1300 and returns at 1800. Dress, Number One with blackouts and burberries.

In the late forenoon of the day, the largest messdeck was cleared for dancing, an adjacent messdeck for food, and one below rigged for the flicks. The cooks baked cakes and cookies, petty officers saved their rum issue, everyone brought out goodies sent from home by their wives and mothers—canned plum puddings, chocolate, or Bovril. We all cleaned into our number one rig. The messdecks were gleaming and all smelly socks and underwear had been emptied from the lockers—the only seating with cushions. The ship's company had formed a rule: the laws of hospitality demanded that there be no wallflowers amongst the Wrens. Sailors lined up single file at the after accommodation ladder. When you were at the head of the line and a Wren came over the side, she was yours for an hour minimum. If she danced off with somebody else during that time, you were free to seek your own bit of fluff.

The hands who had a watch on deck and the duty AA guns-crew looked out over the bleak anchorage swept by rain showers or snow flurries, at rusty, salt-streaked destroyers tugging at their moorings in a chilly wind, at the cold, misty hills. Below was warmth, and light, and food, and a respite from the cold realities of our life. The Leading Telegraphist tended the gramophone and the beat of Benny Goodman's "Jersey Bounce" flooded the messdeck and a comfortable fug from a hundred cigarettes clouded the air. The age-old mating ritual was enacted in the mysterious badinage of the inarticulate young.

"What d'you mean?"

"Oh, I don't mean what you mean," she said.

"No. Honest. I never meant nothin' like that."

"Well, it sounds to me as you'd said it before."

"No, honest."

"Well, I half promised to go with a girl friend."

"Well, she can do without you for one night."

"So can you, you are cheeky, aren't you?"

"No. Honest. It's just . . . Like another chocolate?"

The couples swirled to the rhythm of the big band, but the Wrens couldn't look as glamorous as the girls in Halifax. Their skirts were narrow, thanks to wartime rationing of cloth, and their stockings were black lisle, not silk. And by regulation, they wore blackouts. These were bloomers that went from the waist to just above the knee, where they fitted snugly with strong elastic. Mandatory for Wrens visiting ships, they were. The girls were inspected by a Wren officer before they left the barracks to make sure they had them on. We weren't sure of the philosophy behind the regulation, but perhaps it was suggested by their other name—passion-killers.

The chief Wren of all, the Duchess of Kent, is reputed to have said, when discussing her girls with C-in-C (apropos of their decorum),

"You don't have to worry about my Wrens, sir. They've got it up here," tapping her forehead with her finger.

"I don't care where they've got. My sailors will find it."

The lengthening days were pleasant but made our operations more hazardous. The long winter nights and the gales were our best protection against U-boats and aircraft. From October to March, at the northern end of our operational area, it was totally dark. But now, in spring, the increased hours of daylight changed the nature of our operations against the enemy. We would depart Scapa. If sighted and reported by U-boat or reconnaissance aircraft, our course and speed would not indicate where we were really going. Then, at evening twilight of the night before the strike, we would turn eastward and steam towards Norway at maximum speed. Our main object was to disrupt the enemy's communications.

Hitler was agitated about the vulnerability of the long coastline he had now to defend. Germany, who had cried *lebensraum* for a century, now had perhaps too much. From North Cape to Bayonne is a coastline of some eighteen hundred miles as the crow flies, double that if all the fiords, inlets, and bays where we might land were counted. Hit-and-run raids by Royal Marine commandos kept the German coastal garrisons in a constant state of jitters, and had been doing so since 1940. A classmate of mine from the navigation course at *Kings* had shot a brothelful of Germans, but, with international chivalry and frugality, had not harmed one girl. Now there's an interruption of enemy communications.

From northern Norway to southern France they struck. In 1942, Churchill had told Lord Louis Mountbatten, who was in charge of combined operations, "Your job is to be offensive."

The Germans had uneasy memories of the Zeebrugge raid of 1918, and the sailor who engineered that, Lord Keyes, had been Mountbatten's predecessor: twenty-four hours after France's surrender, our first raiding force was across the channel. In December 1941, commandos struck at Vaagso in south Norway and the Lofoten Islands. A couple of hundred Germans were killed, a hundred taken prisoner, fifteen thousand tons of shipping was destroyed, and an ammunition dump was blown up. It would make anyone nervous. And Hitler had half a million men in his Norway garrison. In February 1942, a radar station was demolished at Brunsval, twelve miles north of Le Havre. In March, HMS *Campbeltown*, still under the command of Lieutenant-Commander Beatty, rammed the lock at St. Nazaire. Commandos blew it up, and *Tirpitz* was condemned to remain in Norwegian waters; this was the only dry-dock on the Atlantic seaboard big enough to receive her. The raids became larger. In August, five thousand Canadian troops landed at Dieppe.

The Home Fleet, whenever possible, added to the anxieties of the German garrison. Besides our protective runs with convoys, we made these offensive sweeps to the enemy coast. A favourite operation was to send over a light cruiser and a destroyer flotilla. On these sweeps our sailing orders invariably read, "The Object of this Operation is to spread alarm and despondency among enemy forces."

Germany's war effort had been materially aided by the acquisition of Norwegian raw and manufactured material. In a steady stream, small coastal convoys crept southward under the protection of the German coast batteries. They steamed inside innumerable islands, large and small, and through still, deep fiords. But there were some open spaces. Whilst Trondheim to Stavanger was almost completely "inland", there was a nice hunting area for us in the Frohavet, to the north, just above Trondheim. But that was four hundred miles further away and we would likely be caught by German aircraft at morning twilight. If the attack was further south, we were both closer to home by morning twilight and would have fighter cover. It's nice to see friendly fighters overhead; on the other hand, it lessened the opportunity to use our guns in AA fire; to me, this was a disadvantage.

But for practice in surface fire, these German coastal convoys were analogous to the shooting-galleries at country fairs, where, with little or no danger, we could knock over clay ducks. Sometimes the enemy convoy would be escorted by a small destroyer or two, smaller than us, and fewer in number. But most of the time these convoys were escorted by M-class minesweepers; these were not to be despised. They were packed with heavy, rapid-firing guns which were devastating if the flotilla came within their range.

Moonless, winter nights were chosen for these operations. On a line of bearing from the cruiser the flotilla would steam in. High in the Director Tower, snug and warm, out of the wind and the spray that lashed the bridge, we would check the lining up of the guns and the firing circuits, test bells, buzzers, and lamps, and calibrate the radars on the shadowy, lean shapes of our consorts, barely visible to port and starboard except for huge, white bow-waves. And below, connected by telephone and speaker circuits, was the gunnery team: eighty-two men, each a vital link if we were to kill Germans that night.

Deep in the bowels of *Sioux*, below the water-line, were the hands in the magazines, waiting to send up a never-ending stream of propellant-charges for the projectiles. Across the handling-room were the hands in the shell-room. They all wore white anti-flash hoods over their heads and shoulders, and white gloves that came up to the elbows. This was to prevent them getting burned if the magazine blew up. Cooks, stewards, storesmen, with one gunnery rating in charge, sat there, contemplating their lot. They were warm and dry, and, until the action started, could flake out on the iron deck and doze; on the other hand, they were locked two decks down by two sets of water-tight hatches. They couldn't sneak a furtive cigarette. Above them were the hands who would receive the propellants and shells from the hoists and shove them out to the 4.7-inch guns—two for'ard and two aft. These hands thought of their lot with satisfaction: they were warm and dry and on the main deck; it was only a few steps to get over the side if we had to abandon ship. And they could smoke. These hands, then, provided the food for the guns. Jammed into the computer-room were fourteen senior and highly skilled gunnery ratings. The disadvantage here was that there was no room to flake out; there was barely room to stand. And you were always under the severe eye of the Chief Gunner's Mate, who was in charge. These hands were the brain of the system. The eyes were the radar operators crouched over their green, luminous scopes. Their absorption would be complete as they watched the mountains of Norway creep closer as the flotilla swept towards the coast.

Their radar scopes showed an exact duplicate of the chart at their side. The Gun Direction Officers (Blind) watched also for the small, slow-moving blips that were not on the chart. That would be the enemy convoy; that would be our quarry. And in one of the small fishing villages on that stretch of coast, a British agent perhaps lay awake wondering if his report had got through and if he would hear the rumble of our guns tonight. The Gun Direction Officer (Visual) stood immobile behind his gun-direction sight and watched the four lookouts, whose binoculars swept back and forth, back and forth. The hands on the gunnery radar dozed com-fortably, knowing that they couldn't measure the range of the target until the search radars found it.

The guns-crew were the clout of the body, the fists; one rating on the telephone linked to the computer-room. They waited their thunderous entrance, huddled together within the gun-shield, par-tially shielded from rattling spray.

Lastly, Father sat in his chair, a muffled figure in sheepskin duffle coat and balaclava; nothing to do—yet. His well-rehearsed team did everything needed to send *Sioux* towards the climax of the night. Simply, death to them or to us. His team went through their well-known lines. He had no script; he would make it up as he went along, after the battle commenced.

Suddenly, the convoy made its entrance, showing now on the search radar. There was the escort moving out to seaward; they had us on their scopes too.

The R/T murmured in a corner of the bridge, the matter-of-fact voice of the Senior Officer's Chief Yeoman.

"Nephews, this is Uncle. Enemy bearing oh-five-nine degrees."

The "Rogers" acknowledged. But we already knew, and had known for nearly half a minute.

"Alarm surface starboard. Follow GDO (Blind)."

The director swung on; gunnery radar measured: "Range six thousand." The computer clicked and whirred and the crew matched pointers. Digital displays rattled, range was matched, deflection and gun elevation were calculated.

The Captain put on his anti-flash hood and his steel helmet, left his chair, and stood in the forward centre of the bridge, behind the main gyro-compass repeat.

"Guns, you can open fire when you see the rearmost escort. GDO (Visual) will put you on."

We were "tail-end Charlie", the last ship, and so took the last escort. You always engage escorts first; then the merchant ships.

"Nephews, this is Uncle. I am illuminating now."

"Uncle" was to seaward of us so as not to block our line of fire. Captain (D) altered us by blue turn to line ahead and parallel to the enemy convoy's course. Behind the convoy the star shell burst, one, two, three, four, five, six; "Uncle" was really pumping them out.

"Follow DGO's sight," said GDO (Visual).

"Director on," from me.

There they were! Exactly as they had looked on the night-practice table in *Excellent*.

"Layer target; trainer target."

"Inclination one-three-five degrees right, speed twelve."

"Have radar range, deflection set," from the Chief Gunner's Mate.

"Rapid broadsides; shoot," I ordered.

Down the line of the flotilla the guns spoke in loud voices, a continual thunder and flash. Twenty-eight 4.7-inch guns.

"Bloody good," I thought; "just as it should be. A textbook action."

They were not destroyers but M-class minesweepers. Three streams of red tracer arched out toward us but fell short. Within two minutes the minesweepers were demolished, wrecked, battered, and sinking; one blew up. The check-fire bells clamoured.

"Shift target, follow GDO's sight; aftermost merchantman."

Director on; layer target; trainer target; inclination oh-nine-oh degrees right; speed seven; have radar range; deflection set; rapid broadsides; shoot.

Every six seconds four shells were hurled to their target. The star shell blossomed back and forth. Searchlights stabbed out from the coast. It didn't matter much; we were nearly finished. The enemy convoy had turned and headed for the shore-line but they had little sea-room—about a mile from the rocks and twenty-eight guns to seaward. They didn't have a chance—which was, of course, perfect from our point of view. In fourteen minutes it was over. A score or so men were in the water; one lifeboat bobbed on the waves.

We turned and withdrew into the darkness as the last star shell spluttered out. Four hours of darkness left. At morning twilight we searched the sky. It was empty, and that was that.

The days lengthened and the convoy season was almost over, the supply line having been switched for the summer months to the Persian Gulf. No more ships would go to Russia until autumn, but there were some empties in Murmansk waiting to be returned. Having delivered USS *Milwaukee* (renamed *Murmansk*), the American crew awaited passage home; in addition, a Russian crew was awaiting passage south to take over the battleship HMS *Royal Sovereign*, which was to be turned over to the Russians as compensation for part of the Italian fleet to which they laid claim.

Rear-Admiral McGrigor, wearing his flag in the light cruiser *Diadem*, was in command of this last convoy of the season. He had with him the light aircraft carriers *Activity* and *Fencer* and sixteen destroyers. Depending upon your point of view, Admiral McGrigor was a good man to sail with or he was not. We noticed that with him we nearly always got into action, whereas with Admiral Dalrymple-Hamilton engagements were few. Some of the actions were, admittedly, between the convoy and the escort—to be exact, between American merchant ships and aircraft of the Royal Navy Fleet Air Arm.

The American merchantmen were nervous of all aircraft and tended to fire upon our own returning aircraft as well as upon the attacking German aircraft. When acting as plane-guard astern of one of the carriers (to pick up pilots who had to ditch), we would sometimes see our returning aircraft driven off by streams of AA fire from merchantmen. Firing guns, like fear, is contagious. If one ship opened fire, others would join it. Picture, then, the wretched pilot approaching the most hazardous part of his sortie—landing on a small, heaving deck. The pilot's absorption is complete: he doesn't want to land on a falling flight-deck, and a rising flight-deck makes the impact that much more severe—he might buckle his landing wheels and go screaming forward on his belly, sparks flying, metal shrieking, and the propeller whanging a frightful staccato on deck. Then red tracer comes burning past his nose. Full throttle, bank, climb. *Sioux* was on the same voice circuit. We heard a savage voice.

"Tell those sons of bitches I'm on their side!"

Once an aircraft was shot down just as it took off. Admiral McGrigor had a way of getting through to those he commanded. He sent a general message to the convoy. "This is a brief course in aircraft recognition. If it has one engine it is ours. If it has two engines it is theirs." But in this operation we got to Russia without warfare of any kind, internecine or other.

Russia to us meant Murmansk, or nearby Polyarnoe, or Archangel in the White Sea. There are many aids to navigation for entering Polyarnoe, but in the spring thaw you can home on the stench, if the wind is from the south. Hundreds of miles above the Arctic Circle and away from the benign influence of the Gulf Stream, which warms Arctic waters all the way to the North Cape, Polyarnoe was cold. Housing consisted mostly of large apartment blocks which had no indoor toilets. The communal privy was at each cross-street between the buildings.

The Murmansk privy was five-sided; a southern exposure was desirable, you got more light—when it was light. Also, the north wind didn't blow directly around your buttocks. Unlike us with our Canadian privies, the Russians in Polyarnoe didn't dig a pit. Rather, there was a step-ladder leading up to a platform perhaps six feet off the ground. You stepped off this onto two steps much as in a shoe-shine parlour. You stood on this (I never did but I was a fascinated observer), leaned your back against the wall, dropped your drawers, and went. Ordure piled up during the winter, since it froze almost immediately. In late April the winter's droppings melted and the stink was unbearable. Then it was carted away by German prisoners. Yes, with a south wind it's not hard to find Polyarnoe.

There was little social life in Polyarnoe, just visiting friends in other ships. We went for long walks; or at least, we walked as far as we could until turned back by a Russian sentry. Sometimes the sentry put a rifle-shot across your bow to let you know you were straying into forbidden territory. Then, with a big grin, he would wave you back. There was no good going to the Red Navy Officers' Club, for, apart from official entertainment, the Russians didn't mix with us—by direction, we knew. The British shore-staff ran a small mess and when the Fleet was in there were always several bottles on the table.

After five days of this, at the end of April, we sailed with a convoy of forty-five ships. Russian Admiral Levchenko sailed with us in *Fencer*. About a day's run out of Polyarnoe we were sighted by enemy aircraft, from Petsamo or Kirkenes, we supposed. It was nice to know that *Tirpitz* would not put in an appearance, but we could expect a barrier of U-boats in the Bear Island passage. Ten took up station. The shadowing aircraft circled. Our fighters damaged one but he transmitted an accurate report of our position. The U-boats pulled in from their barrier to a concentration across our path. High winds, rough seas, and snow squalls made flying difficult but we kept a patrol aloft. The USS *William S. Thayer* was torpedoed by U-307. In the next two days our Swordfish aircraft depth-charged and sank U-277, U-674, and U-959. We would have liked to show Admiral Levchenko more but nothing more happened.

Captain Rose, Royal Artillery, joined *Sioux* in Scapa. He was Bombardment Liaison Officer, BLO. A BLO always worked in conjunction with a FOB, Forward Observation Officer Bombardment. The BLO was in the ship and the FOB ashore. Something was coming up and we were sure it was an invasion of France. We painted for BLO a vivid picture of the horrors of sailing Arctic waters; then, to our intense embarrassment, the weather on the next operation was like a Bank Holiday at Sheerness: calm sea, clear skies, warm.

Admiral Moore took us up to Altenfiord again to see if we could deal *Tirpitz* a death blow. Alas, the Germans had sent up smoke to mask their position and it covered the fiord; we were foiled. We went back to the Shetland Islands to fuel and have another try; the Shetlands are about a hundred and thirty miles north of the Faroes and thus we saved some time. We raised Muckle Flugga Light, and steamed to the tanker anchorage.

We had a day and a night in harbour. Lerwick is the main town and not too distant by boat. What went on in these islands with a total population of less then twenty thousand? How many were girls? What did they do except weave wool and knit Fair Isle scarves and sweaters? We pointed out to BLO that, as a member in good standing of the lecherous soldiery, it was his duty to find out. Were not pillage and rape the specialties of soldiers? It was rape reconnaissance he must concentrate on. Further, there were brother gunners ashore, AA gunners of the Royal Artillery. They were here to protect the Fleet when it came in to fuel.

BLO returned, beaming. The local gunners had for months been making arrangements for a dance where they could meet the local lassies. It was scheduled for tonight. Because the Fleet was in, the soldiers' leave was stopped: they must stand by their guns. Would we substitute for them? We would!

We sailed up to Altenfiord again, feinting a landing on Norway on the way. (Alarm and Despondency.) But when approaching *Tirpitz* we were spotted by a reconnaissance aircraft, the element of surprise was lost, and we knew the fiord would be filled with smoke again. The weather turned vile, and we plodded back to Scapa. Instead of securing to our usual buoy, we were told to secure alongside the base-ship, *Tyne.* Something unusual was brewing.

The King was to visit the Fleet. This caused less fuss than one might expect. He was, after all, a professional naval officer who had commenced his naval schooling at age fourteen as a cadet at the Naval College at Dartmouth. After this he had gone to sea as a midshipman. I remembered seeing a picture of him at Whale Island in his sub-lieutenants' class; he had probably done his spotting drill at the same night-action table as I had. At the Battle of Jutland he had served in HMS *Collingwood* and been mentioned in dispatches. In visiting us he was, then, in a very real sense of the word coming home; coming to perhaps the only place in his kingdom where he was free from the gaze of a curious public, from the probings of a voracious press, and from the demands of a family. In the Fleet he had a measure of privacy not found elsewhere, and he could relax.

"I don't want to paint ship," the First Lieutenant told the Captain; "the hands are exhausted, our starboard side will be against the base-ship and *Volage* will be on our port side. Anyway, there's not time to chip or wire-brush and red-lead. We're a bucket of rust, I know. We've only had eight days in harbour in the last sixty and it's freezing in Russia and raining in Scapa. Moreover . . ."

"All right, all right, Number One," said the Captain; "just wash down the superstructure. But have the hands champher up their tiddley uniforms."

"Why is he coming now?" I asked the Captain.

"Lawrence," the Captain pontificated, "the King of England has three rights: the right to be informed, the right to approve, and the right to advise. He has many duties, one of which is to be seen. And if you don't do something about that scruffy uniform, when he sees you he's going to advise me to log you. But he is visiting us now, I would think, because something big is coming up. If you're fighting for King and country you really are entitled to see the King. Peps you up, inspires you; that's the theory, anyway."

The night before the King was to inspect the ship's company of *Sioux*, I took a boat to the Fleet anchorage, where the big ships were moored, to have dinner with a friend. He was in a heavy cruiser and the officer complement must have been about forty; the wardroom, however, was only half full. We had several drinks, and then dinner; then we sat drinking port and smoking cigars. We talked of school days and of recent operations.

About ten-fifteen he said, "Sorry it's so quiet tonight. The Flagship invited us over. The King is having dinner with Sir Bruce and they're both joining the officers afterwards in the wardroom. It'll be a bit of a bash, I expect."

"That's all right," I said.

"Would you like to go over?"

"Isn't it late?"

"God no! They won't break up till the small hours."

He got a boat alongside and we putt-putted through the drizzle and between the blacked-out hulks of the cruisers, carriers, and battleships.

"Where's *King George V*?" I asked the Coxswain.

"Ahead of us now, about half a mile."

"How on earth do you find your way?"

"Seventh trip tonight."

The monstrous black bulk of the battleship loomed up. Not a light showed. We doubled up the accommodation ladder. A dim light showed the muffled-up quarter-deck staff: Midshipman of the Watch; Officer of the Watch; Quartermaster; various bosun's mates and messengers; a Royal Marine bugler. I thought I could hear a hubbub of voices. "Sounds like yelling," I thought; "strange."

"What ho, what ho," said a cheery voice. "Any more for any more? Come for the bash? You'll be lucky if you can fit in. Snotty, fit these officers in."

The midshipman was Canadian—there were several in the

Flagship; they used to come and visit *Sioux* when they could. He lighted our way forward with a torch and opened the heavy steel door to the after quarters. The din increased. A black-out curtain and another door. "Sounds like an Irish horse-race," I thought.

And there was the wardroom: a heaving sea of sweaty bodies, jostling, pulling, barging about, some prostrate on the deck trying to avoid being trampled, most with another on his back, charging, butting. A few panting bodies refreshed themselves at the bar. Evidently a game of "Horsy-Horsy" was in progress.

The rules are simple. You get another officer on your back—you are horse and he is rider—and you try to pull everybody else down. There are no rules, no sides; everyone is against everyone else, no time-limit except exhaustion. It was evident also that several games of "Dogs of War" had preceded this. There are rules to this game, but not many. Any group of juniors can cry "Dogs of War" on anyone senior. He must then defend himself while the juniors try to de-bag him—take his trousers off. It's a bit one-sided, but it's also quite amazing what a desperate commander can do to a bunch of sub-lieutenants. Many bloody senior bare knees testified to some success. Coats were off, collars torn, bow ties awry. On the fringe of the maelstrom, we edged our way to the bar. In a quiet pool we passed the King and Sir Bruce, as dishevelled and sweaty as anyone.

"Look here, Fraser," panted the King, "I'm senior to you; this time I'll get on your back."

The next day we were briefed by the Commander of the Base-Ship: he briefed two destroyers at once over the loud-hailer system on his bridge.

"Pay attention to me, *Sioux* and *Volage*, and I shall run over the drill for our spontaneous demonstration of affection for His Majesty. This is called 'Cheering Ship', as you already know. Your hats will be off; when I give the command 'Three cheers for His Majesty', you will raise your cap over your head to the full extent of the right arm. I shall then say 'Hip, hip'. You will reply, in a loud, confident voice, 'Hurrah'. Say 'Hurrah' and not 'Hurray'; it sounds better and it carries further. At the same time you will rotate your caps once in a small circle. The same for the other two cheers. That's all, but cheer out loud and strong."

We fell in and waited. The bosun's calls shrilled and HM was on board *Sioux*. He walked slowly forward chatting to the Captain and looking at the troops. Passing down the line he spotted the blue-and-white ribbon of my DSC.

"Where did you get that?"

"The Caribbean, sir."

"U-boat?"

"Yessir."

"Have you got the medal yet?"

"Not yet, sir."

"You should see to it."

"Aye aye, sir."

What a perfectly wonderful idea! I could now get leave to go to London.

The Captain paused when he came to Petty Officer Wiggens, on my right. Wiggens had the blue-and-white ribbon of the DSM.

"This is Petty Officer Wiggens, sir. In charge of our twin Bofors," said the Captain.

"Good morning, Wiggens."

"Good morning, sir."

The King looked inquiringly at the Captain; why had he been stopped here? The Captain explained.

"Petty Officer Wiggens shot down three enemy planes on a recent convoy."

Petty Officer Wiggens repeated, "Three?"

The Captain glared, the King smiled, and that's about all that happened during *Sioux*'s first royal visit. But I think the sailors were glad to have seen the King. We cheered loud and strong and the next day put to sea again, for an AA practice shoot.

In terms of losses, *Sioux* had been lucky so far. In all our actions we had not been hit, except by one 20-mm non-explosive shell which hurt no one. (And this was a godsend. It hit a storeroom. Every single bit of equipment that had been lost or stolen in the past year was in that store-room. It was written off, "lost through enemy action".) Deaths at sea are largely a matter of one here and one there due to "the dangers of the sea". When it is "the violence of the enemy" you lose scores, hundreds, all hands. Our first death had been a leading torpedoman. Returning in a liberty boat one dark and tempestuous evening, he had jumped for the ladder, slipped, fallen into the water, and been swept away by the waves and the tide. He was pulled inboard within a few minutes, but the water was extremely cold and he was dead.

This day, we were to carry out our AA practices against a towed glider target. The glider was about fifteen feet long, had a wing-span of ten feet, and weighed perhaps fifty pounds. Back and forth it sailed over us as the close-range weapons blazed away. Its altitude was about one thousand feet. On one run a projectile parted the towing wire. The nose of the glider dipped and, at a hundred knots or so, it dived. It hit our flag-deck; to be more precise, it hit Signalman White, crushed his chest, and killed him. He was nineteen. A freak accident? They always seem so. But, even without the violence of the enemy, just going to sea is dangerous enough.

A little while previously the First Lieutenant of the *Iroquois* had been walking along the upper deck in a not-very-rough sea, had slipped when a green one came inboard, was battered by it, and died in hospital. Things like this you lived with as a matter of everyday routine. Death was commonplace. But it got through to some. Once, on leaving harbour for another dreary haul up to Murmansk and back, one of the top-men could take no more. With a shout ("Fuck this for a lark") he jumped over the side and started swimming for the nearest ship that was remaining in harbour. Spanking along at a brisk ten knots and with Captain (D) nattering about station-keeping, the Captain merely sent a signal, "Please pick up my deserter. I'll collect him when I get back." The top-man's mess-mates asked, "Who's going to stand the fucker's watch?"

But I knew what was in that top-man's mind, I think. It went much deeper than the dangers of the sea and the violence of the enemy: it was more than fear of death or of maiming. It was analogous to a child's fear of the dark, of the unknown—inchoate, yet frighteningly real. It came from the gut and not the head. It was an atavistic dread that went back eons to when our distant ancestors crouched in cold dark caves in unspeakable terror while Evil stalked outside.

You could wedge yourself in your bunk with *Maclean's* magazine and read of a gentler way of life far away, you could listen to the measured tones of the BBC light orchestra, you could scan home-town papers, months old, and see that the St. Mary's Engineers' Ball was again being held at the Lord Nelson Hotel. Over the muted loudspeaker—Joe was asleep in the bunk above mine—Vera Lynn would belt out that orgy of sentiment and hope:

> There'll be bluebirds over the white cliffs of Dover
> Tomorrow, just you wait and see.
> There'll be love and laughter and peace ever after
> Tomorrow, when the world is free.

But you knew that outside that $\frac{3}{8}$-inch steel bulkhead at your back, primal forces played with frail *Sioux*; and that you would soon go on watch again and see black, white-veined seas towering above you; they came in endless procession. The real world was here. There was nothing else. You were a speck in the cosmos, even less. Yes, I knew what that top-man had in mind.

There were compensations. Marc and Joe and I shared a cabin smaller than my bedroom at home for over two years. In that time we had only eighteen days alongside a jetty, yet there was never a cross word passed between us. Marc had a habit of lighting a cigarette the instant he was awakened. It was a conditioned reflex. Touch him when he was asleep and he would grope under his pillow for cigarettes and matches. The smell of cigarette smoke made me sick. When Marc found this out, at the first touch of the Bosun's Mate's hand upon his foot he would heave himself up, grab his cigarettes, and lurch outside the cabin. In the adjoining flat he would slump on the Confidential Book Locker, eyes still closed, and smoke. On the other hand, I always read before going to sleep. No matter how tired, I read, even if it was only a page or two. It was a sane interlude between the reality that had gone before this moment and the dreams that would follow. But a light, no matter how dim, disturbed Marc. We stood the same watch, and so we arose and turned in together. Therefore, before turning in, I read on the same CB locker Marc would smoke on when we were called again. Marc had married a girl called Mary before he left Canada and he loved the song "For It Was Mary, Mary, Plain as Any Name Can Be". He kept forgetting the words and he couldn't carry a tune, but he loved that song, and so I used to sing it for him. In a screaming gale and swirling snow at three in the morning on an open bridge and ducking the spray that whipped past our heads and clutching the compass to stay on our feet, we sang that song. The signalman and the lookouts grinned: you could see their teeth.

This was no weather for convoys. Captain Rose, our BLO, had been lecturing the gunnery team constantly about the safety of our own troops when we were bombarding and about communications with the Forward Observation Officer, Bombardment—FOB—another Royal Artillery officer who would be ashore spotting our broadsides onto the target. Now we had something else to do besides convoys and hit-and-run raids; we had the invasion of Europe.

seven

Normandy Invasion

In the summer of 1940, after 260,000 British and 70,000 French troops had been evacuated from the beaches of Dunkirk and after Germany had conquered France, Belgium, Poland, Denmark, Norway, Holland, and Czechoslovakia, Winston Churchill had said: "Britain will fight on . . . if necessary for years . . . if necessary alone. . . . We shall go back." On the evening of Monday, June 5, 1944, we did.

This was Operation Neptune, the assault on Fortress Europe over the beaches of Normandy and a prelude to Operation Overlord, the liberation of Europe.

On this Monday afternoon the invasion armada sailed. Our Flotilla and several others had been anchored off Cowes for nearly a week, delayed by bad weather. So it was with cheerful anticipation that we saw the minesweepers get under way: these were the spearhead of the 4,126 ships and landing craft to be flung against the beaches in the assault and the follow-up. This fleet was protected by 1,213 warships, serviced by 736 ancillary craft, and supplied by 864 merchant ships. Nearly 7,000 vessels—seventy-nine per cent British. We were started on our way by the nod of a meteorologist.

Captain (D) quacked like a mother duck, telling the Flotilla we must shave off our beards—if sunk in oily water we would choke; we must wear our good uniforms—presumably, if we were captured, he didn't want the 23rd Destroyer Flotilla looking scruffy; we must don clean underwear—dirty underwear driven into a wound caused it to fester.

Anchors clanked home into hawse-pipes and we steamed sedately into the twilight. I got my head down until we went to action stations. Father, in a jocular mood, sat in his chair. The OOW conned the ship—silent: he had much to do keeping station, watching the dimmed stern light of our next ahead, *Algonquin*, and keeping between the flickering lights dropped by the minesweepers to mark the swept channel. Peter, the navigator, ceaselessly plotted our position, from radar, from fathometer, from dead reckoning, from anything and everything. Baker and I dozed on each other's shoulders. Dawn would be no problem: it was to be rapid-broadside direct bombardment at point-blank range. Overhead we heard the constant drone of aircraft carrying paratroopers who were to secure vital bridges and crossroads behind the assault area. Somewhere up there was the 1st Canadian Parachute Battalion.

By about 0400 on June 6 we could see the coast, a dark blur, flat, featureless except for the church spire of Bernières-sur-mer. On radar, Peter said, the scope exactly matched our chart of the Coursulles area. Our beach, Juno, would be stormed by General Crerar's First Canadian Army.

By about 0500 the drone of aircraft rose to a constant roar, and on shore there were flashes of light from east to west as far away as twelve miles: bright flick, darkness, rumble, boom. Saturation bombing. Seconds after the first bomb, the rumble of detonation; then it was constant, the whole coast flickering.

Morning twilight, wind from the west—twenty-five knots, choppy sea, flooding tide, sunrise 0558, H-Hour 0630; the bombing continued. The Flotilla in line abreast now, about two miles off Juno Beach; and the curtain of night lifted on the biggest naval stage that this world had ever seen.

Fleet destroyers backed and filled—ninety-four of them—as far as the eye could see, across Sword Beach to port, across Juno ahead, across Gold to starboard, and away on west down to the U.S. sector. On our port quarter were *Warspite*, *Ramilles*, and *Roberts* with their 15-inch guns; *Scylla*, *Danae*, *Dragon*, *Frobisher*, *Arethusa*, and *Mauritius* with 6-inch. On our starboard quarter were *Ajax*, *Argonaut*, *Emerald*, *Orion*, *Flores*, *Belfast*, and *Diadem*, all 6-inch. Astern were wave after wave of assault craft. Astern of them loomed ocean liners, each carrying several thousand troops for the second wave.

Overhead Spitfires and Mustangs banked in two-mile circles, spotting for the heavy warships. Above them were more Spitfires, their air umbrella. So far, not a ship had been lost from mines. The minesweepers steamed home through the incoming fleet. The last wave of bombers returned.

We searched the coast. There was the street we were looking for and the building. Both matched our photograph exactly. Our target housed an 88-mm.

"Range oh-four-oh. Deflection set."

"Clock tuned. Deflection set."

To the Captain, "Armament target."

From the Captain, "Let'er rip." (Captain Boak was proving no more a poet than Grubb or King.)

"Rapid broadsides, shoot."

Up and down the coast the guns spoke—over a thousand of them. It was 0600.

Much sand exploded as our first broadside landed, a little to the left. Small corrections were made between broadsides. The guns were in line now, concrete and brick debris flying instead of sand. To east and west the destroyer guns—three hundred of them—were pumping out twelve rounds a minute. Over our heads we heard the whoosh of the 6-inch and the rush of the 15-inch. The din was indescribable. Dust haze and smoke hung over the whole waterfront. Our target crumbled; that 88-mm wouldn't hold up our troops. We shifted target right and kept pumping out rapid broadsides on the scientific principle that anything we knocked down should contain Germans.

The cease-fire bells clamoured. I took my eyes out of the Director binoculars and looked around. It was 0630.

The soldiers were hitting the beaches, along with the tank landing craft, the infantry landing craft, the Queen's Own Rifles, the North Shore (New Brunswick) Regiment, the Regina Rifles, the Royal Winnipeg Rifles. This was the first assault wave. One tank landing craft broached to, some infantry landing craft hit underwater obstacles: spikes, logs, or mines. A rising tide and an onshore wind and churning engines forced them to the sand. Many blew up. Canadian troops streamed ashore. Some enfilading fire splattered down the beach, some mortar fire thucked from behind the front row of houses, some machine-gun fire. Apparently our bombardment was not so devastating as we thought. But our boys sprinted over that bare, unprotected stretch of sand in seconds. Some didn't make it.

Captain Rose had found us another target, further inland. Back to work. We had another bombardment later, but this time with an FOB artillery officer ashore calling the fall of shot. Inexplicably, he went off the air. Rose found us another FOB, who spotted our shells on; then we lost him. His last words were, "Sorry, chaps, I'm about to be captured. Out."

The Canadian troops continued to pour in, but their landing was made more difficult now by wrecked and foundered landing craft impaled on underwater obstacles, and empty landing craft returning. Another wave of paratroopers in Horsa gliders towed by Dakotas: the paratroopers would jump; the soldiers in the gliders would land in small fields close to the strong-point they must take. One Lancaster wobbled uncertainly back from the beaches, mortally wounded and looking for a clear stretch of sea to land in. Amid the hundreds of vessels there was no clear stretch. The Lancaster went in at thirty degrees, splashed, and blew up. A large shell splash off the port side, another, another: this must be the battery at Le Havre. The morning sun glistened off a thousand barrage balloons. The RAF and RCAF filled the sky; there were no Germans. Besides the tank landing craft, giant Shermans putt-putted ashore under their own power, pulled down their canvas skirts—the flotation gear—and churned away to join their mates. A midget submarine, which had lain on the bottom for two days previous to H-Hour, had surfaced to direct them to their targets. Wind from the west, across the beaches, was fifteen knots, the sea still high.

We anchored at short stay. Our troops continued to pour in: Le Régiment de la Chaudière, the Canadian Scottish, the Highland Light Infantry, the Stormont, Dundas and Glengarry Highlanders, the North Nova Scotia Highlanders, the Cameron Highlanders of Ottawa. Over on Sword Beach a bagpipe skirled—they were doing it in style; while some had landed with the first waves, most of the support landed later in the day, the Signals, the Gunners, the Engineers. How my father would have loved to be in that RCE contingent!

We swung at anchor, waiting for a new target, while the troops pushed inland. By ten o'clock all bombardment had moved inland by several miles.

At evening twilight we weighed anchor and swung seaward on anti-submarine patrol. Dönitz had about thirty submarines in the area, and Kranke was sending his E-boats out in force, but our MTBs were dealing with them. Would German heavy forces come creaming down from the north? Not likely. By June 1944 we had destroyed eleven of their heavy ships. What had the Kriegsmarine left? They certainly had plenty of destroyers.

Whatever they had they should throw against us: it is what we would do in like circumstances. But then, *Graf Spee* had run for the River Plate, where we would have sought sea-room. She had scuttled instead of coming out and taking some enemies down with her. Fine thoughts to occupy your mind on a long night patrol, cramped and stiff in the Gunnery Director. On one leg of our patrol the wind blew fresh in our faces; on the other leg the haze from the funnel asphyxiated us. I vomited, but then put on my gas-mask and felt better. The night passed without incident. We anchored off the beach at dawn.

BLO gave us a briefing. As of a few hours ago—early morning, June 7—our troops had pushed inland about five miles on Juno and Gold, about four on Sword. But there was a three-mile gap between Sword and Juno still held by the enemy, and General von Rundstedt had two panzer divisions in reserve. We might today see Tiger and Panther tanks on the beach. What an intriguing thought! Destroyers versus tanks. We knew General Rommel would favour such tactics.

The wind was freshening, twenty knots, moderate waves taking a more pronounced long form, many white horses, some spray. This would hinder the unloading of the constant stream of ships that supplied the build-up.

There was another enemy-held gap of about ten miles between Gold and Utah beaches. American troops at Omaha had only a toehold, two miles inland. Then there was a twenty-mile gap between Omaha and Utah; the Americans were taking a pasting at Utah, barely making it up the cliffs and into the dunes.

We went to defence stations and had breakfast. With the strengthening light the bombardment started again, rumbling up and down the coast. Fire of interdiction, mostly the cruisers. Let a German armoured vehicle venture upon a road and in three minutes the spotter planes would bring down the naval shells upon it; let a Panther stick its nose outside a hedgerow and it would clank into an inferno. No, there would be no enemy movement of troops, guns, vehicles, or tanks during daylight hours. *Sioux*'s guns could reach ten miles inland; the battleship's twenty. And overhead we had our umbrella of Spitfires; above them we could hear the constant drone of Lancaster bombers on their way to targets further inland, these also with their umbrella. Many road, rail, and bridge links to the beaches would be cut today.

I always thought that this day, June 7, was the decisive day. What was Hitler thinking of to allow all this to happen at his doorstep? Was he still asleep?

As far as you could see along the beaches and behind us were an uncountable number of vessels, from small motorboats to ocean liners. A breakwater of sunken ships was forming a lee for those close inshore. And we had towed over huge concrete structures—Mulberries—that slowly settled now to the bottom. A line of them was forming, a mile or more, quays for unloading merchant ships and transports. And from these, roadways were starting to stretch towards the beaches. We had brought our own harbour.

And on the perimeter, from Le Havre to Dover and from Cherbourg to Land's End, was a constant patrol protecting our flanks: among others, fifty Canadian destroyers, frigates, and corvettes—including *Moose Jaw*.

Another night patrol passed uneventfully. We anchored at dawn.

That morning we got a call from the HQ ship, *Hilary*, giving us a target that was holding up some of our soldiers. It was a German-occupied stone farmhouse with a couple of heavy automatic weapons, and apparently our infantry had no tank support. They telephoned their predicament back to Company HQ, then to Brigade HQ, who told *Hilary*. The soldiers then, I suppose, sat in a ditch, brewed tea, and had a smoke. *Hilary* gave us map coordinates and a wave-length to contact a spotting aircraft. This indirect bombardment was carried out from below in the ops room. BLO had our own troops marked on the chart, together with the target. He estimated our shells would be clear enough of our own troops; but if we were to err, it had better be over and not short. We switched to the spotting-aircraft channel and the pilot was already calling us as he circled the farmhouse.

Range was 12,200 yards. Adding a cautious two hundred yards, we fired a full broadside so that the pilot would be sure to see the first "splash". Over and to the right, he said. We corrected deflection, decreased range by two hundred yards, and fired a single-gun spotting round. This was in line and over. Down two hundred. Shoot. In line and barely over. Down two hundred; shoot. In line and short. Up one hundred, rapid broadsides, shoot. The guns stormed away: four 4.7-inch shells every five seconds. The pilot cut in: "You can stop now, old boy, it's a ruin. I can see our own troops moving forward. Out." Time elapsed from the first call from *Hilary* to the last gun: fifteen minutes.

I was curious about the time. Later that afternoon our motorcutter had to go to *Hilary* on some errand or other, and I went along. I wanted to see the Staff Officer, Operations. I told him I was collecting data for HMS *Excellent* and asked if he could trace backwards from the time he had given us our target earlier that day to the time the request for naval gunfire support had

A little white water does not deter the depth-charge party. (*PAC*)

(below) Algonquin refuels in the Shetland Islands between strikes against Tirpitz. (PAC)

(above) The flagship King George V carries Sir Bruce Fraser, Commander-in-Chief of the Home Fleet, on a Russian convoy. Photo taken from the deck of Sioux. (PAC)

(below) The King inspects Sioux before the Normandy landing. (PAC)

Part of the invasion fleet approaches Normandy, June 6, 1944. (PAC)

The 3rd Canadian Infantry Division lands on Juno Beach at Bernières-sur-Mer. (*PAC*)

Dining formally off Normandy, just half a mile from the invasion beach, three days after the initial assault. (*Photo courtesy of Peter M. McEntyre*)

The hard-boiled-egg incident: the officers gather with Cardinal Villeneuve, Lawrence second from left. (*Peter M. McEntyre*)

originated from the company, platoon, whatever, that was held up by the Germans in that farmhouse. He was convinced, but irritated that in the middle of a battle he had to compile statistics. A telegraphist PO phoned back down the line with ill-disguised impatience. As the calls went further inland the impatience evidently increased. But I got the answer: fifteen minutes.

Thirty minutes from the moment our troops got pinned down until they were advancing again. This with God knows how many bombarding ships and spotting aircraft. And when, immediately after getting our target and the aircraft radio channel, we switched to that channel, the aircraft had been calling us. The beauty and thoroughness, the precision and certainty, were impressive. No wonder it had taken years to mount this invasion. You can't do all that staff work in less than a couple of years.

In returning to *Sioux* the motor-cutter was temptingly close to the beach.

"Coxswain, land the cutter over there."

"You mean on the beach, sir?"

"Yes, over there; now smack it about, we haven't got all day."

"Aye aye, sir."

The bow grated on gravel; I jumped out and waded ashore. A furious beach-master (traffic policeman) stormed over.

"What in bloody hell are you supposed to be?"

"Isn't this Sword Beach?"

"Goddamit no. Get off my beach."

We backed out and returned to *Sioux*. But I had landed in Normandy.

The weather was turning foul, the wind freshening, rain falling. We had a stand-down that night and the First Lieutenant said we would dine formally. We donned wing collars and bow ties and met for sherry at five-thirty and dinner at seven. The stewards brought out the best silver and crystal. After dinner the port went round. The Mess President rapped his gavel. "Mr. Vice, the King."

"Gentlemen, the King," said the Vice-President. "The King," we echoed, "God bless him."

A little later the toast of the day.

"Gentlemen, to sweethearts and wives."

We raised our glasses again.

"To sweethearts and wives," we responded dutifully; some adding in a roguish whisper, "May they never meet."

The movie would not start until nine. I lit a cigar and stepped out onto the fo'c's'le for a breath of air. The rain was quite heavy now, gusty. Inland, I could hear the whump of mortars and the rattle of carbines. No wonder the soldiers sang:

> I don't want to be a soldier,
> I don't want to go to war.
> I'd rather hang around Piccadilly Underground,
> Living on the earning of a high-born lady.
> I don't want a bayonet up me arse hole.
> I don't want me ballocks shot away.
> I'd rather be in England, Merry Merry England,
> Rogering all me bleeding life away.

With a sigh of compassion, I re-entered the wardroom, filled my glass, and sank into an armchair. Years later, Alma's brother, then in the Medical Corps, told me he spent that night under his jeep.

The movie was trivial, but afterwards we sang some new songs, led by Leonard Brockington, a civilian, then about sixty and a confidant of the Prime Minister. He was much crippled with arthritis, so bent over that he had to tilt his chair back to look at you across the table. He used to say, "Do you know what they'll do with me if we are captured? They'll dress me in one of your uniforms, parade me throughout Germany, and say, 'This is what the Canadian Navy is reduced to.' " His songs were ballads, some of which went back several centuries. One Elizabethan lyric went:

> Back and side, go bare, go bare,
>   Both foot and hand go cold;
> But, belly, God send thee ale enough,
>   If it be new or old.
>
> I cannot eat but little meat,
>   My stomach is not good;
> But, sure, I think that I can drink
>   With him that wears a hood.
> Though I go bare, take ye no care,
>   I am nothing a-cold;
> I stuff my skin so full within
>   Of jolly ale and old.

He had a strong, true baritone and we roared out the chorus. Our piano player, Able Seaman Waldon, was delighted. He'd tired long ago of our usual songs, which, while the tunes were catchy, had lyrics dealing mostly with seduction, rape, buggery, sodomy, piles, constipation, and the like. Brockington was the first out-sider to live with the sixteen officers and two hundred and eighty men who had been living in the sardine-tin *Sioux* for over a year, and in that year only four days alongside a jetty. He brought home closer. In fact, when he returned to Canada he made over a hun-dred telephone calls, including one to my mother.

The next day we went to patrol the eastern flank off Le Havre. Thinking the shore battery had been knocked out by *Warspite*, we ventured quite close. Then came that particular rushing sound which all hands recognized as large shells homing in. I grabbed my binoculars to see if I could find the wink of red from the next salvo: that would be my target. A fountain of water erupted about three hundred yards away, then the many little splashes of fragments. So intent was I that I didn't notice everyone else was flat on his face. Another rushing wind went overhead. Another landed short but closer. I didn't see this splash develop—just the start of it. A shell-fragment hit my steel helmet and knocked me silly.

Coming back to anchor at sunset we approached HMS *Swift* returning from another patrol. *Swift* took a mine amidships, blew up, and sank. Luckily she was in shallow water and rested on the bottom, but she had broken in half. Most of those amidships died, but those on the fo'c's'le and the quarter-deck were unharmed. They didn't really seem in any hurry to leave, either; they waved us on, so we steamed by and anchored.

I had the morning watch, which always pleased me. I liked the sunrise. That morning, however, there was an overcast and night faded slowly. At an indeterminate point between night and day we heard an aircraft approaching at low level. While we never saw enemy aircraft by day and so fired at nothing, at night the rule was to fire at anything. But was it day or night? I put the Oerlikons and the Bofors on the bearing. Only five seconds had elapsed. I had another two to make up my mind. "Open fire." Six streams of tracer arched out into the cloud, all converging—by luck more than by science—at the same spot. From this cloud came the snout of an aircraft—whoops from the guns-crews—and then the unmistakable wings of a Spitfire. The discipline of the guns-crews was good: they ceased fire before I rang the check-fire bells. Nevertheless, one stream of tracer drifted past the pilot's nose. He did a tight bank around *Sioux*, made the up-you gesture with his fingers, and went this way. Elapsed time: fifteen seconds. The Captain arrived on the bridge in his pyjamas and cap.

"What was that all about?"

"Spitfire, sir."

This didn't make much sense to him but he only grunted and returned to his sea-cabin.

Scuttlebutt had it that we would soon return to Scapa, and, since Canadian troops were by now about ten miles inland, it was probably pukka gen. We went on patrol again towards the Le Havre perimeter at dawn of D plus 6, but kept a prudent distance from the battery.

At 1100 Captain (D) received a message that several German destroyers were slipping down the coast, apparently to enter the River Seine. If we could intercept them! We cranked on thirty-one knots. Ten minutes later we sighted them, steering south. They cleared the point and altered eastward up the Seine. Captain (D) was always anxious to come to grips with the enemy and we were all imbued with his various exhortations: "Sink, burn, destroy. Nothing shall pass," and, "Hit first, hit hard, and keep on hitting." We, too, turned eastward toward the narrowing mouth of the Seine. Captain (D) said, "I'll catch them if I have to go to Paris." Then came the rushing sound, and again, and again. The German shore batteries knew our range within a yard. A brisk breeze blew the splashes over us and we were drenched. Captain (D) said, "Oh dear. Blue one eight. Execute." We turned 180 degrees together and headed home for our anchorage. It had been axiomatic for two hundred years that in duels between ships and shore batteries, the shore batteries always won. Captain (D) had, despite his ferocity, the prudence of a good commander.

A few more patrols passed without event and we steamed back to Scapa. We had helped the Canadian army to land: it was up to the pongos now; God bless them.

eight

Last Action

We were glad to get back to Scapa. Putting already-mixed bottles of gin-and-squash in our Burberrys, we rushed ashore to tell our Wrens that, having firmly launched the invasion of Europe, we were back to concentrate on more serious matters, such as them and *Tirpitz*. We sat in the lee of a haystack and drank the gin-and-squash, the sun set about ten, and, dropping the Wrens at the Wrennery, we caught the last liberty boat back. So much for our Wrens.

Tirpitz was another matter. While we were at Normandy, Sir Henry Moore had succeeded Sir Bruce as Commander-in-Chief. This summer would be a good time to flatten *Tirpitz*, thought Sir Henry, so she could not threaten the autumn convoys. Besides, she held down several of our heavy ships, ships needed to build up a Far Eastern fleet to assist the Americans in operations against Japan. Sir Bruce was going to the Pacific.

We went to Altenfiord for the fourth time. But all the skill and bravery of our Fleet Air Arm pilots could not compensate for old, slow aircraft. *Tirpitz* was again hidden by a protective pall of smoke. The thirty-two U-boats still stationed in northern Norway made the operation risky; but we now had an RAF long-range Catalina air patrol. They sank three U-boats. A flying officer, wounded in one of these attacks, won a VC. Although a few hundred thousand tons of supplies had reached Russia through the Persian Gulf and although there would be no real darkness for another month, our Russian convoys would resume in August. With our carrier-air-patrols the U-boats were at a disadvantage, and Goering still wouldn't give Dönitz the Luftwaffe aircraft needed to make lethal attacks upon us. But there were enough Luftwaffe for us.

Admiral Moore mounted a fifth strike against *Tirpitz*. A five-hundred-pound armour-piercing bomb bounced off the roof of the *Tirpitz's* for'ard turret. A sixteen-hundred pound armour-piercing bomb penetrated both armoured decks but failed to explode. The Fleet retired to the west.

On this operation was an RN carrier manned by an RCN crew, HMS *Nabob*, under Captain Horatio Nelson Lay. On that bright August afternoon, while she was preparing to fuel three destroyers, a torpedo struck her on the starboard quarter. The lights went out, all auxiliary machinery stopped; the engines were stopped, the boilers shut down; ventilation fans were motionless, and the temperature in the engine room rose to a hundred and fifty degrees. *Nabob* sank by the stern about fourteen feet as seawater boiled in; she listed seven degrees to starboard. Boats, floats, and rafts were lowered; she settled another two feet. It looked as if she was going. Captain Lay evacuated two hundred and fourteen men, including ten injured, to *Kempthorne*. *Nabob* settled further. *Bickerton* was torpedoed about a half-mile away and started to settle by the stern. *Kempthorne* was ordered to pick up her survivors as well. *Sioux*, *Algonquin*, and one other destroyer screened *Nabob*. It was a thousand miles to Scapa; through gales and shadowing submarines, we made it.

Admiral Dalrymple-Hamilton took up the first autumn convoy and got the returning convoy back with no merchant-ship losses. Some shadowing aircraft were shot down and two U-boats sunk. HMS *Kite* was sunk; out of her crew of two hundred, nine were rescued.

September, October; the days drew in and the temperature dropped. November, December, ice piled up on the superstructure and darkness was complete. We spent Christmas of 1944 at sea.

This was ridiculous. I reminded the Captain that I hadn't received my DSC and flew south to London.

The Mayfair Hotel was still there, undamaged by bombing; outside the front door, Berkeley Square was still green. I had two hundred pounds in unspent pay in my wallet. Rooms were hard to get but suites were easier; whisky was scarce but champagne was not. Rationing was severe and food was poor, but you could still get breakfast served in your room. At nine in the morning, every morning. I had breakfast sent up—a kipper, cold toast, champagne, and a large pot of strong, hot tea. After five years of war the tea was still plentiful and good. Snug in my bed, my miraculously stable bed, I would sip champagne, placidly watching the sleet hit the window. Warm, dry, rested, safe. Drinks at noon at the Canadian Naval Headquarters on the Haymarket, then to an incredibly crowded pub, the Captain's Cabin; more drinks, then lunch. Then back to the Haymarket, but this time to the Starboard Club to doze in a chair until the five-o'clock crowd came in. Lots of gin here, and the club was jammed by six. Tucked on the corner stool at the bar, with shouting, laughing friends around me, I listened to stories of war from theatres other than my own: fighter pilots, always with unbuttoned jackets; commandos; infantry majors—they always seemed to be majors; captains of motor torpedo-boats—they all had several DSCs; women and girls of all shapes, sizes, and ages—one a countess, I remember. The invasion had caused an easement of air-raids. The nights when fifteen hundred fires burned in London were in the past. But the club was blacked out at dusk and this made everything cozy. In the past also were the dawns when firemen still fought last night's fires, when wardens and rescue parties dug for the living buried, when ambulances rushed wounded and dying to hospitals, when trucks collected the dead, when housewives swept glass from their doorsteps and rubble from their kitchens. But we still had to put up with the flying bombs, the V-1's.

The effect on Londoners was peculiar. After five years of war they were as inured to sudden death as front-line troops. The V-1's came over perhaps as many as three or four an hour: you could see them. But there was nothing you could do. You can't stay in an air-raid shelter all day, and these bombs had been coming over for months. There's no use ducking. You just wait to see where it hits.

I was having lunch at a west-end home one day and my hostess had spared no effort. I knew that what was on the table represented a week's ration; the best silverware was out, a snowy cloth, a week's supply of coal burning in the fireplace, horded whisky and wine plentiful. The conversation was going on in that charming, inconsequential, amusing vein that is peculiar to the English when they are dealing with a colonial and they are not quite sure what he might say.

"And so I said to Dennis, you really are a very naughty boy and it grieves mummy to tell you this . . ."

Sound of a V-1 motor—faint.

". . . but you leave no alternative. Now, of course, what I didn't know, and what his father didn't know, was that the gardener had replaced . . ."

Sound of V-1 motor—louder.

". . . the flower-pots, and Lady Wyatt knew this. So I said to Dennis that I was going to put him in the lavatory until he apologized. I did this and then went out into the garden and when out there I looked up and . . ."

V-1 motor cuts out. Complete silence at the table. Muted rumble of traffic outside. Wine glasses poised halfway to the mouth. Knives and forks suspended over plates. This lasts perhaps twenty seconds; then, about a mile away, *boom.*

". . . and there was this furious, red little face and streams and streams of toilet paper floating out of the upstairs lavatory. Well, my dear . . ."

I knew then that there would always be an England, and that Hitler had gravely underestimated his adversaries.

One morning I rose at seven instead of nine and set out for the Haymarket to pick up Ab Blais at Canadian Headquarters. A staff car drove us to Buckingham Palace and I was expertly shepherded by palace staff into the longest queue I had heretofore seen in England. The Lord High Panjandrum briefed us.

"When you are at the head of the line you will hear your name called. With measured and unhurried tread you will walk forward until you are in line with His Majesty. You will stop, turn, bow, and take two paces forward. His Majesty will then bestow upon you your decoration. If it pleases His Majesty to speak, you will, of course, respond. You are not to initiate a conversation. His Majesty will then shake your hand and you are to ensure that you do not grasp His Majesty's hand too tightly. You will then step back two paces, bow, turn right, and unhurriedly retire. While in this ante-room you may converse in low tones; but when you enter the presence, you are to remain silent."

We stood around in groups, talking uneasily. An ancient captain with two and a half rows of First World War medal ribbons was saying to an equally ancient commander, "Yes, I've known him since he served under me in the Home Fleet in '16. Had to kick his arse a few times, I remember."

Wishing to dissociate myself from those who had kicked the royal arse, I turned to a squadron leader about my own age. I looked at his three DFCS and his DSO. "Not the first time," I said.

"No," he said, "third. But I never seem to get the pukka drill. Duff drill, every time."

"What seems to be the trouble?"

"Always forget to bow when leaving."

Investitures of orders and decorations always start with

orders of chivalry and knighthood. The most ancient and illustrious is the Order of the Garter, dating from about 1350. We
had none that day. My decoration was the lowest awarded, and
so I was at the back of the queue. The head of the queue was two
rooms away, so I am not sure, but I think that the highest that day
was in the civil (as opposed to the military) division of the Order of
the British Empire. I heard that the recipient was in the Ministry
of Supply and in charge of turnips and potatoes; he was made a
Knight Commander. The highest military award that day was the
Victoria Cross. Predictably, the man who won it wasn't there; but
his widow received it for him, and his mother and his children
were in attendance.

My friend the squadron leader stood in front of me, at the
back of the air force DSOs. We chatted as the queue edged forward and we admired the room—large, plush, impressive, with
dead monarchs staring haughtily at us from gilt frames. I was
beginning to feel nervous. Everybody was so obviously impressed
at being here. I had to go to the heads. I conferred with the
squadron leader. He said, "Well, if you don't make it a regular
Morning George (no pun), I expect it'll be all right." Returning to
the queue I felt a momentary panic when I couldn't find my place,
but they had shuffled into another room.

There were perhaps two hundred spectators on the right; on
the left was the King. He looked frail and tired. He and his family
had been here through the whole of the bombings of London. In
perhaps six rows of medal ribbons I noticed two of the First
World War like my father's. I noticed the oak-leaf cluster of his
Mentioned in Dispatches. I wished I'd combed my hair. For some
obscure reason, I'd thought the investiture would be outside and I
wouldn't have to remove my cap. My friend the squadron leader
went forward to get his gong.

I went through it with him: halt, left turn, bow, two paces forward. Now he and the King were chatting. Good! Now they were
shaking hands. So far so good.

And then the squadron leader buggered off. He didn't step
back, he didn't bow, he didn't even turn. He just buggered off. I
heard my name.

"Lieutenant Lawrence. His Majesty's Canadian Ship *Sioux*.
For great gallantry in action with U-boats."

I started forward with my version of a measured and unhurried tread. In six paces I would halt, turn left, and bow. The
squadron leader retreated in front of me; suddenly he stopped
and blushed—at least his ears and the back of his neck did. He

muttered, "Oh my Christ," turned, and hurried back, face scarlet. I stopped a pace away from the King. The squadron leader stopped in front of the King, bowed deeply, and buggered off again at a good clip. I turned left, bowed in what I considered a courtly manner, took two paces forward, and waited. The King, looking after the retreating pigeon and grinning broadly, reached absently for my gong, and, still looking to the left, looped it over the hook on my monkey jacket. I stood motionless. Still smiling, the King seemed to become aware of my presence. He said, "U-boats, eh?"

I said, "Yes, sir."

He said, "Good, good."

We shook hands, lightly, fingers only. And I left.

I took the night train to Glasgow. The train was crowded and I had to stand all the way. Then I caught a naval plane to the Orkneys. As I got closer to *Sioux* I began to worry that she'd been in action while I was away. Nothing charitable about it: it was just that I didn't want anyone to score any successes with my guns.

Nothing much had happened. *Cassandra* was still lying in Polyarnoe awaiting a new bow. All the fleet carriers had sailed for the Far East. *Campania* had been attacked by forty JU88s. Three more U-boats had been sunk. *Sioux* had been only on the fringes of the actions. The convoys were now sailing four weeks apart instead of five. Admiral Dalrymple-Hamilton and Admiral McGrigor took it turn about; thus, one was leaving as the other arrived.

On February 3, 1945, we sailed north with Convoy JW-64 with Admiral McGrigor. On the sixth we were sighted by a meteorological aircraft from Trondheim and from then on were under constant surveillance. Two Wildcats from *Campania* shot down a shadower, but he shot down one of them. On the morning of the seventh a wave of forty-eight JU88s took off. They liked to attack out of the night; so Admiral McGrigor altered the convoy to the east to put their favourite attacking sector astern. At 0745 our radar picked up two flights, one to the northwest and one to the southwest, but the JU88s did not press home their attack. Two Wildcats from *Nairana* set one shadower on fire. During the next two days the shadowers circled. Our fighters flashed out, the shadowers retreated; the fighters returned, so did the shadowers. Their position reports went out with typical German regularity. We still had a U-boat patrol line to get around. And on these two days, the eighth and ninth, the aircraft homed the U-boats. On the morning of the tenth we were south of Bear Island and only two hundred and fifty miles from enemy airfields at Barderfoss.

Watch-keeping was rugged. Four hours on and four hours off during the dark hours at defence stations. Just before dawn we went to action stations, four hours on and stop on. From some empirical formula evolved by the First Lieutenant, Marc and I seemed to get the last four hours of defence stations; then we would be closed up all day at action stations—Marc at the torpedo sight and me in the Director—and then draw two night watches, the last dog-watch and the middle watch. Going aft to our cabin, particularly in bad weather, took valuable sleeping time and so we took to flaking out in the wardroom, which was for'ard and below the bridge. The doctor didn't like this. He was a permanent fixture in the wardroom, snoring in a chair, the wardroom table rigged to receive casualties, and his instruments bubbling gently in the sterilizer. One night we stole some boiling water to make ki and he awoke and went into a rage. He threatened that if we ever got on that operating table as casualties the first thing he would do would be to cut off our balls with an unsterilized scalpel.

This morning of the tenth was good to us. Just before ten o'clock we got a single aircraft on the radar-scope coming in from the south. On the strength of a message from the Senior British Officer in Russia, we believed this to be friendly. But we swung the guns onto the bearing. Nobody was friendly in these waters until he proved it. The plot chanted out the decreasing range. We couldn't get it on gunnery radar. The computer was tuned to plot range—not nearly accurate enough but better than nothing. The bearing was drawing forward, so I set the angle of sight graticules to nine o'clock. Director Layer and Trainer and I looked out over our binoculars. The cloud base was low. The aircraft dropped below it. It was a JU88.

In the Director we all saw it simultaneously.

"Alarm aircraft starboard. Green one-oh-oh. Load. Load. Load. Going left. Speed one-six-oh." I heard the breech-blocks clang shut.

In a few seconds it was in our binoculars.

"Layer on. Trainer on." From below I heard the Chief Gunner's Mate report, "Have radar." Then, "Matching radar rate?" Then, "Clock tuned, deflection set."

"Commence. Commence. Commence," I ordered; and, with a satisfying roar, *Sioux's* guns spoke.

Simultaneous with all this, which took not more than twenty

seconds, the aircraft turned towards us. Our shell-bursts blossomed around him. Adjust the speed; adjust the graticule. He dropped a torpedo. I heard the Captain alter course to comb the spread. At full helm the Captain was throwing the guns off. A hit! By God, we had a hit. One of the aircraft's engines was on fire. He popped up into the cloud. It was finished. Elapsed time? Not more than two minutes. The torpedo passed down the port side. The Yeoman told the Fleet it was coming.

The Admiral moved the destroyer screen to anti-aircraft positions. Weather and light were poor: ten-tenths cloud, in snow squalls a visibility of one mile, between squalls five miles.

At 1019 the main attack developed on the starboard bow. *Whitehall* and *Lark* broke up one formation and shot down three JU88s. *Nairana*'s fighters were off and flying outside the Gun Defence Zone. They got one. Then *Campania*'s fighters got a "probable" and a "possible". Outside the Gun Defence Zone were the dips and loops of dogfights. But the JU88s weren't there to engage fighters: they were there to deliver torpedoes. They bore in. Within the Gun Defence Zone, attacks developed from all directions. It got so that I didn't cease fire when shifting target. The steady, controlled roar of *Sioux*'s guns was stunning, and burned cordite stung my throat. The rubber eye-piece fell off my binoculars and with each broadside I got a sharp rap on the malar bone, the orbital ridge, and the top of my nose as the Directors whipped. *Onslow*, *Orwell*, and *Cygnet* were blazing away, some of their rounds whistling close by. The 20-mm and 40-mm close-range weapons poured it out. With a part of my mind not, apparently, occupied, I noticed that none of my 4.7s missed a broadside. Must remember to congratulate the Gun Captains. Then the after guns cut out. Must be wooded. A quick look over the side of the Director showed that the JU88s were just crossing the bow. Elapsed time, about eight minutes.

There was a lull as the JU88s reformed. Then, in they came again. The water was alive with the creaming wake of torpedoes. To alter course to comb the spread of one was to run into another. The Captain's hard-over turns complicated the gunnery problem. The Admiral altered the convoy ninety degrees away from the attacks. Each roll of the ship set up a clamour of empty brass cartridge-cases clanging to and fro. Suddenly the sky was clear, but the action was not over. As the Wildcats and Swordfish returned to land on, the convoy opened up again. The Admiral was vexed but his report was written with restraint. He said that this "showed a quite inexcusable lack of fire discipline even taking into account the bad visibility, low cloud, and the pace of events. There is little resemblance between a JU88 and a Wildcat, and none with a Swordfish."

He was right. A Swordfish has two wings, a JU88 one. Wildcat and Swordfish have one engine, a JU88 has two. Add to the dangers of the sea and the violence of the enemy "the stupidity of friends". Nevertheless, only one of our fighters was shot down (by the Germans, not us), and the pilot was picked up. We totted up the Fleet's score later: seven certain, four probable, eight damaged.

We seemed to have slipped through the U-boat screen. No doubt they would gather outside Polyarnoe for our exit.

Icing, high winds, heavy snow squalls, and short visibility hampered us all the next day. I sat the long hours in my Director, cold, cramped, reliving the action. With startling clarity I could remember each detail of the engagement: how the aircraft looked, his angle, his speed, his turns, other aircraft in relation to him, my spotting orders, where the bursts were, when we shifted target—I could run it through my mind like a movie. I was completely happy. I would do much better next time.

But it didn't clear. The next day, the twelfth, the Russian escort met us. They always met us on the last day, never further out. Three of our escort detached with the Archangel section. We arrived at Kola Inlet that night and proceeded up the harbour in pitch blackness and snow squalls. It was after midnight when we tied up. We lost an escort as the last merchant ship got safely in. *Denbigh Castle* was torpedoed. You couldn't rely on the Russians to keep even the harbour entrance clear of U-boats. We'd given them some submarine-chasers but it didn't do any good. The Russian air force was ineffective, too. Two merchantmen were sunk the next day by the same U-boat that torpedoed *Denbigh Castle*. We heard that the Russian papers headlined the glorious Soviet Navy once again bringing a convoy safely into the northern ports, but it might have been a bitter rumour. We were just glad to turn in that night knowing we wouldn't be awakened by the action-stations bell. Convoy JW-64 was over.

Next morning we ate breakfast in a wardroom with fresh air blowing through it. It was one of the major pleasures of life to raise the deadlights and open the scuttles. Most of us worked until eleven, and then, since it would be dark again at three in the afternoon, leave was piped.

I was about two hours astern of the rest, for I had to make out my "Quarterly Return of Ammunition Expended", summarize endless columns of "Maximum and Minimum Temperatures of Magazines and Shell-Rooms", and generally concoct the multiplicity of reports which people who sit behind desks consider essential to the waging of war.

The only officer left aboard, besides the Officer of the Day, was a new sub-lieutenant who had joined the ship before we sailed. Summers was lying on the wardroom settee reading the *Weekly Intelligence Report*. When I suggested he would be more use to the ship getting a bit of exercise and relaxation, he reluctantly went to lock the book away and get his greatcoat. "I thought I'd finish that first and then go," he said defensively. "It's hard to get time at sea."

I was annoyed at the implied reproach; at sea, when off watch, most of us spent as much time as possible in our bunks—it shortened the trip. I stifled a snotty retort, however, and just grunted, "Come on then."

He was the best type of sub-lieutenant one could expect in a war now five years old. He had just left university and, considering the very drastically shortened wartime courses in Gunnery, Torpedo, Anti-Submarine, Navigation, and Communications which he had just completed, he knew quite a lot. All he needed was a year or so at sea.

After a two-mile walk around the drab town we pushed open the doors of the Royal Navy Mess, only to meet our First Lieutenant struggling into his greatcoat. "We're recalled," he said bitterly. "Oh, isn't this a lovely war! Check the men's canteen on your way back."

As I approached the men's canteen—Summers had gone straight back—I saw the Shore Patrol stamp in. The Chief Petty Officer roared for silence and eventually got it amid many good-natured cries of "Have a beer, Chief". The sailors had been there several hours. The ship's companies of four destroyers were ordered back to their ships. For some reason we weren't going out with our own Captain (D) but with Captain (D) of the Zs: *Zambesi, Zealous, Zest*. The uproar recommenced, but the sailors gulped their drinks and filed out complaining loudly. They were noisy, but the iron bond of discipline held them in every waking moment.

An hour later we sailed out of Kola Bay.

A few miles away, on the port side, the coast of Russia slipped quickly past, then Finland. We were making thirty knots. Just before dawn, the clouds cleared and the other destroyers showed up clearly, three slender shapes splitting the Arctic seas into mountains of spray, their superstructures and the thin fingers of their guns etched sharply against the pale luminosity of the restless Northern Lights. They looked deadly and efficient, as machines of destruction should, yet strangely beautiful too.

By daylight we rounded North Cape and were steaming down the coast of Norway.

At first light we closed up at action stations: the enemy had airfields at Hammerfest. Over the intercommunication system the Captain told us the purpose of this operation. Five hundred people, mostly women, children, and old men, were stranded on the small island where they lived. The Germans had stove in all their boats and taken all their food. Starvation threatened, and the plan was simply to dash in, embark them, and return to Polyarnoe. Summers was visibly excited.

In the forenoon watch, course was shaped for Soro Island. The sun would not rise until 0933, but the sky to the south'rd was a bright pearly white, lightening the slate-grey water. Summers and I were in the control tower. He reached in front of me and picked up the voice-pipe to the bridge. "Bearing red three five. An object. Far," he shouted. I was ruffled that I had not seen it first; furthermore, it was I who normally passed reports.

The Director Trainer swung us around and I adjusted my binoculars on a small white dot of land. As we approached, it grew and its base widened. A similar white dot appeared to port and then two more to starboard. As the ships rolled over the curve of the earth, the dots grew taller and their bases joined, disclosing a fair-sized island. Pinnacles shot up rapidly on either side and behind, and soon the whole coastline was visible. Inland, the mountains rose, peak after peak.

As we steamed into the shadow of a deep fiord and up its still, black waters, the battle ensigns fluttered to the mast-head; I felt the familiar tightening across my stomach at this signal that action might be joined at any moment. Summers seemed positively exultant. "Wait until you've seen your first bomb hit," I thought. The Captain's face looked tired and his steel helmet gave him a grim look. Only the gurgle of the water against the sides, and the quiet orders of Peter, the Navigation Officer, broke the silence. I could hear the rasp as the Captain rubbed his chin. We all wore the white anti-flash masks.

The shore-line was jagged and forbidding, but suddenly, as the sun rose, the highest peak was tipped with red, and then, as if a reservoir had been tapped in the skies, a scarlet light spilled down the cliffs running gently from crag to crag. The dark waters caught the brilliant hue, the tension lifted a little, and the world seemed a happier place.

The fiord widened. From behind a large outcropping, scattered huts clinging to the base of the mountain came into view. A figure bent over a net straightened and stood rigid for a moment, then, waving wildly, bounded down the slope. Other figures appeared and soon the two wooden piers were jammed. The anchor pendants dipped, four anchors splashed, and the cables roared deafeningly through the hawse-pipe, leaving a red haze of chipped rust over each fo'c's'le. Boats pulled swiftly to shore and embarkation commenced. Summers took our whaler. He had strapped on a forty-five. There was no need of it.

In half an hour we were snugged down again. Arms and ammunition were landed for seventeen young men who were staying. Anchors clanked home; the ships swung, formed a column, and steamed swiftly for the open sea. Soon the mountains were dots on the horizon; then, one by one, they dropped from sight.

Summers was disappointed. I settled down thankfully and pulled up the hood of my sheepskin. Summers remained erect, exposed to the freezing wind, his binoculars sweeping relentlessly back and forth, back and forth, as though willing an enemy to appear.

Back in Polyarnoe the Norwegian men, women, and children were transferred to merchant vessels. Convoy RA-64 sailed the next day with thirty-four ships.

The previous year had been a good year for killing U-boats in Arctic waters; twenty-two were sunk. So far none had been bagged this year; but, cruising just outside Kola Inlet was U-425. With her were several other U-boats, and local conditions were all in their favour. The departure of the convoy was confined to a forty-mile passage running eastward along the shore before turning north. This was known to the enemy, and U-boats were stationed every few miles along it. So close to harbour was *Denbigh Castle* when first torpedoed that we thought she must have hit a mine. The efforts of the Russian minesweepers were notoriously feeble. But no; she had been torpedoed. The Russian air-patrols were daylight only and quite ineffective. Russian forces, both marine and air, did the bare minimum and had no offensive spirit. We had. Admiral McGrigor ordered four destroyers to dash out ahead of the convoy, sweep the forty-mile channel, and then sweep back. From time to time we dropped a depth-charge. The night before, *Lark*, *Lapwing*, *Alnwick Castle*, and *Bamborough Castle*, two sloops and two corvettes, carried out an anti-submarine search to Longitude 35°E. U-425 was caught and sunk.

RA-64 sailed at 0745, February 17. Russian tugs were standing by to bring in damaged ships. A few Russian escorts were to follow the convoy until dark, but they steamed around aimlessly. At 1024, *Lark* had her stern blown off. About an hour and a half later the merchantman *Thomas Scott* was torpedoed and sank. During the night *Bluebell* was hit by a torpedo and blew up. There was one survivor. The Russians towed *Lark* back into harbour.

The next day, the eighteenth, the weather deteriorated and flying was stopped. A gale blew up, perhaps sixty knots, gusting to more. A heavy swell arose. By the nineteenth the convoy had scattered. On the morning of the twentieth the gale abated and we set about rounding up stragglers, a gruelling task but a matter of some urgency, for we were being shadowed again. By the middle of the forenoon watch twenty-nine ships were back in station, leaving four stragglers. *Zambesi* noted it had taken her twelve hours' continuous steaming at high speed over an area of nearly one thousand square miles to round up nine stragglers.

I was up in my Director again, awaiting events with a thudding heart bursting with anticipation. An hour later some thirty aircraft arrived. We were still steering west and they were on the port bow. The wind was strong and the sea still rough but *Nairana* flew off fighters. The Admiral altered the convoy to south to put the attack on our quarter. And in came the JU88s, some on the bow and some on the quarter.

Again the air was filled with the smoke of a hundred guns and the acrid smell of burned cordite. The mustard-yellow smoke whipped in front of my binoculars. The weaving JU88s were practically at sea-level. They would steady momentarily to drop their torpedo. Summers did well. His orders were clear and firm and accurate. Here was action at last! An ocean for a battlefield. A determined foe that knows all the tricks. A willing foe and sea-room. Comrades in twenty other ships wheeling and forming on the orders of our Admiral to meet each new attack. In our own ship, two hundred and eighty shipmates welded into a beautiful fighting team: the stokers, eyes intently on their steam gauges; the engine-room artificers curbing forty thousand horsepower to obedience of the Captain's wishes relayed through the jangling engine-room telegraph and revolution indicator; shipwrights and electricians of the Damage Control Party waiting to render first-aid should the ship be wounded; wireless operators and radar operators sending the constant stream of information they received to the guns and the operations room; the gunnery-control ratings feeding wind, drift, roll, pitch, range, and a dozen other variables into the computer, which churned out elevations and deflections to the guns, whose noses point expectantly in the air.

The breech-blocks clang shut; a roar as the broadside leaves and the four deadly black flowers blossom in the sky. The heavy bass of the big guns, the melody carried by the more rapid bam bam of the Bofors, and the chattering Oerlikons playing a vicious counterpoint drum out, in heavily accented notes, the cacophony of battle. Forty minutes later the attack had been beaten off. No casualties. *Onslow, Zealous, Bamborough Castle, Rhododendron, Lapwing, Sioux*, all scored. Some "probables", some "possibles", some "damaged". With a heavy heart I confess that *Sioux* got only one "damaged". It was not quite over. When the fighters returned to land on, the convoy opened up on them again. They were landing with a wind over the deck of seventy knots, quite enough for a pilot to think about.

By that evening another straggler came back into the fold; now we had thirty-one out of thirty-three. The next afternoon, another came home. The last, the *Crosby Noyes*, we never saw again. (She plodded along, hundreds of miles astern, but was lucky enough to make Scotland safely.) The remainder of the day we were shadowed. We had HF/DF bearings of U-boats but it was really too rough for them to attack. On the twenty-second another gale blew up, seventy to eighty knots.

It's difficult to describe wind and sea of this primeval force. *Nairana* was rolling forty-five degrees either way. That afternoon *Sioux* rolled to fifty-six degrees. Marc had a good grip on the compass-stand but most of the rest of us on the bridge ended up in an untidy heap on the port side. With massive seas looming over our heads, *Sioux* picked herself up, hesitated, dipped slightly again, lolled for a full six seconds—a very long six seconds—and righted herself. She was a good girl, *Sioux*. "God bless Samuel White's shipyard," I thought. We were all soaked through, with two hours more of the watch left, and the temperature at thirty-one degrees.

In the evening it got worse. The convoy was hove to and scattered. We worried about our Norwegians. All hands felt paternal

towards them. Their condition and fate were frequently discussed. What would they do when they got to Scotland? How were
the women and children minding the motion of the ships?

In the convoy, abused engines broke down, cargoes shifted,
decks split, steering gear went wonky, ice-chipped propellers
thrashed. Merchant ships dropped astern and sometimes stopped.
There was little we could do to help. The seas continued at awful
heights, spindrift streaming from boiling crests. *Sioux* shuddered as wave after endless wave pounded her thin sides. Summers positively enjoyed that gale. He kept chattering about the
size of the seas: "Look at that one, look, look."

On the morning of the twenty-third it was still blowing a full
gale and we were down to twenty ships. By evening we were back
up to thirty-one. But the one straggler, *Henry Bacon*, never made
it. She was attacked by part of a formation of nineteen torpedo
bombers and sunk. *Zambesi, Zest,* and *Opportune* went back to
rescue survivors and got sixty-five, including all the Norwegians.
Between thirty and forty of *Henry Bacon*'s crew gave up their
seats in the lifeboats to the Norwegian women and children.
There just wasn't enough room in the boats for both crew and
passengers. Those that gave up their seats were lost; all in the
boats were picked up.

The gale continued on the twenty-fourth with gusts up to
seventy knots. Convoy speed was about three and a half knots. We
occasionally heard the chatter of the U-boat's radio but no attacks developed. That afternoon there was a burial in the convoy.
We didn't know if it was a death from strafing or perhaps a fall
from the ship's violent motion. The casualty was a small boy, a
Norwegian. A dozen or so figures collected on the poop, and
through my binoculars I could see them taking off their hats and
bowing their heads in prayer. When they raised their heads a
small bundle sewn in white canvas slipped over the side and
splashed into the sea. The group broke up and dispersed. Two remained and they stood at the taffrail gazing astern. When
darkness came an hour later, they were still there, staring back.
Summers was silent when we went off watch. There was a
thoughtful look on his face and I knew he'd set foot on the long
road the rest of us first trod five years before.

The gale continued on the twenty-fifth. We inched our way
south. On the twenty-sixth the wind, though continuing strong,
veered to the northwest. Convoy speed increased to seven knots
for a few hours. At midnight of the twenty-sixth I was relieved of

my bridge watch and started aft to my cabin. For several days the crew had been using the cat-walk, which led aft from the bridge, above the for'ard torpedo tubes, around the funnel, and across the Bofors gun-deck, above the after torpedo tubes, to the after canopy, which housed the sick bay, a petty officers' mess, a seamen's mess-deck, and two officers' cabins. This cat-walk was perhaps fifteen feet above the upper deck, which for the past week had been constantly swept with white water and sometimes with green, and had, therefore, been deemed unsafe and closed to traffic. The abatement of the wind and the dropping of the sea had prompted me to open the upper deck for traffic about a half-hour earlier.

I stayed awhile chatting with the Captain, who was sharing a pot of coffee with the Navigator and the Petty Officer of the Watch. Thus, it was about twenty past midnight when I set off for my bunk: the Middle Watchmen were all closed up; the First Watchmen by now were all turned in. The upper deck was deserted. I undogged the steel door at the break of the fo'c's'le, stepped outside into the whistling, rushing dark, slammed the door, dogged it up again, grabbed a lifeline, and set off in lurching steps. I was abreast of the for'ard torpedo tubes when *Sioux* gave a peculiar lurch. Not a roll, not a pitch, although she was doing both of those, but a sag as well. She was going sideways into the sea, not over it. She rolled to port, dipped, and slid further to port. I flung away the lifeline and hurled myself toward the for'ard torpedo tubes, hoping that being five feet higher off the deck would help. But no. I was picked up and swept aft, submerged face down. My knee hit metal and the pain caused me to shout. I took a mouthful of water. I remember looking up and seeing the funnel. I don't think I was over the side but I was many feet off the deck. For several seconds I was tossed and tumbled. I felt metal and grabbed; felt it with my other hand and grabbed again. *Sioux* heaved up. I was face down on something when the water subsided. The icy shock of the water—temperature forty degrees—hit me for the first time. I didn't tremble or shiver, I heaved. My fingers were locked over a lip of metal and over a flange. I raised my head and looked around cautiously. I was on the after torpedo tubes, about fifty feet further aft from where I'd started my early-morning dip. With many a wary glance at the seas I slid off the tubes, undogged the watertight door to the after canopy, slipped in, dogged the door again, and stood in amazement in the warm air, gazing at a tranquil scene illuminated by red night-lights. I started to lecture myself: "Eternal vigilance is the price of safety." To hell with it, everyone gets knackered some time. I went down to the cabin flat, stripped, towelled myself dry, donned pyjamas, and turned in. It was the first time in five years of war that I'd worn pyjamas at sea. I felt somehow that this balanced the books.

Late that afternoon we sighted Scapa Flow. For two weeks we had been through the worst weather hitherto encountered by an Arctic convoy, at speeds from hove-to to seven knots, averaging three knots. Twelve of the destroyers had to be docked for hull repairs. Not *Sioux*; we entered harbour, sliding by the Port War Signal Station which was manned by Wrens. The telescopes and binoculars of all our signal staff were fixed on the Station. Signal-lamps chattered, we hoisted our pendant numbers, the challenge and reply satisfactorily completed. Then the informal signalling began: three small handkerchiefs waved to us—two white, one red. A signalman looked decidedly chock-a-block and snapped shut his telescope.

Convoy JW-64 put the total of goods delivered to Russia at over four million tons, including five thousand tanks and seven thousand aircraft. Of the 811 merchant ships that had sailed, 720 completed the voyage, 33 turned back for various reasons—usually weather damage—and 58 were sunk. A total of 829 officers and men of the Allied merchant navies died. Of the escorts, 18 were sunk: a total of 1,944 officers and men died.

In the convoys from Russia the ships were largely in ballast. Russia had nothing to export. But 29 ships, both naval and merchant, were sunk for a grand total of 105 ships sunk. Nearly 5,000 men dead. For four million tons of supplies, including five thousand tanks and seven thousand planes, it was a bargain. (It is difficult to conjecture what the Soviet army and air force would have done without these supplies, what the course of the war would have been, how much longer it would have lasted.) Compare it to, for instance, land battles in 1914 with 754,000 casualties, in 1915 with 1,549,000, all to gain a few hundred yards of mud.

Some of the great names of the United States Navy had been in the Home Fleet to help cover these convoys: the USS *Washington*, *Wasp*, *Tuscaloosa*, *Wichita*. USN destroyer officers had raised glasses in our wardroom. (No bourbon? Rye-on-the-rocks, then. No ice? Just straight then.)

These convoys were a four-thousand-mile voyage up and down

a long coastline held by the enemy and from which he could sortie submarines, surface-craft, or aircraft at will. The German had the power to interdict completely the passage of our convoys; but for Goering's impregnable ignorance of the co-operation essential between navy and air force and but for Hitler's crippling restrictions on his naval commanders, many more of our bones would be lying at the bottom of the Arctic. The enemy had the initiative, and for about twenty-eight days at sea—with a three-day turn-around in Kola—we anxiously awaited his thrusts. We were limited to the north by the ice field, our arrival point was well known, and our arrival time was predictable. Had Hitler not imposed his "no-risk" policy on his battleships and cruisers, it would have been catastrophic for us.

As it was, we did all right. In 1942, *Bulldog, Beagle,* and *Beverley* drove off the *Hermann Schoemann,* z24, and z25 (which had twice the fire-power of our forces); drove them off five times. In 1943 Vice-Admiral Kummetz was at sea with the pocket battleship *Lützow,* the heavy cruiser *Hipper,* and five destroyers. This force could have annihilated the convoy but for timid handling by the German commanders. In a series of skirmishes, in smoke-screens and snow flurries, in the gloom of the Arctic twilight, Captain Sherbrooke, vc, kept the powerful force at bay with just five destroyers.

But the weather was the greater and ever-present danger: frequent gales of unusual violence, ice which could smash a propeller or accumulate on the top hamper, darkness and snowstorms. Running rigging and exposed machinery had to be constantly chipped; maintenance was difficult. Our aircraft were operated on a schedule of twelve hours' flying and twelve hours' maintenance. The for'ard-ends of flight-decks—sixty feet above the water-line—were sometimes bent up from the seas. One carrier took a green sea the entire length of the flight-deck.

In the end it all came down to the human element, the reactions of a man pushed to the limit of endurance and beyond, sometimes far beyond. Merchant seamen were put to the test time and again; the skill and seamanship of their masters passed belief. In fog, ice, snow, storm, darkness, and enemy attack, not a single merchant ship was lost through collision.

These men and the crews of their convoys performed extraordinary feats under appalling conditions, conditions that did not improve measurably even when they were at berth at Scapa Flow.

Take the food, for instance. After five years of war, rationing was stringent. Small and hard brussels sprouts, large and hard turnips, and soft, shrivelled potatoes formed the main part of our diet. There was meat of a sort. It was tough and often hard to identify. We regarded our dehydrated eggs and powdered milk and talked of better days.

We were sitting thus one evening after dinner and drinking port (my anodyne). The Captain knocked on the door. "May I come in?" he asked. We rose and he came around and sat on the bench in front of our electric fireplace.

"Cardinal Villeneuve is visiting the Fleet," he said. "He's from Quebec. We're the only Canadian ship in harbour and the Commander-in-Chief has told me that the Cardinal will be coming over here tomorrow morning for a couple of hours." He turned to the First Lieutenant. "Now look, Number One. This bucket looks more like a Greek freighter than a man-of-war. Oh, I know it's not your fault," he added hastily as the First Lieutenant looked outraged, "but get her cleaned up as best you can."

He swung around to the Torpedo Officer. "Marc, you're a Catholic. Come to my cabin after breakfast and brief me on the protocol. What do you call a Cardinal, anyway?"

"Your Eminence," said Marc.

"Now," the Captain continued briskly, "what else? Oh yes. Brown. Where's Brown?" Brown was his steward and he appeared quickly from the pantry. "Bring some of my good sherry in here tomorrow. For noon. And I want some hors d'oeuvres."

"Hors d'oeuvres?" asked Brown in amazement.

"Yes," said the Captain, "hors d'oeuvres. Can do?"

"Well . . ." said Brown uncertainly.

"Good," said the Captain, "that's that. The rest of you have a good long look at your men's tiddley uniforms. I don't want them looking like scruff. Well, I'm off. And Brown, I want *good* hors d'oeuvres." There were sinister undertones in his voice. Brown looked after him helplessly as he went out the door.

I was Officer of the Day, and a little while later Brown came up to me and asked for the motor cutter to go ashore. "At this time of night?" I said. "Whatever for?"

"Captain's business," he answered evasively.

Brown returned a couple of hours later with a small package, walked swiftly through the wardroom to the pantry, and shut the door behind him.

At breakfast the next morning there was an air of suppressed excitement in the pantry. The First Lieutenant looked curiously at the stewards a couple of times but said nothing.

At ten-forty the ship's company fell in on the quarter-deck and the officers stood around the accommodation-ladder chatting. After a few minutes the Commander-in-Chief's barge swung around the headland and pulled rapidly towards us.

"Fall in," said the First Lieutenant. We milled around.

"Come on," impatiently. "Dammit. Do I have to teach you how to fall in? Seniors on the right. Juniors on the left."

The barge pulled alongside the ladder and His Eminence came over the side. The Captain saluted.

"Good morning, Your Eminence. Welcome aboard."

"Good morning, Captain. Thank you."

"The troops are fallen in aft, Your Eminence. I thought you would like to speak to them first. Then we can make a tour of the ship and you can talk to some of them individually. There are many from your part of Canada.

"I would like you to meet my officers," he continued, and then took His Eminence down the line and introduced us all.

The First Lieutenant moved out after he had been introduced, and, facing aft, called the ship's company to attention. His voice had lost the penetrating power and snap that parade-ground instructors drill into us from an early age, and, in unconscious recognition of the occasion, had taken on an almost clerical note.

His Eminence talked for about ten minutes and then walked around the ship, stopping frequently to chat with sailors en route.

At about a quarter to twelve we filed into the wardroom. The three stewards in their white coats stood expectantly, poised for action. On the sideboard was a decanter of sherry and fourteen glasses and in the middle of the bare, polished table, theatrically illuminated by a wayward beam of sunlight slanting through the scuttle, lay a large wooden tray of hors d'oeuvres. The mystery of Brown's trip ashore last night and the excitement in the pantry this morning was explained.

Small green cabbage leaves formed a periphery upon which were spaced biscuits and what we all knew must be the last of the Captain's anchovies; inside this, like the spokes of a wheel, were orange slices of carrot; on this were set small triangles of bread covered with a dubious-looking dark-brown fish paste; then another ring of cabbage upon which was a profusion of rectangles and squares of red and white cheese. And inside this were *three hard-boiled eggs*. Fresh! Exactly as the hen laid them!

Two were halved and, pointing north, south, east, and west, formed a white-and-gold setting for the third. This was whole and stood upright in the geometric centre of the tray, balanced on a small mount of salt.

We all stared. Brown edged forward protectively. The other two stewards passed sherry.

"Well," said the Captain, "may I repeat, Your Eminence, how glad we are that you could visit us. Your health."

We sipped. All were edging away from the Cardinal towards the table. The Captain looked at us, perplexed. We stopped. Brown swept forward and grabbed the tray. He advanced on the Cardinal. We moved back in with him. Conversation was jerky.

Brown offered the tray to His Eminence. We watched in agony. His hand hovered, undecided, and then chose cheese. All eyes switched to the Captain. He chose an anchovy. I was next and as the tray came in front of me I reached for the egg. Brown pulled the tray back. I reached further. Brown pulled the tray back further. I picked up a carrot. Brown continued around, his eyes burning with warning, and if any hand strayed too near the centre he pulled the tray back.

Our manners returned. It occurred to us all simultaneously that we should not take an egg until the Cardinal or the Captain did. It was equally clear that the few on their left would be the only ones to get an egg. Now began a great jockeying for position. Soon we were spread out in a long tail to the Cardinal's left—a tail that had a tendency to bunch up at the base. Conversation was sporadic and strained. The Captain's expression changed alternately from glares at us to sudden smiles as His Eminence turned towards him. He had divined what was the matter but had decided, evidently, that he also should not take an egg until the Cardinal did; and the dignity of his position forbade his trying to get on the other side of the Cardinal where the rest of us jousted for position.

Such is the power of naval discipline, however, that we ended up roughly in the order of our seniority, much the same way as we had fallen in at the accommodation-ladder to greet our guest. The seniors, of course, were closer to the Cardinal, and to the eggs.

As the moments passed we broke into slightly more relaxed groups but never wandered far away from the imaginary tail-bone. Four times the tray was passed; each time His Eminence chose cheese or an anchovy; so did the Captain, and so did we.

It was arranged that when our guest was to leave, the Captain would take him to his cabin to collect his coat, and while they were there we would get our hats and gloves and fall in again by the accommodation-ladder.

We went through the door with a last regretful look at the eggs. The First Lieutenant shepherded us out but we hung back to make sure that he didn't scoff them. In sibilant whispers (the Captain was half-listening), the First Lieutenant drove us onto the upper deck.

Now the jockeying for position started again. The age-old rule "Seniors on the right, juniors on the left" had been discarded: the right flank was the one furthest from the wardroom. And we had all made a mental note that the first back in the wardroom would get the eggs. The left flank was closer to the wardroom and all the seniors managed to get there more or less in order of their seniority.

The Captain, when he passed, was obviously furious. But his anger was a periodically experienced hazard that could usually be weathered. A fresh egg was a gustatory delight that had not been experienced by any of us for nearly two years.

The barge roared away. We stood, quivering, unable to move until the First Lieutenant dismissed us. Doug walked slowly up our ranks, smiling a little. Then, getting well forward of us, closer to the wardroom, he gave the order, "Officers. Dis-miss."

Before the last syllable was out he had swivelled and was pelting along the upper deck. We broke ranks and followed in thundering pursuit. In the wardroom companion-way he was overtaken and hauled down. Vigorously we pulled, pushed, elbowed, clutched, and shouldered our way in. Marc was first. "Where are they?" he roared.

The tray could be seen through the pantry hatch. Some anchovies were left, some cheese, some cabbage. But no eggs.

Brown looked gently at our flushed, dishevelled group.

"Do you mean the eggs, sir?" he murmured. "I shared them with the rest of the stewards. I thought none of the officers wanted them. You all refused them four times. I'm very sorry, sir."

The visit had another sour side. We had perhaps thirty or more French Canadians in Sioux. Our Prime Minister, Mackenzie King, had finally, reluctantly, introduced conscription into the army. We didn't have conscripts in the navy. Our soldiers had been fighting in France, Holland, and Germany for nearly a year, in Italy for nearly a year and a half, in Africa for nearly two. Casualties were mounting and replacements were in short supply. We heard that Mackenzie King had been booed by Canadian soldiers when he had inspected them in England. Conscription was not popular anywhere, but less so in Quebec. It was not their war, Quebecers said, despite U-boat sinkings within two hundred miles of Quebec City. We heard that some French-Canadian intellectuals mocked the war effort. One university student rode a motorcycle through the streets of Montreal in a German uniform, it was said. Our French-Canadian shipmates didn't comment. But that day, as some hands gathered in a messdeck to meet Cardinal Villeneuve, a Winnipeg seaman said to a Trois Rivières seaman, "Ask him when we're getting some more Frenchmen over here so we can finish this fuckin' war."

In fact, despite the general good humour, there was a growing irritability in *Sioux*, not serious, but noticeable. We were all drinking more than we had been. One officer had to be chided for attempting to disrobe a visiting female entertainer in a wardroom (he was chided as lacking a proper sense of time and place). Our Paymaster was reproved for being disorderly. To be reproved for that in the Home Fleet one has to be very disorderly. He said, "I always drink more than I should."

We said, "Well, stop one drink short of it."

He said, "I don't know how much to stop one drink short of."

So we carried out trials. For three evenings in succession we watched him. We gave him our considered judgement. As a rule of thumb he could drink one bottle between pre-dinner drinks about six and bed around midnight. Saved! Each evening he poured a bottle of gin into a jug and filled it with water. When that was empty he turned in. No more trouble. The doctor sat in the corner of the wardroom settee for longer and longer periods singing "Red River Valley". Marc was singing "Mary, Mary" with added fervour. Our ebullient Roy had taken to staying aboard in Scapa, was receiving more letters than usual from Canada, and had marriage in mind, we suspected. Certainly I had the same thoughts. Many of the ship's company had two-year-old children they hadn't seen.

We sailed again in the middle of March for Murmansk: two light carriers, a light cruiser, and nineteen escorts. The days were lengthening, the weather was fine, and we were routed three hundred miles west of Trondheim and Barderfoss airfields, so no air attacks developed. The U-boats didn't find us until we were off Kola. There a snow-storm stopped flying at the most dangerous period and *Lapwing* and two merchant ships were sunk.

In an unprecedented display of friendliness, a flotilla of Russian destroyers invited forty officers of the Fleet to lunch. I was *Sioux*'s representative. *Algonquin* was represented by her captain, Lieutenant-Commander Desmond Piers. There would be about six British guests in each Russian destroyer.

We were greeted at the after accommodation-ladder with the punctilio of navies all over the world, and escorted to the wardroom. There we were introduced. This took on the aspect of me-Tarzan-you-Jane. The Officer of the Watch spoke English, but he went back up to the quarter-deck. The Russian names were strange to the Canadian ear and not easily remembered. Exhibited again was that peculiar English trait which springs from a centuries-old and deeply-ingrained belief, first, that anyone who speaks other than English is being slightly ridiculous and probably rude, and, secondly, that if you speak English slowly enough and loudly enough, any fool should be able to understand. We sat down. I managed to situate myself next to the Russian First Lieutenant; he could speak some English. The Russians were beaming at us in obvious and genuine good-fellowship. We beamed back. No drinks were offered. The Russian doctor, obviously their leading socialite, said, "Unterzeeboten, *blam*." We all laughed as he threw his hands in the air expressive of a depth-charge explosion. Encouraged by his success he held up two fingers. "Unterzeeboten, *blam, blam*." I felt bound to respond, "Der Cherman aircraften, *bang, bang, bang*," and I demonstrated air-bursts by exploding my fingers outwards in the air. A Russian sub-lieutenant crouched, an index finger extended in front of each eye, hands vibrating: he was an Oerlikon, *"Pom, pom, pom, pom, pom . . ."* The din of battle continued. It was interrupted by a cough at the door. There stood the Captain, four rings, Captain (D). All rose in silence.

Now, in the Canadian navy we rise, in a relaxed sort of way, when the Captain comes in, and we remain standing until he asks us to be seated. This he invariably does immediately. Not so in this Russian destroyer. First of all, the Russian officers were rigidly at attention, staring fixedly into space like a lot of wooden soldiers; and secondly, the Captain surveyed us all, deliberately, for quite a few seconds. Both hands in jacket pockets, thumbs to the front, cheroot between his teeth, one highly polished shoe on the combing. He surveyed us through the smoke of his cheroot, and then came forward.

We sat down at the table, twenty-two of us. Soup was served, a thick soup, heavy with potatoes. A white arm reached in front of me and deposited a tumblerful of vodka. Not vodka and water, vodka. Not a small glass, a tumbler. I looked apprehensively at this and started slurping my soup as quickly as possible. The Captain tapped for silence. "Gentlemen," he said, "you know why today you are here?"

"Da, da. Red Navy Day."

"Quite so. We are late, but that is so. I ask you then to drink a toast to the Red Navy."

And before we could raise our glasses he had downed his. Bottoms up. Empty. Six, seven ounces. We did the same. How the sombre pall of that Arctic day lifted! What an easy language Russian was, really, when you put your mind to it. I finished my soup and reached for the bread. I finished the bread just as an arm reached in front of me and deposited a tumblerful of rum. Not rum and water, rum. Not a small glass, a tumbler.

Debbie Piers took his cue. He turned to the Russian captain. "With your permission, sir. The British Navy." He downed his rum. Bottoms up. Empty. We did the same. Debbie said, "Very good rum. Mind if I have a drop more?" And he sipped another rum during the next course. A tumblerful of gin was now served, but we coasted on it during the next two courses, fish and meat. No bottoms-up. I ate as if my life depended on it. But the Russian doctor opposite me kept proposing little toasts. We toasted my home, his home; my mother, his mother; my dog, his dog. Talk was general and noisy and merry, certainly fluent; each spoke in his own tongue but comprehension of the other was not lacking.

I fought to keep my eyes focusing and ate steadily, everything in sight. My stomach, which had rebelled and rolled uneasily at the first cascade of vodka, seemed to have accepted its lot and settled down for an afternoon's drinking. But co-ordination was getting sloppy and locomotion would go next. Coffee came and I drank cup after cup. Nearly three hours passed.

My God, this was the life!

The doctor caught my eye, raised his glass, and we both sipped. Each time I put my glass down it was topped by a steward. It hadn't been empty for hours: it hadn't even been half-empty. I noticed the doctor's glass didn't need refilling and the realization dawned that he was taking a mouthful and spitting it back in. The rules of the game were clear. Our Russian hosts were out to scupper us. Fair enough, if they could. But I noticed the Russians were drinking in relays: when talking to us they drank; but, when we were talking to somebody else, they ate. That meant that the odds were three to one. Suddenly I felt truculent. I addressed the Russian captain. "You will excuse me, comrade Captain, sir, if I point out that your doctor doesn't drink with me. He sips, yes. He swallows, no. In my country this is a serious breach of faith."

"In mine also," said the Captain. "How many drinks my doctor he is behind please?"

"Two."

The Captain raised two fingers to the stewards and two tumblers of gin were placed in front of the doctor. We started our chant "So drink, chug-a-lug, chug-a-lug, chug-a-lug. So drink, chug-a-lug, chug-a-lug." He downed one. Loud cheers from all. "So drink, chug-a-lug, chug-a-lug, chug-a-lug. So drink, chug-a-lug, chug-a-lug, chug-a-lug." He downed the other. He looked around the table with the expression of a man who has seen his duty clear before him and has discharged it well. He said something, muzzily; his eyes glazed; his head lolled; he was out. First blood to our side. The stewards hauled him off.

The Political Officer drank little and spoke little.

The table was cleared and small three-ounce glasses were placed before us. More toasts; and important toasts were always "dodna"—bottoms up. Stalin! Churchill! Roosevelt!

"Say, Debbie, tovarich. Shall I mention Mackenzie King?"

"No."

A mandolin was brought out, then another; bright, throbbing music. We didn't know the words but we could stamp and clap. Stamp and clap we did. I made motions that I wanted a fiddle; the mime for playing a fiddle is international. A steward disappeared below and found one. Alma had always said I had a unique problem as a violinist. Under four drinks I was too nervous to play and over four my fingers got all muddled up. That, you will agree, leaves little time to perform. But not that day. I'd never tried to play before after drinking a whole bottle, or more. The "Garry Owen" set everyone prancing around. We danced The Lancers with great gusto. My nimble fingers flashed up and down the fingerboard: my bow, with strong, broad strokes, was perfectly synchronized; the notes were true and mellow and forcible. Or so it seemed to me.

A Russian sub-lieutenant flung himself at Debbie, determined to kiss the visiting captain. With a girlish shriek Debbie took to his heels. Around they went, over tables, chairs, settees, the sub-lieutenant gaining. We cheered them on. With coy glances over his shoulder and imaginary skirt held high, Debbie squealed at every leap. He was too good: the sub-lieutenant sank down exhausted.

My God, here's the Russian Gunnery Officer with another vodka. Well, if he can, I can. . . . Spaceeba. . . .

"Here's your morning tea, sir. Time to turn out. Here's your tea, sir. You've missed breakfast. Time to turn out. Cable party will be piped in fifteen minutes. The First Lieutenant said to tell you you've been in your pit for twelve hours and . . ."

"All right," said Marc, "I'll get him up."

And we sailed again from Kola.

The Admiral practised a ruse-de-guerre. We knew the U-boats would be stationed along the swept channel that ran eastward. But a new channel had been swept running practically due north of Kola Inlet. Nine U-boats were stationed along the old route. The Admiral sent four destroyers storming up it, dropping depth-charges and firing star shell. The enemy were deceived and the convoy sneaked out the back door, by the new route. U-boats never made contact again. The enemy aircraft never found us either. Oh, perfidious Albion! All ships arrived safely in Scotland.

By 1945 the tide of the war at sea had definitely turned in our favour. The tenacious attempts of the U-boats to sever the main artery of the Allies—the sea lanes—had nearly succeeded. But where three years ago they'd been sinking three-quarters of a million tons of our shipping monthly, the average tonnage sunk during these last months was down to fifty thousand tons.

Germany had built over eleven hundred U-boats, and over seven hundred had been lost. Of 40,900 men recruited into the U-boat arm, 28,000 had lost their lives and 5,000 had been taken prisoner.

But they had been effective: the British Merchant Navy had over 30,000 killed. However, in the last four months of 1944 only twenty-four ships had been sunk by U-boats, while fifty-five U-boats had been destroyed. But, incredible as it may seem, there was still a chance that Dönitz could snatch the initiative again, and again achieve supremacy. The new Type XXII and XXIII U-boats were more than a match for any escorts we had, and they were coming into service faster than we could sink them. But we were now building merchant ships faster than the U-boats could sink them. The escalation of this trend and the extrapolation of the graphs raise interesting conjectures. Allied bombing of the Dortmund, Ems, and Mittelland canals had disrupted the U-boat-building program for some months. But by April 1945, twelve Type XXI U-boats were ready to go to sea and another ninety-one were out on trials. If speculation is the fancy of the scholar, it is intriguing to wonder what would have been the outcome of the war if Hitler had waited in 1939 for Dönitz to build up his U-boat fleet. Dönitz, you will remember, didn't want war until he had 129 U-boats, but had to start with only twenty-two operational.

The high seas had long swept clear of surface raiders; no merchant raiders had dared put out for nearly two years, and the last raider at sea was sunk in October 1943. *Atlantis, Komet, Orion, Widder, Pinguin, Michel, Thor, Kormoran, Stier,* all were sunk, interned in foreign ports, or had limped home to Germany, never to sail again. They had joined the famous *Vulkan* of the First World War in history and legend. Of the German warships, *Prinz Eugen* had been, since August 1944, supporting the German army on the Eastern Front by furnishing fire support. *Leipzig* had been rammed and cut in two by *Prinz Eugen,* and never returned to ocean service. *Hipper,* after being driven off by Captain Sherbrooke in the New Year's Eve battle of 1942, needed major repairs and never sailed again. *Blücher* had been sunk in Oslo Fiord in 1940. The pocket battleship *Spee* was a gaunt monument in the River Plate. The other two pocket battleships, *Lützow* and *Scheer,* were training ships in the Baltic, practising for a battle that never came. *Gneisenau* had been damaged by a bombing attack after her spectacular dash up the English Channel and never put to sea again. *Scharnhorst* had gone down under the guns of the Home Fleet. In building *Tirpitz* and *Bismarck,* Raeder had produced two of the finest battleships in the world's navies. *Bismarck* had been pounded to a wreck by the guns of the Home Fleet. That left *Tirpitz.*

Hers was a melancholy history. She and *Bismarck* had been constructed under the 1936 building program: eight 15-inch guns and twelve 5.9-inch, forty AA guns; heavy armour; thirty-one knots and an eight-thousand-mile range; 42,900 tons. (Hitler had wanted 80,000 tons and 20- or 21-inch guns. Raeder had patiently explained to the corporal some facts of maritime life, such as harbour depths and docking facilities.) *Tirpitz* had arrived at Trondheim in January 1942. The presence of this mighty ship had affected Home Fleet strategy for three years. Every operation had to be planned with her possible sortie in mind. Battleships, carriers, and cruisers had to cover each convoy.

In March *Tirpitz* sailed against an outbound and an inbound convoy. In weather too tempestuous for an air search she was reported by the British submarine *Seawolf*. Admiral Tovey in *King George V* was covering the convoy; with him was the battlecruiser *Renown*, the aircraft carrier *Victorious*, heavy cruisers, and light cruisers. Admiral Ciliax was in *Tirpitz* and had, of course, a destroyer screen. Ciliax and Tovey never met. *Tirpitz* came within seventy-five miles of the convoy but in those gloomy, storm-lashed latitudes contact is difficult. The aircraft of *Victorious* found *Tirpitz* eighty miles from the Fleet. They attacked: no hits. Two were shot down. *Tirpitz* laid a smoke-screen and went home.

In July, *Tirpitz* and *Hipper* sailed to rendezvous with *Sheer* and *Lützow*; ten destroyers would accompany them. Three destroyers and *Lützow* ran aground but the remainder met in Altenfiord. Convoy PQ-17 was the target. Then the German force returned to harbour because an extraordinary event had occurred. In the face of the threat from this German surface force, PQ-17 had been ordered to scatter. The First Sea Lord had considered that single ships could best avoid destruction. But aircraft and U-boats found PQ-17 and sank twenty-four ships. Lost were nearly one hundred thousand tons of miscellaneous war supplies, in addition to 210 aircraft, 430 tanks, and 3,350 vehicles. The mere presence of *Tirpitz* in northern waters was responsible for this loss. She could have stayed in Altenfiord and never come near the convoy and the result would have been the same.

In those days Rommel was knocking on the gates of Cairo, and units of the Home Fleet had to be sent to the Mediterranean. American ships came to help with Russian convoys, but then Admiral Chester Nimitz needed them in the Pacific. Even after his victory at Midway his fleet was inferior to the Japanese.

During the spring and summer of 1943 *Tirpitz* lay in Altenfiord, greatly affecting the war even though fuel was so short that she could only sail about twice a month for brief trials and gunnery practices. In Trondheim she had occasionally been attacked by long-range bombers; up here she was safe from this threat. She was the most dangerous battleship in the world. Her mere existence affected the balance of sea-power in every ocean. A daring attack by manned torpedoes had failed when the short-range "chariots" sank only five miles from their quarry. In September *Tirpitz* sortied with *Scharnhorst* and bombarded the weather station on Spitzbergen, a nice enough little jaunt, one supposes, and a bit of gunnery practice. In September 1943, when RN midget submarines attached four two-ton charges to her hull, the crews surrendered and were picked up by one of *Tirpitz*'s boats. Captain Hans Meyer did all he could: closed watertight doors, ordered steam raised, swung the bow one hundred and fifty feet by working his cable, began to swing the stern, sent for a tug. But, with our men aboard, the charges exploded. The main engines were damaged, two turrets were jammed, the rudder was twisted. And the St. Nazaire dry-dock was not available to her. Seven hundred workmen were sent from Germany and slowly she was repaired. But the extent of the damage was then unknown and she continued to be a restraint on our movements. In February 1944 she was missed by bombs from a Russian heavy-bomber raid. In April we in the Home Fleet hit her, and again she was repaired. In July and again in August we hit her.

The Norwegians called her the "Lonesome Queen". For over two years she lay in bleak fiords behind her anti-torpedo nets. If we thought our life harsh, what must it have been for *Tirpitz*'s crew? At least we were moving. I could imagine the endless, sterile, pointless drills as month followed month and year followed year with never a chance to unleash the deadly power of a beautiful fire-control system. The finest of Zeiss optical range-finders with never an enemy to take a cut on, her great guns always mute.

In September British heavy bombers flying from Russia hit her with a twelve-thousand-pound bomb. Her sea-going days—such as they had been—were over. She was moved to Tromso to escape the Russian advance and to be used as a floating coast-defence battery. In October, Bomber Command went for her again, but because of the weather scored only a near-miss. In November, her smoke-screen was incomplete and six-ton bombs ripped open her hull for a hundred feet. She listed, a magazine blew up, and she capsized, drowning nearly a thousand men.

Her death was a lesson in history repeated from the First World War and was an echo of the fate of the German High Seas

Fleet. In both wars we contained heavy German ships only at great cost in ships, men, money, and time; and the creator of the High Seas Fleet—Grossadmiral Alfred von Tirpitz—was perhaps vindicated in that his concepts nearly brought the Allies to their knees. *Tirpitz*'s influence had been enormous and far out of proportion to the forty-six rounds she fired at the weather huts of Spitzbergen. Vindicated also was the British policy of building not necessarily bigger ships or better ships, but more ships.

The Canadian soldiers we had landed on Juno Beach were doing well. God bless their little khaki socks! On the BBC news each night we followed the progress of the Third Canadian Division. When they were checked on the Falaise road we mourned, and then rejoiced as they went forward again. Past Ypres (what memories for some of them!), northeast through Bruges and Ghent, into Holland. General Crerar had been given the important but unspectacular task of clearing the western flank. As sailors we were glad to see the ports of Le Havre, Dieppe, Boulogne, Calais, Dunkirk, Ostend, and Zeebrugge in Canadian hands. Nine months later our soldiers were crossing the Rhine into Germany from the west and the Russians were driving on Berlin from the east, perhaps with some of the tanks the Arctic convoys had brought to them.

This, then, was the justification and the fruition of over five years of hard fighting to get supplies through to our soldiers. For wars are won, in the final days, by Sam the infantryman with a musket in his hand. When Hitler had looked westward from the French seaports now held by Canadian soldiers, the only barrier still before him had been the long lines of battered cargo ships and tankers plodding along from Trinidad, Curaçao, Aruba, Guantanamo, New York, Boston, Halifax, St. John's, Reykjavik, Akureryi, Londonderry, Glasgow, the Orkney Islands, and Murmansk. That's about ten thousand miles of convoy route and I'd sailed every cable of it. Germany's finest seamen had been unable to break this supply-line. Hitler had contemplated invasion of England in Operation Sea Lion but with his strange prescience had allowed the plan to wither. But with the implacable bulk of the Home Fleet between him and the beaches of England, perhaps prescience is not the word, perhaps common-sense is better. Our sea-lanes had transported vast reservoirs of war material into the hands of the men now using them in Europe: food, oil, guns, tanks, and aircraft. The American naval historian Alfred Thayer Mahan had written of such an operation when talking of the armies of

Napoleon and the ships of Nelson in a similar campaign waged nearly a hundred and forty years before:

> Those far distant, storm beaten ships upon which the Grand Army never looked, stood between it and the domination of the world.

The war in Europe was not yet over, although it was obvious in the winter of 1944-45 that we were going to win. That left another war to finish, the one in the Pacific.

We heard that the United States fleet did not particularly want us out there. Who could blame them if this were true? Admiral Ernest J. King had been Commander-in-Chief of the USN Atlantic fleet in 1941, the "short-of-war" period before Pearl Harbor when the USS *Kearney* and the USS *Reuben James* were torpedoed. In 1942 he became Chief of Naval Operations. Besides supporting the war in the Atlantic and the invasions of Africa, Sicily, and Europe, he had built up the shattered Pacific fleet. Since the disastrous Battle of the Java Sea in February 1942, Admiral King had engineered quite a few decisive engagements, some more successful than others: the Battle of the Coral Sea, the Battle of Midway, the Battle of Guadalcanal, Tassafaronga. The leap-frogging began in the spring of 1944: Bougainville, the Gilberts, the Marshalls, Leyte Gulf. The Battle of the Philippine Sea was the greatest carrier battle of the war and made our Russian convoys look like child's play. After three days' fighting the Japanese fleet had only 35 serviceable planes out of the 430 it started with: in one day Vice-Admiral Jisaburo Ozawa lost 346 planes from ten carriers in ten minutes. At Okinawa the USN radar pickets survived three thousand kamikaze attacks.

But from our point of view we had Singapore to avenge, and, closer to Canadian thoughts, the Canadian garrison at Hong Kong, who had had many killed, wounded, and imprisoned. Lord Louis Mountbatten's forces were fighting in Burma still. Yes, we owed it to our American allies for their help in the Atlantic and the Mediterranean to fight in the Pacific.

Admiral King thought that Sir Bruce's principal job should be the liberation of Indonesia and surrounding areas. After all, we had lost these lands. But Winston Churchill, with his infallible instinct for the centre of the stage and the main spotlight, insisted, for prestige reasons, that the Royal Navy be in at the death of Japan. We heard that an RCN light cruiser would be going as well. Since March 1944, the Royal Navy's Pacific fleet had been fighting around Sakashima Gunto. Vice-Admiral Sir Bernard

Rawlings was in *King George V* and his fleet included the carriers *Indomitable, Victorious, Illustrious,* and *Indefatigable.* Sir Bruce joined later in *Duke of York.* I met him after the war at *Excellent* and he said that the weather was much better in his new command: "Quite as dangerous as the Home Fleet, perhaps more; but not so wretched, not nearly so beastly."

We never sailed again to Russia. I've quite forgotten what we did in those last weeks in the Home Fleet, but it was just messing around the Orkneys and the Faeroes. One drizzly evening we entered harbour. There was a variety show at the canteen ashore and nearly all hands had planned on meeting someone there. But we never got ashore. While we were fuelling, the Captain bustled into the wardroom.

"We're going home," he announced.

"Home?'

"Home. Halifax."

"When?"

"Now. At least, when we've finished refuelling."

There was a strange silence, not the exuberance we'd always thought would accompany this long-awaited news. I believe we were regretting having to miss that evening's show. But then, the goodbyes would have been painful. And what was there to say except goodbye? Three hours later we steamed out of Switha gate for the last time. Nearly everyone was on deck, looking back. Looking back at a shabby collection of Nissen huts, ugly barracks, a Wrennery, a wet canteen, a dry canteen, some stores. We all had our private thoughts but I think all of them included someone we knew we'd never see again.

Hard steaming brought us to the Azores Islands, the latitude of southern Spain. We put in at Ponta del Gada to fuel. Such sun! Such warmth! We shed Arctic clothing and chattered like magpies. But it was after leaving the Azores that our spirits rose to a frenzy. For the first time in two years the compass-card was reading West. Not North to Murmansk, not South to Scapa Flow, but West to Halifax.

One evening about supper-time we pulled alongside Jetty Five in the Halifax Dockyard. There were about ten people on the dockside to meet us. The ship's company poured ashore. The Chief Engineer blew down his boilers, the subdued roar of the ventilation fans ceased, and *Sioux* lay at rest in a home she had never seen before. She had carried us a hundred and twelve thousand miles.

Epilogue

The European war receded into the background. Now, all hands were talking about the war against Japan. *Sioux* would refit and sail as soon as possible to join Sir Bruce in the British Pacific Fleet. Our "chummy-ship", *Algonquin*, would sail with us. *Huron*, *Haida*, and *Iroquois* were returning from Europe and after refit would join us. One of our cruisers, *Ontario*, was transiting the Mediterranean and would join the British Pacific Fleet in a few weeks; our other cruiser, *Quebec*, was already there.

The Captain recommended me for transfer to the permanent force: from the Royal Canadian Naval Volunteer Reserve to the Royal Canadian Navy. I was ordered to proceed to National Defence Headquarters for an Interview Board. (You always "proceed" in the navy.)

On the Board, next morning, was my Manning Commander, now a Captain, fuller and redder in the face, and bleaker in the eye. I don't remember many of the questions. But one, ominously, was, "What will you do if we don't accept you?"

I said, "Write."

"Write what?"

"I don't know yet. I'll go back to university first. Perhaps I'll write of this Board, ha ha."

A frosty silence greeted this light sally. The questions had been shallow and perfunctory. They'd made up their minds before I'd even appeared. I was told to return after lunch. I returned at three and knocked on the door. My legs were rubbery.

"Come in."

I entered. All three were smiling broadly. The Manning Captain rose, eyes not bleak but twinkling. What an attractive old sea-dog he was, to be sure. He stuck out his hand.

"With very little hesitation we have accepted you." Very little? "Congratulations, Lawrence. Welcome to the Band of Brothers. We are sure you will always be a credit to the Service."

The navy's cornucopia had not yet discharged its last treasure. Doug Bruce had decided not to go to the Pacific but to finish his law studies. I was to be appointed First Lieutenant in his place.

The First Lieutenant, not the Captain, is the centre of all things. He is the Executive Officer. Each head of department—engineer, gunnery, torpedo, ordnance, electrical, signals, navigation, asdic, supply—has his regular staff who work under him every day; so have the fo'c's'le, top, and quarter-deck officers. But unusual, out-of-routine tasks have to be arbitrated by the First Lieutenant and extra hands supplied. "Guns" must debark ammunition for testing. The Paymaster must embark victuals. Harbour training must be frequent on the attack simulators. The Dockyard Bosun wants to get at the rigging and the Dockyard Engineer wants to get at the steering engines in the tiller flat and the Chief Bosun's Mate wants to chip and red-lead and the Ordnance Officer wants to carry out quarterly maintenance routines and the Signals Officer wants to dry bunting. Most jobs need extra hands and all impinge, slightly or greatly, upon other departments. The XO is the focal point for all requests, complaints, demands, threats, pleas, from above and below. Heads of departments assure him of dire consequences if what they want today is not done today with exactly the number of extra hands they have asked for. The Captain's pressure is less direct, but remarks like "The whaler is looking a little scruffy, isn't it, XO?" can only be interpreted as "Scrape, scrub, and paint the whaler."

The signal log is a constantly unfolding chronicle of the ship's life: when the tugs will take you in tow and where they'll drop you; who's going to hospital and who's coming back, and who's going to detention or returning from detention; draftings to courses; other ships' movements and intentions; RPCs for drinks at noon; the rig-of-the-day for special functions—sporting and social; demands for stores, spare parts, water, fuel, and lube-oil of a dozen varieties; weather reports, accident reports, fuel and water-consumption reports; results of examinations; incidents that the Admiral views with pleasure and those he views with concern, or worse, *grave* concern.

All the trades you find practised in a small, thriving community you find in a destroyer; besides the obvious ones of electrician, mechanic, cook, waiter, shop-keeper, there are also those more humble and obscure: plumber, lamp-trimmer, clerk, butcher, sailmaker, postman. Besides being valuable and indispensable members of the over-all organization of the community, they are all their idiosyncratic selves, with private dreams of how they may ascend the promotion ladder, which jobs they like and which they abhor. Somehow, the XO has to consider pregnant wives, sick children, families dispossessed by the bailiff, dying mothers, brothers' weddings, bill collectors' threats, and truant sons and daughters; he must weigh telegrams from a parson, a family doctor, a local MP, all of whom insist that a sailor must return home immediately. The gamut of calamities is extensive: auto accidents, foreclosed mortgages, hail-beaten oats and rust-ruined wheat, frozen wells and scalded aunts, amputated limbs, rats in the basement and bees in the attic.

The new Captain joined. After a month or so I pointed out that I hadn't taken leave for over a year, hadn't seen my parents for over two. Could I go now? Yes, certainly; I must take leave for the good of the Service, as often as was possible. I was to go immediately. The Mate of the Upper Deck could look after things while I was gone.

I stopped in Montreal to visit friends on the way back to Halifax. I was by myself one day in the Normandie Roof, sipping a reflective beer, when the news broke: Germany had surrendered unconditionally. The European war was over. May 7, 1945. Five years and eight months before, Dönitz's U-boats had made their first kills. Now they would be popping up all over the oceans of the world flying the large black flag of surrender.

The Normandie Roof went wild. I was in mufti and so went unnoticed. At the next table to me was a corpulent army captain from Quebec. I had been half listening as he expostulated about the difficulty of getting spare parts—whether for himself or the army I wasn't sure. He wore a single ribbon—the General Service Medal—without the silver clasp that signifies service in an area of combat. His table filled rapidly with exultant civilians. All bought him drinks: he had about eight rum-and-cokes lined up. "Well, boy. You did it. You did it. You beat the bastards," his new-found friends shouted, and clapped him on the shoulder and shook his hand—both hands. The captain nodded in a self-deprecatory fashion. Victor beamed paternally over the beginning of yet another successful and profitable evening.

Amid these Normandie Roof rejoicings I felt solitary. It was true I rejoiced also, but I could find nothing in common between my rejoicing and that of these boisterous people. I left and returned to Halifax.

Sioux was looking better and better. I was proud of her. The ship's company was beginning to coalesce into a family again. One able seaman in the new draft had been brought back after beating up half the shore patrol with his feet. Evidently he was a student of karate. "How did you do it?" his admiring shipmates asked.

"I can kick pretty high," he replied modestly.

Since we were going to work under the American navy, I reread the biography of Commodore John Paul Jones, USN. His views on the qualities necessary in a naval officer led me to yet another examination of conscience:

Coming now to view the naval officer and in relation to those under his command, he should be the soul of tact, patience, justice, firmness, and charity. No meritorious act of a subordinate should escape his attention or be left to pass without its reward, even if the reward be only one word of approval. Conversely, he should not be blind to a single fault in any subordinate, though, at the same time, he should be quick and unfailing to distinguish error from malice, thoughtlessness from incompetency, and well-meant shortcoming from heedless or stupid blunder. As he should be universal and impartial in his rewards and approval of merit, so should he be judicial and unbending in his punishment or reproof of misconduct.

But at 0245, on the morning of August 6, the B-29 *Enola Gay* took off from Tinian, flown by Colonel Paul W. Tibbets. At 0815, over the headquarters of the Japanese Second Army at Hiroshima, an atomic bomb was toggled out. On August 9 a second atomic bomb exploded over Nagasaki. These was much shuffling of feet amongst the Japanese war-lords in Tokyo, understandably. They had a long history of success. Anami, Umezu, and Toyada were urging Emperor Hirohito to fight one last battle to save national honour. Baron Suzuki's cabinet, including Togo as foreign minister, advocated speedy peace—with honour. Anything to save face. On August 14, Japan surrendered.

The honed fighting-edge of *Sioux*'s ship's company was blunted. How could it be any different? But they were good hands. *Sioux* started to empty as the reserve sailors returned to their homes inland. With a diminished crew the messdecks seemed unbelievably spacious. The hands were relaxed, and cheerful, and obeyed orders with alacrity. I had leave piped every day at

1530, make-and-mend on Wednesday afternoon, no work on Saturday. Why bother, now? I dimly foresaw the long years of peace stretching ahead, personally fulfilling perhaps, but professionally arid. One night there was a farewell mess dinner for me in Sioux which turned into quite a bash. You may believe that. It looked a little peculiar, a little formal, when the officers attended the forenoon muster in their mess-kit—wing collars and bow ties. Then we trooped back to the wardroom for a breakfast of eggs and bacon and beer.

We sang a final verse of "Come Inside, You Silly Bastard, Come Inside". Then the new First Lieutenant told the officers to shower, shave, shift into the rig-of-the-day, and get to work. The stewards had stowed my gear in a staff car. I walked solemnly and rather deliberately along the upper deck of Sioux. Quite a few of the old ship's company had gathered and I shook hands with all of them. I looked back as we drove off the jetty. Sioux was tugging gently at her mooring lines in the slight chop running down from Bedford Basin. She was clean, and gleaming, and had lost the dejected air of a ship refitting. She was looking vindictive again, and ready. Ready for what? Her upper deck and superstructure were filled with seamen quietly going about the daily chore of catering to her needs. On a bosun's chair, reeving a new halyard at the truck of the mast, was a young signalman, White's replacement. I had served Sioux as best I could; others would do the same.

The memories of the broken bodies and the wasted lives were becoming dim. The brutality of the Third Reich, its insane plan for world domination, its gas ovens which "purified" the human race of six million Jews, are today dispassionately discussed by historians and are not a particular feature of school curricula. Other millions who died, alone and broken, are not mentioned now. They live only in the memories of portly men passing into old age. Soon their extinction will be complete. But the threat to what most of the world held to be honourable and decent was real, removing the threat was not easy, and to have played a part in overthrowing unspeakable horrors is, perhaps, no small thing. On Remembrance Day each November and on Battle of the Atlantic Sunday each June, Alma and I and a few others gather at the war memorial; others do the same all across Canada. But the number grows fewer each year and the young stare curiously when they happen by. Perhaps that's as it should be.

But I cannot forget Rammy Nairs and Bud Boyer, friends from my square-bashing days in 1939, who went down with their ships:

we had frolicked away many a beery evening in the Crow's Nest and I can't imagine not seeing them again. Chief Petty Officer Bingham had drowned also, he who had seemed so indestructible. And I remember good things too. By 1945 our crackling torpedo gunner, Pat Budge, had risen to lieutenant, driven his own corvette, *Sorel*, been appointed First Lieutenant of *Huron*, and picked up a Distinguished Service Cross. His promotions were to continue until he reached Admiral. "Herr von" Pullen must have seen many scuppers run red with blood; he had driven *St. Francis*, *Ottawa*, and *St. Laurent*, and had picked up the Order of the British Empire. "Chummy" Prentice ended with two DSCs and a Distinguished Service Order.

With the war over it became incumbent upon me to choose the branch of the navy in which I would specialize: torpedo, anti-submarine, signals, navigation, fighter-pilot, or gunnery. The electrical branch was out: I didn't have enough education and a B SC was a prerequisite. The supply branch was out too; they were beginning to require a B COM. Why these branches would require their officers to waste those years in a university when they could have been at sea learning their profession was more than we salt-horses could understand. But they weren't real sailors anyway; driving a ship and firing weapons was the real art of the sailor. I chose gunnery. They say the only reason any officer chooses to specialize in gunnery is so he will never again have to sail in the same ship with a gunnery officer. They say we are an aggressive and an abrasive group of men, overly addicted to duty.

I said goodbye to my wife—Alma, of course—and Mother and Father and sailed from Halifax in *Aquitania*, bound for HMS *Excellent*. I hadn't fared so badly in a bloody war; what had a sickly season in store?